ROOTS

AND

RITUALS

Bihari Kayastha Traditions in Hinduism

By

BISHAKHA SINHA

Roots and Rituals © Copyright 2023 By Bishakha Sinha

For more information, email chatwithbsinha@gmail.com

Publishing Consultant: Thanx A. Mills, LLC | www.thanxamills.com

DISCLAIMER

There is no religious advice in this book, or the materials produced by its sponsoring organization. Any statement shouldn't be construed as a substitute for your ability to evaluate religious claims based on a rational evaluation of the evidence. Any misunderstanding or misuse of information in articles posted in this book shall not be the responsibility of the authors or publications sponsored in this book.

Furthermore, we are not responsible for any loss, damage, or injury caused or alleged to be caused, directly or indirectly, by any action or behavior precipitated by information in this book.

Especially if you act on statements predicting future events and these events do not materialize.

We hope you find the information in this book helpful. If you choose to read any posted article, you should be aware that the results of implementing the ideas advocated in that article will vary from person to person.

Application of the ideas contained therein is not guaranteed to produce any result. We are not responsible for any factual or scientific errors in the materials posted or publications advertised. Misuse or erroneous interpretation of biblical texts is also included here. The material presented here, and the stories shown are only illustrative examples.

By carrying out the beliefs contained in the materials and stories, some individuals have said that they achieved their goals. Readers should be aware that information about events occurring in current and former mission lands is based on stories related by missionaries. Modifications may include but are not limited to, changing the purported facts, doctoring the photos, and inventing direct quotations.

Despite being achievable for some, the results mentioned by some individuals, such as their chances of going to heaven, should not be interpreted as those that you may achieve.

Readers need to understand that the information contained in the postings and advertisements is simply an indication of what the authors think and feel about certain religious matters and is not meant to be taken literally. Any statement or claim should be evaluated using your common sense. There is a lot of public domain content and images compiled from various sources.

DEDICATION

To Mom and Dad,

You have been the guiding light of my life with your unwavering love and boundless support. Throughout my life, you have instilled values and wisdom in me that I have incorporated into this book. It has been your sacrifices and encouragement that have fueled my journey, and I am grateful for the foundation you have laid for me.

Thank you for being my biggest cheerleader, my greatest source of inspiration, and my pillar of strength.

With deep appreciation for all that you have done and all the love you have given to everyone, this book is dedicated to you.

With love and gratitude

TABLE OF CONTENTS

FOREWORD

H induism. Amidst constant change and uncertainty, Hindu philosophy and spirituality offer us a profound source of insight, solace, and understanding.

In addition to being a religion, Hinduism encompasses a rich tapestry of practices, beliefs, and traditions that have evolved over millennia.

The author of this book has endeavored to unravel the essence of Hinduism, bringing forth its ancient wisdom and contemporary relevance. This book thoughtfully and comprehensively explores Hindu philosophy, mythology, rituals, and spirituality. Hinduism offers profound spiritual insights that transcend boundaries and speak to the human condition that goes beyond scholarly examinations.

According to Hinduism, all aspects of life are ruled by the divine, truth is sought, and inner peace is cultivated. Diversity is celebrated, interconnectedness is respected, and self-realization is aspired to. With this book, you will be guided through a journey that explores Hinduism in all its facets, including its sacred scriptures, such as the Bhagavad Gita and Upanishads, as well as its multitude of deities, rituals, and practices.

Globalization has made it more important than ever to appreciate and understand the beliefs and practices of different faiths. A person seeking spiritual growth, philosophical insights, or a deeper connection to the world around them will find much to benefit from Hinduism's rich history and timeless teachings.

To fully experience the wisdom found within these pages, I encourage you to read this book with an open heart and mind. Hopefully, it will inspire you to explore further, to ask questions, and to embark on your spiritual journey.

A valuable resource for newcomers to Hinduism as well as those seeking to understand this profound tradition, this book deserves commendation for its dedication.

With heartfelt blessings,

Pandit Keshav Joshi, Atlanta, USA

PREFACE

My Grandma (Dadi) always said "No matter where you go in life,
you will always be remembered by your roots.
So, know it and be proud of it!"

❧

Hinduism is one of the most intricate and enduring traditions in the vast tapestry of human spirituality. A tradition that extends far beyond religion, embracing philosophy, culture, and an understanding of the self.

Hinduism reminds me of the profound connection we share with these ancient teachings on this journey through its heart. This exploration is more than an academic endeavor for me; it is an immensely personal journey into the roots of my own identity. As a child, I was immersed in Hinduism's sights, sounds, and stories. My first encounter with this tradition came through the melodies of bhajans sung by my grandmother, the scent of incense wafting through our home during pujas by my mother, and the timeless tales of Hindu gods and goddesses.

Although life had taken me far from those early years, I felt a growing desire to reconnect with them. In many ways, I was motivated by a desire to understand the significance of the practices and beliefs that had shaped both my family and me.

My love for my heritage and reverence for it are reflected in this book. The purpose of this essay is to share with you the profound richness of Hinduism, to peel back the layers of myths and rituals, and to reveal the timeless wisdom at its core. Here, we will travel through the Vedas, the Upanishads, the Mahabharata, and the Ramayana. We will explore dharma and karma, the pantheon of deities, and meditation's transformative power. In addition to analyzing these teachings academically, we will discover their profound relevance to our modern lives.

In Hinduism, we are taught about the interconnectedness of all things, the pursuit of truth, and the importance of self-realization. As a result, we are encouraged to embrace diversity and respect the sanctity of life in all its forms. By exploring these ancient texts and practices, I invite you not only to learn but also to reflect, question, and discover your connection to this remarkable tradition.

I hope you will find this book to be a bridge between humans and the wisdom of the ages and one that reconnects you with heritage, which has touched us all in some way or another. As a seeker of spiritual truths, an explorer of cultures, or simply someone seeking to better understand your roots, I hope that this journey through Hinduism will be as transformative and enlightening for you as it has been for me. It is important to me that the next generation knows about our traditions and values.

With humility and gratitude,

Bishakha

EMBRACING HINDU FESTIVALS AND TRADITIONS

❧

My Journey of Growth

As a CHILD, in a household steeped in Hindu traditions has been a profoundly enriching experience. The festivals, rituals, and customs of my culture have not only shaped my cultural identity but have also instilled spirituality and values in me. I celebrated Hindu festivals and traditions, which shaped my character and worldview. In this book, I explore my journey of celebrating these festivals and traditions and share that journey with you

1. The Tapestry of Festivals

Hinduism is characterized by festivals, each with a unique significance and ritual. From the joyful celebration of Diwali, signifying the overcoming of darkness with light, to the devotional fervor of Navratri, dedicated to the divine feminine, I have been fortunate to participate in many celebrations. Not only have these festivals provided moments of joy and togetherness, but they have also imparted invaluable life lessons.

2. Family and Community Bonds

Commonly, it happens for Hindus to celebrate festivals with their extended families and neighbors. Community is reinforced through these gatherings, insisting on the importance of belonging and unity. Instilling values of love, respect, and empathy for others, the shared rituals and festivities create a powerful bond.

3. The Rhythms of Rituals

Spiritual growth and discipline are achieved through rituals, which are the heartbeat of Hinduism. There is a sense of reverence and mindfulness that is engendered by these daily rituals at the family altar to the elaborate ceremonies that occur during festivals. In addition to reminding us of the importance of transcending the materialistic pursuits of this world, they serve to remind us of the spiritual dimensions of life as well.

4. Spiritual Growth and Reflection

As a result of celebrating Hindu festivals, I have discovered myself and grown as a person. Meditation, prayer, and introspection have taught me the importance of cultivating a strong spiritual foundation. Through these moments of reflection, I have been able to gain clarity and purpose, which has guided me through life's challenges and victories.

5. Universality and Inclusivity

There is no doubt that one of the most profound aspects of Hindu festivals is their inclusivity. Embracing love, compassion, and unity, they welcome people from all backgrounds and beliefs. Diversity and appreciation for different perspectives and cultures have been encouraged by this spirit of inclusivity.

Growing up and celebrating Hindu festivals and traditions has been a transformative journey for me, which has helped me shape not only my cultural identity but also my values and outlook on life in general. I have grown as an individual through the tapestry of festivals, the bonds of family and community, the rhythms of ritual, and the moments of spiritual reflection. As a result of these experiences, I have come to appreciate the profound wisdom and universal values offered by Hinduism, providing a guiding light on my journey of self-discovery.

This legacy book can also include personal insights, anecdotes, and reflections in addition to established customs. It gives you a more intimate understanding of how our family or community has lived and cherished these traditions. As a means of inspiring future generations, this book that contains traditions can serve as a source of inspiration for those who follow in the footsteps of their predecessors. It is a lasting tribute to a community's cultural richness and depth to leave this book as a legacy.

As a result, it can encourage readers to explore their heritage, value their roots, and perhaps even take on the responsibility of further preserving and evolving these traditions as they continue to grow. It is a gift that keeps on giving, ensuring that the legacy lives on for generations to come.

1

ABOUT HINDUISM

⚜

A rich cultural and philosophical heritage distinguishes Hinduism as one of the oldest and most diverse religions in the world. The Indian subcontinent is where it originated over 4,000 years ago, and it is now widely considered to be the fusion of several different cultural, religious, and philosophical traditions. Hinduism is not only a religion but also a *way of life*. It is a cultural heritage that provides insight into the way of life in each aspect of life. *'Sanatana Dharma'* is another term used to describe Hinduism.

Hinduism is characterized by the following key characteristics:

- There is no single founder or scripture for Hinduism; it is a diverse religion. The Hindu religion allows for a great deal of individual interpretation with no universal definition or doctrine.

- Dharma is the concept of duty, righteousness, and morality. There is a range of expectations based on an individual's age, gender, caste, and occupation.

- Karma - A belief in the cycle of cause and effect, whereby one's actions (both good and bad) influence one's future.

- Samsara - The cycle of birth, death, and rebirth determined by karma. Breaking free of this cycle is the goal.

- Hinduism is often viewed as a polytheistic religion, but it also acknowledges monotheism in its belief in Brahman, the ultimate reality. The ultimate reality is manifested in different deities, each representing a different aspect. It is believed that Brahma (the creator), Vishnu (the preserver), Shiva (the destroyer), and Devi (the goddess, often referred to as the Divine Mother) are some of the most important deities.

- Having complex roots and involving a variety of practices, as well as a multitude of deities, the religion has a varied history. Worship and traditions are carried out in the places where people belong and where they have a strong sense of belonging.

♦ The Vedas are the oldest and most authoritative scriptures of Hinduism. A hymn, a ritual, and a philosophical teaching make up a Hindu ritual.

♦ Upanishads are philosophical texts that explore the nature of reality, self-awareness (Atman), and ultimate reality (Brahman).

♦ The Bhagavad Gita is a dialogue between Arjuna and Krishna that deals with moral dilemmas and duty.

♦ A variety of Hindu practices aimed at self-realization and spiritual growth are known as yoga and meditation. Meditation techniques and various types of yoga (physical, mental, and spiritual disciplines) are included here.

♦ In Hindu society, social classes are organized into hierarchical systems known as castes. In modern times, however, the caste system has been subject to much debate and reform, as it is no longer a fundamental aspect of Hinduism.

♦ Hindus believe in reincarnation, in which the soul is reborn in different bodies through many lifetimes. There is only one goal, which is to achieve Moksha or be freed from the cycle of birth and death, and union with the ultimate reality of being that everything is.

♦ Diverse religious paths and practices are generally accepted in Hinduism. Different people approach spirituality differently, and there is no one "right way" to reach the divine.

♦ Hinduism celebrates many festivals, including Diwali (Festival of Lights), Holi (Festival of Colors), Navaratri (Nine Nights Festival), and more. It is common for these festivals to be tied to legends and religious rituals.

I think it is important to point out that Hinduism is an extremely diverse religion, with a wide variety of sects, philosophies, and regional variations. Consequently, interpretations and practices may vary widely among its adherents. Aside from that, there has also been a significant movement within Hinduism in recent years to promote social reform, gender equality, and greater inclusion within the religious community.

2

DEITIES WORSHIPPING

❧

To trace the origins of Hinduism, one must look back thousands of years, which makes it one of the world's oldest organized religions. As a result of different cultural and religious developments over a long period, it has been difficult to pinpoint precisely when the worship of deities in Hinduism began, as it has evolved over the years through the development of various cultural and religious elements. It is thought that Hinduism originated in the ancient Indus Valley civilization, which existed around 3300–1300 BCE in what is now Pakistan and northwest India. There is archeological evidence of early religious practices during this period, including symbols associated with deities.

Moreover, it can be assumed from historical documents and archaeological evidence that image worship in Hinduism has been present for approximately six to five centuries before Christ. Hinduism evolved significantly during the Vedic period, roughly between 1500 and 500 BCE. Among the earliest known Hindu scriptures are the Vedas, which are an ancient collection of religious texts that constitute Hinduism's earliest religious texts.

It was during this period that Vedic gods like Indra, Agni, and Varuna were prominent in religious practices.

The Hindu religion evolved and incorporated many beliefs, practices, and deities. The worship of images of deities such as Vishnu and the Goddess had become an important element of the worship of various deities by the early centuries of the Common Era. This sort of worship would have taken place both at home and in the temple and were both assumed to be sacred occasions.

There was a gradual evolution in temple design, and it developed into a variety of intricate designs. Temple worship involved making an image of a holy person by strict iconographic guidelines and having it served by dedicated priests.

During the consecration of the image, flower, and food offerings, anointing, and bathing of the image, oil lamps, incense, bells, and processions with the image, a daily program, which followed the customs of the royal court for all the gods involved, were all carried out in a very elaborate manner. Hindu religious thought developed around the concept of a pantheon of gods and goddesses. Brahma (the creator), Vishnu (the preserver), Shiva (the destroyer), along with numerous other gods and goddesses, each with their attributes and stories, are among these deities. It is important to keep in mind that Hinduism is incredibly diverse, with different regions and communities within the broader Hindu tradition having their interpretations, practices, and emphasis on specific deities that are unique to their region or community.

Various deities have an animal associate (vahana) that helps to identify them and to express the specific features of those deities; this was accomplished by using an artistic device that would attribute several body parts, such as hands and heads, adorned with weapons and other objects, to the images of these deities. Stories describe the origin, role, weapons, and other attributes associated with the image, especially in the Puranas - an ancient Sanskrit sacred writing containing Hindu legends and folklore, the oldest of which dates from the 4th century.

In addition to the forms of worship offered in the temple, which includes both personal prayer and various rituals performed by priests, the deity may be worshiped at home as well, either through personal images, or family images handed down to the next generation, or by practicing meditation (dhyana). Meditation can include highly specialized kinds of visualizations of the deity being invoked, in which the deity is often portrayed as a communicator with the worshiper through the medium of meditation.

Besides worshiping the deity in Hinduism, pilgrimage is also one of how the deity can be worshiped.

There is a strong belief that pilgrimage is a very important part of creating a sacred landscape, and of showing that all things belong to the deity and that it is under its control.

The pilgrimage is a way of showing this. A sacred ford or crossing-point between heaven and earth is reached on every pilgrimage undertaken by Hindus, through which they can work through the sorrows of this world and reach that threshold of liberation. As the Hindu sacred landscape has evolved, many *tirthas (worshiping places)* have developed across it.

3

ORIGIN OF LIFE

In Hindu cosmology, the time of creation, preservation, and dissolution of life are cyclical cycles determined by ages known as "Yugas." Creation, preservation, and dissolution continue in an eternal cycle. According to Hindu mythology, Brahma, Vishnu, and Shiva, collectively known as the Trimurti, created the universe.

- **Brahma** is believed to be the creator of the universe. Often, he is shown with four faces, which symbolizes the fact that he can see far ahead and possesses a wealth of knowledge. In some texts, it is stated that Brahma is the creator of the universe and all living beings within it as well.

♦ In Hinduism, **Vishnu** is seen as the preserver. The universe is believed to be sustained and protected by him. In times of crisis, Vishnu descends to earth through various avatars, including Rama and Krishna.

♦ **Shiva** represents destruction or transformation. Often, he is depicted in a meditative posture, symbolizing the ultimate detachment from the material world, which represents the ultimate finality. Shiva's role is to cause the dissolution of the universe, followed by a period of rest before the cycle of creation begins again.

Hindu mythology includes a rich tapestry of allegorical narratives about Brahma's family, which are described in various ways in various texts.

Brahma is traditionally believed to be married to Saraswati, a goddess of knowledge, music, art, and learning, who is Brahma's consort. Many depictions of her have a veena (musical instrument) and a book in her hands. It is believed that Saraswati represents creativity and wisdom. Other divine couples, such as Shiva and Parvati and Vishnu and Lakshmi, are often depicted together as Brahma and Saraswati.

The Manasputras are thought to be the creation of Brahma, according to some texts. The beings were created directly from Brahma's mind to assist in the creation process.

In Hindu mythology, Daksha is among the Manasputras and, as such, is regarded as an influential figure in terms of her daughters. The deity had several daughters, some of whom married various deities and sages. Known also as Dakshayani, Sati was Shiva's first wife. Parvati, the second wife of Lord Shiva (also known as Uma), was Sati's reincarnation.

The worship of Lord Brahma in contemporary Hinduism is less widespread than that of Lord Vishnu or Lord Shiva. Lord Brahma is relatively less worshipped by the masses than other deities, as he is more often considered a symbol of creativity rather than an active deity.

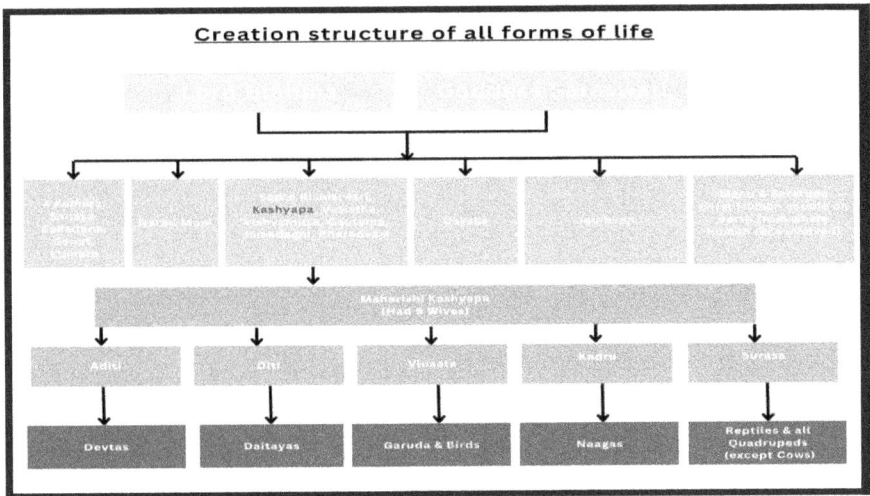

Creation structure of all forms of life

4

ABOUT 33 MILLION
GODS IN HINDUISM

∽

"**33** million gods" is often used colloquially to convey Hinduism's diverse and vast array of deities. Considering Hinduism's diverse beliefs and practices, it is important to understand that it is a complex religious tradition. Each god, goddess, and divine entity has its attributes, stories, and symbols. There is a vast pantheon of deities that are worshiped by millions of people worldwide. While it is difficult to pinpoint an exact number, it is often estimated that there are around 33 million gods in Hinduism.

These gods and goddesses are believed to possess various powers and attributes, and each deity is associated with specific aspects of life, nature, or cosmic forces. The number 33 million is often used symbolically to represent the vastness and diversity of the Hindu pantheon rather than a literal count of individual deities.

Overall, the gods and goddesses in Hinduism play a significant role in the religious and spiritual lives of millions of people, offering guidance, protection, and blessings in various aspects of life.

The 33 Koti Gods are typically divided into three main groups:

8 Vasus: These are elemental deities that are associated with different aspects of nature. Invoked for protection and well-being, they are considered benevolent spirits. Here are the names of the eight Vasus:

1. **Dhara (or Prithvi)**: Represents the Earth element.
2. **Anala (or Agni)**: Represents the Fire element.
3. **Anila (or Vayu)**: Represents the Wind element.
4. **Apa (or Varuna)**: Represents the Water element.
5. **Dhruva (or Dhara)**: Represents the Pole Star.
6. **Soma (or Chandra)**: Represents the Moon.
7. **Prabhasa (or Surya)**: Represents the Sun.
8. **Pratyusha (or Nakula)**: Represents Dawn.

There are 11 Rudras in the universe. These are forms of the god Shiva that are associated with various aspects of destruction and transformation. In addition to being powerful, Rudras are known for being both fierce and benevolent.

Here are the names of the eleven Rudras:

- **Ajaikapada**: form of Lord Shiva as a one-footed goat. "Ajaikapada" literally means "the one-footed goat."
- **Ahirbudhnya**: This Rudra is often associated with serpents and is sometimes regarded as the deity of the netherworld.
- **Virupaksha**: His name means "having a deformed eye," and he is sometimes depicted with three eyes. Virupaksha is associated with cosmic vision and perception.
- **Aparajita**: The undefeated one, symbolizing Lord Shiva's invincible nature.
- **Bhima**: Represents immense power and strength, reflecting the formidable aspect of Lord Shiva.
- **Mahān**: The great one, emphasizing Lord Shiva's vastness and cosmic presence.
- **Shambhu**: This name signifies auspiciousness and is often used as an epithet for Lord Shiva.
- **Ugra**: Meaning fierce or terrifying, this name highlights the formidable and awe-inspiring aspect of Lord Shiva.

- **Bhava:** Signifies the nature of becoming or existence. Bhava represents Lord Shiva's role in the cycle of creation, preservation, and destruction.
- **Kapali:** Meaning "the one with a skull," Kapali is often depicted wearing a garland of skulls, symbolizing the transcendence of mortality.
- **Rudra:** The name Rudra itself means "the howler" or "the roaring one." Rudra is one of the most common names associated with Lord Shiva and is used to refer to his fierce and dynamic aspect.

The 12 Adityas are solar deities, including well-known figures such as Lord Surya (the sun god) and Lord Varuna (the god of cosmic order and water). There are several cosmic principles and natural phenomena associated with them.

Here are the names of the twelve Adityas:

- **Mitra:** Often associated with friendship, contracts, and agreements.
- **Varuna:** Regarded as the god of cosmic order, water, and the celestial ocean.
- **Aryaman:** Represents nobility, contracts, and partnerships.
- **Bhaga:** Associated with wealth, prosperity, and happiness.
- **Ansa:** Often considered the deity of the moon.
- **Dhata:** Seen as the creator or bestower of existence.

- **Indra**: One of the most well-known deities in Hinduism, associated with thunder, rain, and kingship.
- **Vivasvat (Vivasvan)**: Often identified with the Sun itself, representing light and radiance.
- **Tvashtha (Twashtri)**: Regarded as the divine craftsman and architect of the gods.
- **Savitar**: Represents the creative power of the Sun and is often invoked in rituals.
- **Pushan**: Associated with the safekeeping of flocks and herds.
- **Martanda**: Sometimes referred to as the "dead egg" or the "egg that is not opened," symbolizing the end of the inauspicious phase of the Sun.

A total of 31 can be calculated by adding these three groups. In addition, there are two other categories:

The two most important gods in the Vedas are Indra and Prajapati. While Indra is the king of the gods and the ruler of heaven, Prajapati is a Vedic deity associated with the creation process. There are 33 concepts, including the Self (Atman) and Brahman (the ultimate reality).

33 koti gods = Eight Vasus + Eleven Rudras + Twelve Adityas + Indra and Prajapati (08+ 11 + 12 + 02 = 33)

I think it is important to note that this concept originates from ancient Vedic texts and is not widely discussed in the contemporary Hinduism community. The interpretations of different texts and traditions may also differ. Therefore, the list of gods in the Vedic cosmology does not represent a literal tally but rather the categorization of different aspects of divinity.

5

THE TEN FORMS
OF LORD VISHNU

~

Hinduism believes that Lord Vishnu has ten primary avatars (incarnations) known as Dashavataras. Lord Vishnu took these various incarnations in different epochs to restore cosmic order and protect dharma (righteousness). Lord Vishnu has ten forms:

These are in order: Matsya, Kurma, Varaha, Narasimha, Vamana, Parashurama, Rama, Krishna, Buddha, and Kalki.

- Matsya (The Fish) - In this avatar, Lord Vishnu takes the form of a fish to save the ancient scriptures (Vedas) and the sage Manu from a great flood.

- Kurma (The Tortoise) - Vishnu, took form as a tortoise to support Mount Mandara, used to churn the cosmic ocean for the nectar of immortality (amrita).

- Narasimha (The Man-Lion) - Vishnu took on a half-lion, half-man form to protect Prahalad from Hiranyakashipu, who had the boon of not being killed by either man or beast.

- Varaha (The Boar)- Lord Vishnu incarnated as a boar to rescue the Earth from Hiranyakashyap, who had submerged it in the cosmic ocean.

- Vamana (The Dwarf)- Vamana (The Dwarf): In this avatar, Vishnu appeared as a dwarf Brahmin to subdue Bali, the powerful demon king.

- Parashurama (The Warrior who had an Axe) - The Brahmin warrior Parashurama incarnated as Lord Vishnu to rid the world of corrupt and oppressive Kshatriya rulers.

- Rama (The Prince of Ayodhya) - When the Treta Yuga began, Vishnu took the form of Lord Rama, a prince of Ayodhya, who defeated Ravana and established dharma.

- Krishna (The Divine Cowherd) - Krishna is the most famous and beloved avatar of Vishnu, who appeared in the Dwapara Yuga to guide humanity through the Mahabharata war and teach spiritual wisdom through the Bhagavad Gita.

- ◆ Balarama (The Elder Brother of Krishna) - Balarama is Vishnu's ninth avatar. Known for his strength, he played a major role in Krishna's life.
- ◆ Kalki (The future Warrior) - This avatar of Vishnu is believed to appear at the end of the current era, the Kali Yuga, to restore dharma, destroy evil, and usher in a new age of righteousness.

Each of these avatars represents a different aspect of Lord Vishnu's divine intervention and his role in maintaining cosmic order. There may be other avatars or variations of the Dasharatha recognized by some traditions.

6

Karma and Reincarnation

✋

Essentially, karma means "deeds or acts," but it also describes the law of cause and effect more broadly. Consciousness is governed by the law of action and reaction, which is known as karma. According to Sir Isaac Newton, in physics-the study of matter and energy-every action produces an equal and opposite reaction.

With the same force that you exert on your material, it is molecularly pushing you back with the same force you exert on it. The concept of karma is based on the belief that every mind thought, emotional, and physical act, no matter how insignificant in comparison to its impact on the individual, is projected into the soul substance and eventually returns with the same impact on the individual.

Every Hindu expects to work towards attaining moksha. Although he or she does not consider it to be a necessary part of this life, he or she does not expect it to come immediately.

A Hindu knows that this life is not the last and they don't try to deceive themselves into thinking that this is the last. Despite seeking and achieving profound spiritual realizations, they still understand that much work remains on earth and that only mature, God-realized souls can reach Moksha.

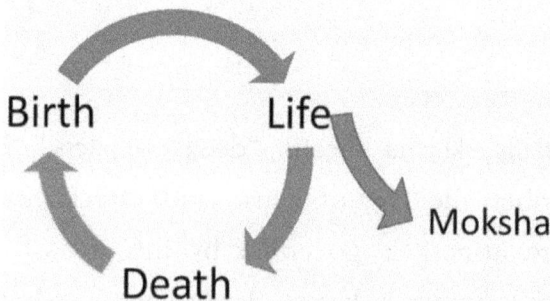

Birth Life

Moksha

Death

7

THE FOUR STAGES OF LIFE

◦∕∕◦

Hinduism believes that life is divided into four stages. Every man should ideally go through these stages, which are called "ashramas":

1. Brahmacharya – Bachelor, this is the student phase of life
2. Grihastha – Married life phase and duties of maintaining a Household

3. Vanaprastha – Retirement phase and handing over responsibilities to the next generation.
4. Sannyasa – Phase of giving up material desires and prejudices. Wandering Ascetic Stage

Brahmacharya – Bachelor, student phase of life

The guru provides formal education about art, warfare, science, philosophy, scriptures, etc. In the past, the average lifespan was 100 years, so this is the first quarter or 25 years of your life. A young male leaves home at this stage to study with a guru and gain spiritual and practical knowledge. He is called a Brahmachari. During this period and is prepared for his future profession.

Grihastha – The Married Family Man:

There is a second phase of one's life (between 25 and 50 years of age) that begins when one gets married and is responsible for taking care of his family and earning a living to support and raise his children. It is at this stage that Hinduism supports the pursuit of wealth (artha) and sexual pleasure (kama), provided certain social and cosmic norms are followed. During this period, the children of this man are in the Brahmacharya stage of development.

Vanaprastha – Retirement stage:

During this stage of a man's life, he no longer serves as a householder. A third stage of life occurs between the ages of 51 and 75 approximately. As the person moves into this stage, he or she hands over responsibility to the next generation. His children have grown up and established their own lives, and he has become a grandfather. His wealth, his security, and his sexual pleasures are all sacrificed at this age. If his wife is allowed to accompany him, he must maintain very little contact with his family during his stay. An elderly person is indeed forced to live a very harsh life because of this type of situation. There is no wonder why this third ashrama has become almost obsolete in recent years.

Sannyasa – The Wandering Recluse:

To achieve this stage, the man must give up all material desires and detach himself from all the material relationships in his life. It was supposed that he was devoted to God. As a sanyasi, he does not have a home, he does not have other attachments; he has renounced all desires, dreams, fears, hopes, duties, and responsibilities. As a result, his worldly ties are broken, all his worldly ties are broken, and his only concern becomes finding moksha, or liberation from the cycle of birth and death, and becoming one with God.

At this point in time, the previous generation has entered the Vanaprastha stage, whereas the generation that came before them has entered the Grihastha stage. There is no end to the cycle.

THE EPOCHS OF HINDUISM

ccording to Hindu cosmology, time is organized into cycles called "Yugas," which represent According to Hindu cosmology, time is organized into cycles called "Yugas," which represent different stages of the development of mankind as a society and as a culture. Each Yuga represents a different stage of this development. The Hindu epochs are grouped into four main Yugas, which are called the Mahyugas or Chatur Yugas. They are as follows:

The Yugas consist of four phases: Satya Yuga (golden age), Treta Yuga (silver age), Dvapara Yuga (bronze age), and Kali Yuga (iron age). As the moon waxes and wanes, the yugas follow a cyclical pattern.

Satya Yuga –

♦ According to Hinduism, it is the beginning of the Yuga cycle. It is also known as Satyug, which means the age of truth or sincerity.

♦ It is calculated to be the longest of all four Yugas, having been preceded by the Kali Yuga and followed by Treta Yuga.

♦ Truth and humanity were the hallmarks of this Yuga. It included knowledge, penance, and meditation.

♦ In this Yuga, work was at its purest. During this Yuga, the Sanatana Dharma (eternal religion) was established.

♦ Lord Vishnu takes an avatar in each Yuga; in Satyuga, he incarnates as Matsya, Kurma Varaha, and Narsimha.

♦ During this era, it is believed that the average human lifespan began at 100,000 years and then gradually decreased to 10,000 years.

♦ There would be no illness in this era. The personalities of the people did not clash. There were no flaws in each other's personalities, and no one suffered from sorrow, violence, ego, hatred, anger, lethargy, and jealousy.

Treta Yuga –

- This is the second of the four Yugas, also known as the Silver Age.

- The Satya Yuga precedes it, and the Dvapara Yuga follows it.

- Treta is a Sanskrit word that means "a collection of three things," so in this Yuga, people experienced three avatars of Vishnu were the fifth, sixth, and seventh, respectively, of the four avatars of the previous Yuga.

- Vamana, Parashurama, and Rama are the successive incarnations of Vishnu in Treta Yuga.

- During this Yuga, mining and agriculture were the essential factors of livelihood.

- Humanity became more focused on worldly possessions and less spiritual.

- Deserts and oceans were created by climate change so frequently and in such a ratio.

- The Treta Yuga saw virtue decline to a quarter of what it had been in the previous Yuga.

- There was a decrease in the average lifespan of humans from 1000 to 10000 years.

- It is important to note, however, that despite its seemingly adverse effects, this Yuga was also a source of knowledge about universal magnetism, which helped humans comprehend the true nature of the Universe and the forces of matter.

- In the Treta Yuga, Rama was Lord Vishnu's avatar in the Ramayana, one of the two major epics of Sanskrit literature.

Dvapara Yuga –

- During the Dvapara Yuga, also known as the Bronze Age, humankind was tainted with dark and evil qualities. Compared to their ancestors, they weren't as strong.
- Discontentment and fighting were common among humans. There was a widespread outbreak of diseases. It was common for humans to fight each other and to be dissatisfied.
- At this time, spiritual and divine beliefs also declined, and people became more competitive and pleasure-seeking as a result.
- Atharva Veda, Sama Veda, Rig Veda, and Yajur Veda were the four Vedas divided into four groups during Dvapara Yuga.
- No one was wholly truthful because divine knowledge and intellectual spirits ceased to exist.
- As a result, humanity was plagued by diseases, ailments, and other varied desires.
- Most Brahmins had a basic understanding of two or three Vedas, but it was rare for them to study all four Vedas in depth. Different actions and activities resulted from this distinction and categorization.

- Upon realizing their misdeeds, they would perform penance by organizing yugas to gain worldly benefit and divinity. Humans lived on average for a few centuries.
- Virtue and sin were divided equally during the Dvapara Yuga. The average human height was seven cubits, and the average lifespan was 1000 years.
- During the Dvapara Yuga, Mahabharata was the second of the two major epics in the Sanskrit language, after Ramayana.
- Lord Krishna, the eighth avatar of Lord Vishnu, was born during this era. Similar to any other avatar, He took this avatar to teach love and establish Dharma.

Kali Yuga –

- In Sanskrit, "Kali" means conflict, quarrel, or strife.
- The fourth Yuga, or Iron Age, is the worst of the four Yugas. This cycle is preceded by Dvapara Yuga and followed by Satya Yuga.
- According to Shastras and Vedas, Kali Yuga is characterized by conflicts and sins, and we are currently living in it.
- A Yuga associated with Kali is not to be confused with the Goddess Kali. Kali Yuga is known as "the age of Kali (demon)," "the age of vice and misery," "the age of darkness," or "the age of quarrel and hypocrisy."
- There is only one-quarter of virtue in the Kali Yuga, and the rest is taken over by sin.

- It refers to the reign of Kali, the demon, and Kalki, his nemesis, the tenth and final avatar of Lord Vishnu. According to the Vishnu Puran, Kali is the adverse manifestation that is working towards "the end" or rather towards the eventual rejuvenation of the Universe through entering the Satya Yuga.

- In Hinduism, Gautama Buddha is regarded as the ninth avatar of Lord Vishnu, which also occurred during the Kali Yuga.

- The average human lifespan is about 100 years, and human stature is reduced to 3.5 cubits. Human lifespan is expected to drop to 20 years by the end of this terrible Dark Age.

These Yugas are symbolic and not meant to be taken literally. Each Yuga presents unique challenges and opportunities for spiritual growth, reflecting the cyclical nature of human civilization and the understanding of time. There is also a larger unit of time known as a "Manvantara," which consists of 71 Mahayugas. Before the beginning of the next Manvantara, there is a transition period known as Sandhi Kala.

9

GOTRAS

Originally from Sanskrit, '*Gotra*' is believed to be equivalent to lineage in Hindu culture. As the term implies, it refers to the group of people who are related through an unbroken male line to a common male ancestor or patriline. A gotra describes one's ancestry and is an integral part of Hindu culture. Vedic scriptures are believed to have originated the concept of gotras. The concept of gotras is rooted in the Rigveda, one of Hinduism's oldest and most sacred texts.

Gotra is a Rigvedic term that simply means "cow pen" or "herd of cows." According to the Rigveda, the hymns contained in the text were composed by rishis (sages). Sages had disciples who followed their teachings and carried on their spiritual and social traditions. Eventually, these lineages evolved into the gotra system as society became more organized. According to mythology, each gotra represents a distinct lineage of descendants of a specific rishi.

There are several important functions served by the gotra system in Hindu society:

The primary function of gotras is to regulate marriage within Hindu communities.

Marriage within the same gotra is considered illegal by Hindu tradition because the gotra plays an important role in marriage. Genetic defects are often caused by marriage within the same gotra.

Identifying with a gotra also means identifying with its spiritual and cultural values. There is a shared heritage, customs, and traditions associated with the lineage of the rishi.

Knowledge of one's gotra may be important in certain situations, especially inheritance and legal disputes.

Ancestral lineage preservation: Gotras help preserve records of ancestral lineages, ensuring that individuals can trace their roots back to a specific rishi.

Brahmins first attempted to classify themselves into different groups through the concept of Gotra.

Some well-known gotras include:

- **Bhrigu**: Associated with the sage Bhrigu.
- **Vatsa**: Associated with the sage Vatsa.
- **Kashyapa**: Associated with the sage Kashyapa.
- **Gargya**: Associated with the sage Gargya.
- **Gautama**: Associated with the sage Gautama.
- **Vishwamitra**: Associated with the sage Vishwamitra.
- **Bharadwaja**: Associated with the sage Bharadwaja.
- **Katyayana**: Associated with the sage Katyayana.

There are many more gotras, each associated with its lineage and sage.

I believe it is important to point out that even though gotras hold significant cultural and social significance for traditional Hindu communities, their relevance and application may differ in modern times because of technological advancements. Within Hinduism, different sects and regions have different interpretations and practices related to gotras.

However, it was indeed a good way for our ancestors to avoid genetic diseases.

10

My Roots

❧

Bihar is a state located in the eastern part of India that is known for its rich history, culture, and contributions to Indian civilization. Bihar has some interesting aspects you might find interesting:

There is a great deal of historical significance to Bihar. It is associated with the Mauryan Empire, which was one of the first and most powerful empires in ancient India. It is believed to be the birthplace of Lord Buddha.

Buddhism is one of the world's most important religions, and Bodh Gaya is one of the most important pilgrimage sites for Buddhists all over the world. Siddhartha Gautama gained enlightenment and became the Buddha here.

University of Nalanda and Vikramshila: Among the oldest and most prestigious universities in the world, Bihar was home to Nalanda and Vikramshila. Scholars from different parts of the world flocked to these learning centers.

There is a rich cultural heritage in Bihar. It is known for its folk dances such as Jat-Jatin and Bidesia, and its traditional music such as Maithili and Bhojpuri.

There is something unique and simple about Bihari cuisine. There is a great deal of popularity for dishes such as litti chokha, sattu, tilkut, and khaja, among others.

The state of Bihar celebrates numerous festivals with great fervor. One of the most important festivals in the state is Chhath Puja, a festival dedicated to the Sun God.

Bihari languages such as Bhojpuri, Magahi, Maithili, and Angika are widely spoken there. A lot of people speak Hindi as well. It should be noted that Bihar has a strong literary tradition, with writers such as Ramdhari Singh 'Dinkar,' Phanishwar Nath 'Renu,' and Ram Vilas Sharma hailing from this state.

Bihar has several tourist attractions, including Rajgir, Vaishali, Patna Sahib, and Kesaria Stupa, in addition to Bodh Gaya. Several cultural heritage sites are in the state of Bihar, including the ancient ruins of Nalanda, Rajgir, and Vaishali, which offer a glimpse into the glorious past of the state.

In the Gaya District of Bihar State, Haridaspur is a small village or hamlet in Paraiya Block, where my father and forefathers belong. I strongly recommend that if you visit Bihar and explore its historical sites, cultural events, and natural beauty, you do so to reconnect with your roots. It is also beneficial to connect with local communities and learn more about their lifestyles.

11

About Kayastha

Kayastha- kaya- ('principal, capital, treasury') and -stha ('to stay')

Kayastha (also called a Kayastha) is an Indian community that can be broadly classified by the regions in which it was traditionally located on the Indian subcontinent—the Chitragupta Vansh Kayasthas of North India, Chandraseniya Kayastha Prabhus of Maharashtra, the Bengali

Kayasthas of Bengal, and the Karanas of Odisha. It is important to note that all of them were traditionally considered to be part of the "writing castes", who had traditionally served as administrators, ministers, and keepers of records for the ruling powers.

Kayastha origins are thought to be complex, and there are several theories concerning the historical background of this community, including the following:

Kayasthas are a hybrid caste with both Brahmin (priestly) and Kshatriya (warrior) lineages. Their original purpose was to perform administrative and record-keeping duties for the Kshatriya rulers, according to this theory.

Lord Chitragupta's creation of the Kayastha community: One of the prominent legends associated with the Kayastha community is the belief that the community was created by Lord Chitragupta, the divine accountant of the god of death, Yama (the god of creation). This legend says that Lord Chitragupta assigned various responsibilities to different groups of people, and the Kayasthas were responsible for record-keeping, writing, and administration.

In ancient texts, inscriptions, and documents, the Kayastha community is referred to historically. Kayasthas, for instance, is mentioned in ancient Indian dynasties like the Gupta Empire (4th to 6th century CE).

During the medieval period, the Kayastha community gained prominence as administrators, scribes, and accountants in several kingdoms and empires throughout India. As record keepers, financial managers, and administrative overseers, they played an important role.

I would like to point out that there are different interpretations of the history and origins of different communities, including the Kayastha, based on different sources and cultural perspectives, and therefore they may vary from one another. As time has passed, the Kayastha community has also diversified into a variety of sub-groups and sects, each with its own unique practices.

Various legends and historical interpretations surround the origin of the Kayastha community. In Hindu mythology, Lord Chitragupta, the divine accountant of the god of death, Yama, is one of the most prominent and widely accepted figures.

The legend goes as follows:

A long time ago, Lord Brahma, the creator of the universe, was in the process of creating the four Varnas (castes) - the Brahmins, the Kshatriyas, the Vaishyas, and the Shudras. He realized, however, that there was a need for a separate caste to handle administrative and record-keeping tasks. To fulfill this need, Lord Brahma created a new caste called the Kayastha. Chitragupta was created from a feather from his own body. As the divine accountant, Chitragupta was responsible for keeping track of each soul's deeds (both good and bad). To assist Chitragupta in his duties, Lord Brahma created the Kayasthas. Among their primary responsibilities was assisting Chitragupta with meticulously recording human actions. A variety of administrative functions were also assigned to them. It is traditional for the Kayasthas to wear the feather of Lord Brahma on their earlobes or as an ornament to symbolize their divine origins. As per this legend, the Kayastha community served various rulers and kingdoms in India as scribes, accountants, record keepers, and administrators over time.

Even though the legend has widespread acceptance, it is important to note that it is a mythical account of the origin of the Kayastha community. Several ancient texts, inscriptions, and documents also mention the Kayasthas, indicating their importance in the administration and clerical functions of ancient India.

According to some Hindu traditions and folklore, it is believed that Lord Chitragupta had two wives: Dakshin and Nandini. The Dakshin goddess is often revered as a separate entity and is associated with prosperity, wealth, and blessings. In various forms of worship and devotion, Dakshin is depicted alongside Chitragupta.

Nandini: Another name associated with Lord Chitragupta's wife is Nandini. Her symbolism is considered sacred and auspicious, often associated with abundance and fertility.

12 sons began to build a dynasty called Chitraguptavanshi Kayasthas, which is a branch of the Vansha (dynasty). These sons were Saxsena, Mathur, Gaur, Nigam, Asthana, Kulshrestha, Suryadwaja, Bhatnagar, Ambastha, Srivastava, Karna, and Valmiki.

12

THE 16 SANSKARS
IN KAYASTHA TRADITIONS

∽

"The 16 Sanskaras" are a set of life rituals or sacraments that are significant to Hinduism and mark various stages of a person's life from birth to death. It is important for a person's spiritual and social development to engage in these rituals. Even though the 16 Sanskaras are not exclusive to any caste, many Hindus, including those belonging to the Kayastha faith, follow them.

Several objectives are believed to be achieved by these rituals, including:

A Sanskara is said to facilitate the evolution and development of an individual's spirituality. In many Sanskaras, rituals are used to purify and cleanse the individual, both physically and spiritually. It is symbolic of new beginnings and purity to perform ceremonies like Namakaran (naming ceremony) and Annaprashan (first feeding of solid food).

Sanskaras play an important role in integrating individuals into their cultural and social communities. People establish a sense of belonging and identity within their communities by participating in these rites of passage.

Sanskaras are often used to impart moral and ethical values through teachings, prayers, and blessings. As a result, they serve to instill important principles and guide individuals in making ethical choices.

Upanayana (sacred thread ceremony) and Vivaha (wedding ceremony) mark the assumption of specific roles, duties, and responsibilities within society. A Sanskara is often accompanied by prayers and blessings from elders and religious figures. A blessing is believed to invoke divine protection, guidance, and support for the individual as they face life's challenges.

A Sanskara is performed with the belief that it will help align a person with nature and cosmic forces. Ceremonies like

Garbhadhan (conception) are performed to invoke positive cosmic energies for the unborn child's well-being.

An individual's connection with the divine is believed to be established through offerings, prayers, and rituals involved in Sanskaras. In this way, they serve as moments of spiritual communion and devotion. One's commitments and obligations are reminded by them.

In an individual's life, Sanskaras mark significant transitions and transformations. Symbolizing growth, maturity, and evolution, they symbolize the passage from one stage to the next.

Sanskaras are divided into 16 categories as follows:

- Garbhadhan is the first sacrament performed at conception. The prayer is intended to invoke blessings of health and virtue for the child.
- A Pumsavana is a ceremony conducted during pregnancy to ensure the well-being of the fetus.
- The Simantonnayana ceremony, also known as Godhbharai, is celebrated during the seventh month of pregnancy.
- The Jatakarma ritual is performed when a child is born. A newborn is protected, and well-being is assured through various ceremonies and prayers.
- Namakaran: This is a naming ceremony during which the child is given a name. Usually, it takes place 6 or 12 days after birth.

- The Nishkraman ritual involves taking the child outside for the first time, usually to a temple.

- A child's first solid food is known as Annaprashan. Around six months is the typical age at which it occurs.

- Chudakarana: This is the ritual of cutting the first hair of a child to purify him or her and promote healthy hair growth.

- In Karnavedha, the baby's ears are pierced, symbolizing the opening of spiritual channels.

- Vidyarambha is the beginning of formal education. A child is introduced to the alphabet or other forms of learning.

- The upanayana ceremony marks the beginning of a boy's formal education and spiritual learning.

- A wedding ceremony is called a Samavartana, which is also called a Vivaha or a Kanyadaan. As a married person, it marks the beginning of a new chapter.

- In Vanaprastha, a person gradually withdraws from worldly responsibilities and prepares for a life of contemplation and spiritual practice.

- In Sanyasa, attachments and responsibilities to the world are renounced to devote oneself to spiritual needs.

- The Antyeshti ceremony takes place after a person dies and is followed by cremation.

- Shraddha: It is a ritual performed to remember and honor deceased ancestors. Typically, it is done on special occasions or anniversaries.

In Hindu traditions, including among Kayasthas, these Sanskaras are considered essential for leading a well-rounded and spiritually fulfilling life.

Sanskaras form an integral part of Hindu culture and tradition. From generation to generation, they preserve and pass down ancient customs, rituals, and knowledge.

GARBHADHAN –
CEREMONY OF CONCEPTION

"Gifting womb" is known as Garbhadhan.

Hinduism recognizes 16 sacraments, including Garbhadhan. A child's conception is marked by this ceremony. Garbhadhan derives from the Sanskrit words garbha, which means womb, and dhan, which means donation or implantation. Prayers and rituals are performed during the Garbhadhan ceremony to invoke blessings for a healthy and virtuous child. It is commonly believed that the parents' atmosphere, thoughts, and actions at the time of conception can have a significant impact on the unborn child.

The Garbhadhan ceremony can be conducted in the following ways:

According to Hindu astrology and calendars, the ceremony is usually performed during an auspicious period.

Parents may invoke the blessings of deities associated with fertility, childbirth, and protection of the unborn child. Prayers may be offered to Lord Shiva, Goddess Parvati, Lord Vishnu, or specific forms of the Divine Mother. Invoking positive energies and seeking divine blessings may be achieved through the recitation of sacred mantras and chants by the parents and officiating priest. This sanskar is meant to bring harmony, respect, love, and a promise between the newlyweds to always respect and love each other.

The ceremony may include various offerings like flowers, fruits, and other symbolic items. Parents may pray for virtues such as wisdom, compassion, and strength for their children. During the ceremony, elders may offer their blessings for a healthy and virtuous child.

At the time of conception, a spiritually and morally wholesome environment is emphasized, and the ceremony emphasizes purity of thought, intention, and action.

Although Garbhadhan ceremonies are significant in Hindu tradition, their practices vary based on regional and cultural influences. Individual beliefs and preferences may also be considered in modern interpretations and practices. Garbhadhan is an auspicious and sacred event, representing the beginning of parenthood and the creation of a new life.

After the couple has been united in holy matrimony, this sanskara is performed. A human's first known rite begins before conception and is the first known act of a human being. To ensure newly married couples cleanse their minds of any negative thoughts, this ritual was enacted. Thus, causing problems during the conception process.

PUMSAVANA –

WELLBEING OF THE FETUS

$$\mathcal{C}\!\mathcal{P}\!\mathcal{O}$$

"Pumsavana" depicts the first bond between mother and child.

Pumsavana is one of the 16 Sanskaras (sacraments) in Hinduism, associated with the second trimester. The term "Pumsavana" is derived from Sanskrit, where "Pum" means male and "Savana" means to give birth. Pumsavana is a ritual aimed at ensuring the well-being of the fetus, with a particular focus on the development of male qualities.

The unborn child can be protected by the blessings of deities associated with fertility, childbirth, and childbirth.

According to Hindu astrology and calendars, the ceremony is usually performed during a specific period that is considered auspicious for the second trimester of pregnancy.

The ceremony emphasizes the importance of purity of thought, intention, and action during pregnancy, as it is believed that a morally and spiritually wholesome environment is beneficial to the baby.

In general, Pumsavana represents the care and attention given to an unborn child's well-being. Ensure that the mother's diet is healthy and balanced to promote proper fetal development. When a mother or family discloses pregnancy news to others.

SIMANTONNAYANA –
GODHBHARAI

⁂

G odhbharai, also known as Simantonnayana, is one of the 16 Sanskaras (sacraments) in Hinduism.

"Simantonnayana" derives from Sanskrit, where "Simanta" means parting of the hair, and "Upanayana" means leading.

Simantonnayana is a ceremony that celebrates both the mother and her unborn child's well-being. In addition to offering blessings and good wishes for a healthy delivery, friends and family come together to celebrate. After the seventh month, the baby and mother are believed to be in a safe phase. There are some families that celebrate it at the end of the eighth month.

Instead of a Godhbharai ceremony, some families perform a puja after the baby is born.

The Simantonnayana ceremony can be conducted in the following ways:

65

The ceremony is usually performed during the seventh month of pregnancy, which is considered an auspicious time for celebrating the mother and child's health. New clothes, jewelry, and other decorative items are traditionally presented to the mother on this Day. Parting her hair with a special comb symbolizes the opening of new energies and blessings.

It is common for the mother to be showered with gifts, such as clothes, jewelry, and items for the baby. The gifts are intended to express love and support for the expecting mother. Additionally, they may chant or recite specific mantras.

Celebrations and feasts: The guests are often provided with a festive meal or feast, which provides an opportunity for joyful celebrations and socializing.

Practices and rituals associated with Simantonnayana may vary from region to region and from culture to culture within Hinduism. This ceremony may have different customs and traditions in different communities.

During the late stages of pregnancy, the ceremony places a strong emphasis on the female reproductive system and the well-being of the mother, ensuring her comfort, happiness, and overall health throughout the process.

The mother and the unborn child are blessed and prayed for by family members and friends.

JATAKARMA –
THE NATAL RITES

⌘

Jatakarma is a ritual for *welcoming baby to this world*. It is derived from Sanskrit, where "jata" means "born" and "karma" means "ritual action" or "duty. Jatakarma literally means "the ritual of the born" or "the duty after birth".

Hindu rituals such as Jatakarma are performed shortly after a baby's birth. Specifically, this samskara refers to the bonding that occurs between a father and a newborn baby.

The purpose of Jatakarma is to protect the child from negative influences and ensure their healthy development.

The father performs this Sanskara before cutting off the newborn's umbilical cord. As part of the Jatakarma ritual, the father touches the baby's lips with honey and ghee to welcome him. The child's tongue is marked with ghee (clarified butter), and darbha grass is touched to their ears. The baby is wrapped in old clothes and only after chahthi/barhi pooja starts wearing new clothes. The first cloth for the baby is sent by the maternal family, which is what babies wear at their chahthi/barhi ceremony. Gifts are given to baby by his father or uncle who could do this ceremony in the absence of father.

NAMKARAN - CEREMONY FOR NAMING THE CHILD

❧

naming ceremony, also known as Namakaran Sanskar, is one of the most important Hindu rituals performed upon the birth of a child. During this ceremony, the newborn is formally named, which is a significant event in Hindu culture and is used to establish the child's individuality.

A Namakaran ceremony is usually performed on the sixth or twelfth day after a child is born, but regional customs and family preferences may vary. Parents choose a suitable name for their child in consultation with elders or priests. Names are often chosen carefully with religious or cultural significance in mind.

Ceremonies and rituals

Before the ceremony, the child and mother are usually bathed and dressed in clean, new clothes. To obtain the blessings of various deities for the well-being and prosperity of the child, offerings are made to them. Priests or family members chant Vedic hymns and mantras to invoke divine blessings.

Some traditions mark the tongue of the child with honey, ghee (clarified butter), or a mixture of honey and ghee. This is done to symbolize good fortune and sweet speech.

Family elders offer blessings and good wishes for the child's future, including parents, grandparents, and other relatives.

In celebration of the new phase in a child's life, he is often offered honey or some other sweet substance.

During the ceremony, the chosen name is announced and used for the first time. Recently, it has become very common to need the baby's name before discharging from a hospital, so this ceremony can also be performed in the form of Chahthi or Barhi.

The Namakaran Sanskar is a joyous and festive occasion that brings together family and friends to welcome the new member of the family and pray for their well-being and prosperity.

BIRTH CEREMONY - JANAM CHAHTHI/BARHI

When to perform this ceremony

When a baby is six days old (Chahthi) also, in a few Kayastha families, when the baby is 11 or 12 days old (also called as Barhi), this ritual is performed.

Significance of this ceremony

It was believed that on the 6th day after the birth of a child, Vidhaata (Goddess of destiny) would enter the house around midnight on the 6th day to write the destiny of the newborn on the baby's hand. This is a must celebration for all the babies except for when it needs to be celebrated.

Exception for celebrating this ceremony

Six days after the birth of the child, this ritual chahthi ceremony is performed. A child's religious functions are also performed after 27 days of birth when he or she is born in Gand Mool Nakshatra.

Interestingly, out of the 27 Nakshatras, six of them are Gand Mool Nakshatras. They are Ashwani, Jyeshta, Magha, Ashleha, Moola, and Rewati. According to their astrological significance, each of these Nakshatras has an impact on human life. A child born in Gand Mool Nakshatra is considered unlucky for the father, mother, maternal uncle, child, and maternal aunt. Shanti Prayog should be used to neutralize these ill effects. If a nakshatra repeats within 27 days, or multiples thereof, this should be done.

According to legend, Sant Tulsidas and Kabirdas were born under the Gand Mool nakshatra. Despite hardships in the beginning, they quickly gained popularity among the public.

In Bihar, a father is forbidden from seeing his child's face for 27 days (which is no longer possible).

It is also recommended that food be cooked with 27 different types of water at 27 different quantities. Panditjee should perform havan and ceremony.

POOJA INGREDIENTS

New clothes for newborn baby

New clothes for new born's mother

Gifts for Bua (Father's sister)

Sup or soop (The bamboo products used in rituals and are biodegradable)

Red color pen – 1

Blank white Paper - 2

Diya- metal - 1

Wooden Plank

Yellow Cloth

New clothes for baby

New clay Diya - 1

Cotton wick

Mustard seeds

Red color

Ceremony Rituals

- No need of fasting for this ceremony
- This ceremony is celebrated either in evening or night
- Nail cutting for baby and baby mom before pooja
- Place all food offering on a plate filled. Another 6 bowls fill with Yogurt, Ghee, Sugar, Kheer, Milk, Rice flour
- Mix rice flour/ wheat flour, haldi with water in a paste form and place 6/11 handprints by Bua on a yellow cloth and place on the wall near pooja place
- Wrap newborn baby in new clothes from maternal family and place on the sup and place near Pooja place
- Keep all food offerings near the newborn baby
- Bua needs to place kajal (steps to make this is below) to the baby's eye. A black spot is also applied to the baby's forehead in this ceremony to ward off evil.
- Light Ghee Deepak in pooja place
- Folk songs/geet are sung, and everyone enjoys dinner
- A cash gift or piece of jewelry is usually presented to the baby at this time. Relatives and friends are usually invited to celebrate the baby's birth.
- Next day all the offered food are given as prasad to family members

Kajal making process during ritual

This ceremony is done by Fua (Father's sister also called Bua) or by sister incase fua is not available.

Ingredients

Pure Ghee

2-4 saffron threads

4-6 Almonds

Sandalwood paste

1 tsp Ajwain Seeds

Cotton as wick / red cloth

Copperplate

Spoon

Empty container/ Kajroti

Almond oil

1 burning lamp

2-3 small bowls

Process for making the kajal -

Fill the burning lamp with pure Ghee and place the bowls on either side to support the copper plate after dipping the cotton in the sandalwood paste. Roll the sandalwood-clad cotton with the crushed almonds and ajwain seeds to form a wick. Now that the wick is lit, place it beneath the copper plate so that the soot can be collected. Once the wick is finished, carefully remove the copper plate, and scrap the black soot in an empty container or Kajroti.

Now, take a few drops of the Almond oil and mix it in the soot until you get the desired consistency.

Use this kajal to put on the baby and baby's mom.

TRADITIONAL FOOD ITEMS MADE FOR POOJA OFFERING

Dal puri, Pua, mixed vegetables or 5-7 types of vegetables, Mithai, Kheer and any vegetable food or rice can be offered and kept near the pooja place.

In addition, fish is also made for this ceremony.

NISHKRAMAN – FIRST OUTING FOR SHOWING THE SUN

❧

Nishkraman literally means "going out, coming forth."

Nishkraman is a Hindu ceremony that celebrates a child's first outdoor experience. Hinduism considers it to be one of the most important samskaras (rites of passage). The ceremony marks the child's formal introduction to the outside world.

When should Nishkraman be performed:

Nishkraman is typically performed when the child is a few months old, usually in the third or fourth month. Family preferences and regional customs may determine the specific timing.

In the Nishkraman ceremony, the child is blessed and protected from natural elements and external influences as they step out into the world for the first time.

Children and parents are usually bathed and dressed in clean, new clothes before the ceremony.

First-outing offerings are made to various deities to seek their blessings for the child's safety, health, and prosperity. As a child observes and hears things in this world, impressions are formed in his or her mind. As a result of this ritual, the baby's mental development begins.

Priests and family members chant Vedic hymns and mantras to invoke divine blessings.

To experience the world beyond the home for the first time, the child is taken outdoors, often to a local temple or a place of natural significance. A child's well-being is blessed by the elders in the family.

As a symbol of this new experience, the child may be offered a taste of honey or another sweet substance.

As soon as the child returns home, the ceremony is complete.

It symbolizes the child's first steps into the external world and is a significant event for the family. In this moment of joy and celebration, family members come together to offer blessings and good wishes for the child's future.

ANNAPRASAN –

FIRST FEED WITH SOLID

$$\sim$$

"Introduction to solid foods"

In Sanskrit words "Anna," which means food, and "Prasan," which means initiation.

An Annaprasan ceremony is performed when the baby's first teeth begin to appear or when the child is six months old.

When a baby eats solid food for the first time, typically cooked rice, it marks his or her introduction to solid foods. The baby has so far only been nourished by breast milk. The purpose of this ceremony is to bring the child good health, radiance, and physical strength.

Steps for this ceremony -

- ◆ This ritual is done on 4th month of baby birth
- ◆ It is auspicious to do Satyanarayana pooja on this day. Date can be consulted by Panditjee.

- During the ceremony, the baby is dressed in traditional attire, and a small blessing is performed to seek blessings from the deities. Parents also wear new clean clothes for the ceremony.
- Kheer is prepared and in a katori (silver or steel made bowl) and with a spoon Panditjee or family elder feeds kheer to the baby
- Later all the elders and family members feed the baby the same kheer

Ingredients -

- A silver spoon and silver bowl for the baby to lick food
- Kheer made of rice or Rava (Suji)
- Honey
- Ghee
- Holy Basil leaves (Tulsi)
- Holy Ganga water

Annaprasan items should be chosen very sincerely. After all, the baby is fed for the first time. Indian Rice Kheer recipe is exclusive for baby's Annaprashan Ceremony. Milk and rice are the Kheer ingredients.

Fun games to be played -

The religious ceremony is often followed by a fun game where several symbolic items are placed on a banana leaf or a silver tray which your baby can then pick from.

The objects include:

- ◆ books symbolizing learning
- ◆ jewels symbolizing wealth
- ◆ a pen symbolizing wisdom
- ◆ clay symbolizing property
- ◆ food items symbolizing a love for food

Family and friends have a great time cheering the little one while he makes his choice. It is believed that the object your baby picks up from the tray represents his area of interest in future.

CHUDAKARAN –
ARRANGEMENTS OF
THE HAIR TUFT

❧

A child's first haircut is called '*mundane sanskara'*.

The sanskara represents a new phase of life, where the baby's hair is cut and his nails are trimmed, symbolizing cleansing, renewal, and growth. In addition to enhancing our appearance, the hair on our heads protects us from harmful elements in the environment. As a result of this sanskara, new hair grows that is strong and clean.

This ritual is performed when a child is in an odd year 1,3,5. The ceremony can be held on any auspicious day or family wedding provided by Panditjee.

Women who have (worshipped kuldevi-Milan) prepare food offerings with a lot of cleanliness and prasad is prepared early in the morning. The women preparing the food should take bath and wear new clothes. The food offerings include dal puri and kheer. The mango leaves should be placed on top of the thali near the pooja place, followed by dal puri and kheer. The number of diyas lit are 7,11 or 21 in count. Only family members of the father's family (same Kul) consume this offered prasad. Rest family members can have other food or prasad.

Mundan ceremony process

- The day begins with Kul-devata/devi pooja performed by the elderly woman of the house
- Both mom and kid wear new clothes
- Ideally, the barber comes to the house. Alternatively, the mother and Bua go to the salon and Bua cuts the first strand of hair.
- Hair is later removed from the kid's head by the barber. A strand of hair is left on the boy's head, while the full head of hair is shaved on the girl. Save the strand of hair as a keeper for the kid.
- Bua applies haldi and yogurt to the kid's head later at home.
- It is time for the kid to take a shower and put on new clothes
- Gifts are given to Bua
- Satyanarayana pooja can be done as well.
- Remaining other prasad is taken by all invitees with food.
- Songs and dance can be performed.

KARNAVEDHA –
PIERCING THE EARLOBES

❦

arnavedha is a Hindu ritual in which a child's ears are pierced, also known as *Karnavedham or ear-piercing*. In Sanskrit, the word "Karnavedha", which translates to piercing the ear, derives from the words "karna" which means ear and "vedha" which means piercing.

It is typically performed during early childhood, usually before a child turns one year old, and is considered significant in Hindu culture. In addition to its cultural and religious significance, the ceremony is believed to have several benefits as well.

Karnavedha is a deeply ingrained cultural tradition in Hinduism that is performed as a rite of passage for children.

It is believed that piercing the ears at specific points can promote general well-being and maintain a balance of bodily energies. Karnavedha is also performed for aesthetic reasons in addition to cultural and religious significance. There is a scientific explanation for this sanskara as well. Acupressure points are located on the ear lobes. Many neurologists have shown that the earlobes and the brain's hemispheres are connected through intensive research. Therefore, piercing ears helps in developing intelligence and enhancing immunity against respiratory infections, hernias, and hydrocoele.

Piercing the ears is considered to enhance spiritual and sensory perception by some.

In many Indian cultures, earrings are considered an essential part of traditional attire as a form of adornment.

According to regional customs and preferences, the ceremony is usually conducted by a priest or a knowledgeable elder in the family. Generally, ear piercing involves chanting mantras, observing certain rituals, and piercing the ear.

Although Karnavedha is a common practice in Hindu culture, it may not be followed by all Hindus, and practices may vary according to individual beliefs and regional customs. To gain a deeper understanding of cultural or religious practices, always consult with knowledgeable sources or spiritual leaders.

VIDYARAMBHA –
LEARNING THE ALPHABET

❧

"Start of the learning venture"

Vidyarambha, also known as Aksharabhyasa, marks the beginning of a child's formal education in Hinduism. Vidyarambha is derived from the Sanskrit words "vidya" (knowledge) and "arambha" (beginning), meaning "beginning of learning."

Depending on regional and familial customs, this ceremony is typically performed at the age of three or five. The ceremony is considered auspicious and is conducted with great reverence. Vidyarambha primarily aims to introduce a child to the process of learning, particularly in the context of the alphabet and basic mathematics.

The Vidyarambha ceremony generally consists of the following

Usually, the ceremony begins with the child seeking blessings from elders, especially from the family's spiritual leader. Saraswati is the goddess of knowledge and learning in Vedic tradition. During Saraswati Puja, a puja (worship) is performed to the Hindu goddess of knowledge, music, arts, and learning. For the child to have a successful and prosperous educational journey, devotees seek her blessings.

On a bed of uncooked rice or sand, the child is guided to write the first few letters of the alphabet or a simple mantra (such as "Om" or a relevant verse from a sacred text). An elder or a teacher may guide a child's finger. The role of a mentor in the child's education can be emphasized when a respected teacher or elder helps the child write the first letters.

The distribution of Prasad, which is blessed food or other offerings, signifies the divine blessings for the child's education. Vidyarambha is a cultural and religious event for many Hindu families, and it is believed to prepare a child for formal education.

UPANAYANA –

LEARNING THE ALPHABET

❧

'*Upa'* means '*close'*, while '*Nayana'* means 'to *bring'*. An upanayana is a sacred Hindu ritual that marks the beginning of formal education and spiritual initiation for a young boy. "*Thread initiation*" or "*sacred thread ceremony*" are other names for it. Upanayana literally means bringing closer to the guru or Divine.

A sacred thread is worn diagonally across the boy's body during the Upanayana ceremony (usually made of cotton or a specific type of thread). The boy's pursuit of knowledge, spiritual growth, and the beginning of a new phase in his life are symbolized by this thread. A child's intellectual and mental development is recognized as being the supreme sanskara in it.

A qualified priest performs the ceremony, which consists of chanting mantras (sacred verses), offering offerings to the fire (agni), and receiving blessings from elders. It is expected that the boy will begin formal education after this ceremony, particularly in Vedic scriptures and other sacred texts.

Historically, Upanayana was associated with boys of certain castes, but in modern times, there has been a shift towards inclusivity, and families from diverse backgrounds may choose to perform Upanayana.

PRAISHARTHA:
FIRST STUDY OF THE VEDAS

In Vedic terminology, Vedrambha or Praishartha means 'beginning of Vedic studies'

Vedarambha signifies the initiation of Vedic study, as opposed to Upanayana, which marks the start of education. According to his lineage, each student masters one of the Vedas in this sanskara. This is also called: Vidya sanskar/ Upanayana Sanskar / Khali Chuhana.

This ritual is done when kid is 4.5 - 5 years old

Procedure

The child wears new clothes on this day. Preferred color is yellow, and I avoid colors like black or total white outfit.

The kid sits on a stool. Panditjee or any elder of the family makes kids write on slate with chalk/paper-pen. Upon completion of the ritual, all women in the house give the baby a gift.

All the guests give their blessings and place aachhat (white rice) on the child.

The kid receives blessings from all God and then from all the elders.

Everyone eats later (lunch/dinner)

Keshanta/ Ritushuddhi: Cutting the hair

The word 'kash' means hair, while the word 'anta' means end. In this sanskara, the student first shaves his beard after reaching maturity, typically when he has a small amount of hair on his face. When a girl starts her menses for the first time, the Ritushuddhi ceremony is performed.

From childhood to adulthood, the sanskara marks a significant transition. This is the point in life when the student acknowledges the changes that have occurred both psychologically and physically.

Samavartana - Graduation ceremony

'Completion of graduation'

Samavartana, also known as graduation or returning home ceremony, is a Hindu ritual that marks the completion of formal education, typically associated with the end of Vedic studies.

It is often considered the counterpart to the Upanayana ceremony, which initiates a boy into formal education. Samavartana marks the completion of that education. A student's transition into adulthood and life outside of the classroom is an important event in their life.

The Samavartana ceremony is performed for the purpose of seeking blessings from parents, teachers, and elders. As part of the ceremony, gifts may be presented to the teacher, the sacred thread may be ceremonially removed, and prayers for the student's success in the future may be offered.

In old times, it meant returning home from the house of the acharya. Earlier, when the gurukul system was the norm, students left their guru and gurukul after completing their studies. Samavartana sanskara refers to this departure. It signified that the student was ready to move on to the next stage of his or her life.

Regional and family traditions can affect the specific customs and rituals associated with Samavartana. Although Samavartana has deep roots in Hindu tradition, its practice may vary in modern times, and not all families will observe it in the same way.

VIVAHA -

MARRIAGE CEREMONY

❧

Hinduism's most important sanskara is vivaha, which means marriage. The wedding rituals and ceremonies generally begin with the engagement of a couple and end with the Homam or Nishekam ceremony. There are several days of colorful celebrations.

Do you know anything about Bihari Kayastha weddings?

If so, then you're already aware of its vibrant and colorful nature! Traditional and rustic weddings are very popular among Biharis. Soon-to-be married couples are required to observe a variety of rituals. A traditional Indian wedding involves several colorful ceremonies that reflect the true spirit of the bride and groom's families.

In earlier times, weddings took place over a month and were celebrated as a long festival by the groom and bridegroom's families. However, due to the constraints of modern time, the duration has been reduced, but the customs and rituals remain.

There are three main categories of Hindu wedding rituals in Bihar - pre-wedding rituals, marriage rituals, and post-wedding rituals.

Kuldevta/Kuldevi pooja -The first wedding card is presented to Kuldevta/devi/ or any Isht devta who is worshipped. When possible, it is recommended to perform the pooja at Kuldevta or Kuldevi' s place where they are worshiped, otherwise, the process can be performed at a temple as well.

Pre-Wedding Rituals
and Ceremonies

Satya Narayan Katha

The Satyanarayana Katha is an integral part of any Bihari wedding. The bride's parents organize this Katha. Everyone from the groom's side takes part in the elaborate prayer service or pooja. Priests narrate Kathas and light havens. The diya remains lit during the entire marriage ceremony.

Cheka Ceremony

A formal engagement ceremony is held at the bride's home. After consulting an astrologer, either 7, 9 or 11 members accompany the groom on a visit to the bride's house. During the exchange of rings, the groom's parents visit the bride's house with him. During this visit, they carry a lot of gifts or shagun like jewelry, clothes, dry fruits, and sweets. After both families have settled down, the bride and groom exchange rings. On the following day, the groom's family and the bride visit the groom's house with rings and shagun. On this day, they exchange rings, and this ritual is known as Cheka, which is the exchange of rings on this day.

HALDI KUTAI CEREMONY

Following the engagement, the Haldi ceremony takes place.

During the Ubtan ceremony, married women (suhasinis) grind turmeric into a paste for application to the bride's body.

Women sing traditional and popular songs during the grinding of turmeric, creating a festive atmosphere. The bride's house also holds a similar ceremony.

The entire process of beautifying the bride is called Haldi Kutai.

TILAK

Visiting the groom's house: The bride's brother visits the groom's house to mark the marriage alliance's acceptance with a Tilak Thaal. By doing this, the bride's family shows that the alliance has been accepted. The bride's brother is accompanied by an accountant, barber, laundryman, and other servants.

To celebrate the alliance, the bride's brother applies tilak to the groom's forehead, then gifts him jewelry, clothes, and sweets. As part of the puja ceremony, Turmeric (Haldi) is placed on the groom and made to sit in the puja ceremony wearing yellow dhoti. The yellow dhoti is sent by the family of the bride. Additionally, he gives him Haldi paste and the groom's wedding day clothes. As part of the formal send-off, a lavish dinner is served along with gifts for the bride's family, the special bridal attire, the Nath (nose ring) and maang tikka (part of bridal jewelry worn on the forehead).

Process from Bride side - 5-7 members (1 pandit, 1-2 servants) and 3,5,7(any odd number) Brother and any other male family members are sent to the groom's family.

Below items are sent along with the family: 5 or 7 Pudiya – sindoor placed on newspaper and folded with red thread (mouli)

Groom's clothes, dhoti/suit, bedsheet, gold ring, copper bowl (kasa) or silver (chaandi) ka katora, paan, Dhan – 5 kg, Haldi, kasauli, Patmori, sweets and any other furniture, bed, cooking set, Almirah (if applicable)

Process from Groom side as return items -lagan clothes are sent from groom's family along with multiple gifts for bride

Sweets and or fruits

MANDAPPACHADAN

It is during this Bihari wedding ritual that the mandap, or the wedding altar, is set up. As part of a Bihari wedding, bamboos are usually used for the construction of the mandap, and banana trees and mango leaves are used to decorate it.

Setting up pandal: Traditionally, a mandap (pandal) is set up in the courtyard for the wedding. A Mandappachadan is usually composed of bamboo and decorated with mango leaves and banana trees, but it is no longer popular today with modern facades with decorated lights and large canopies. A traditional house, however, consists of a mandap with harish (a symbol of good agriculture) made of wood in the center.

HALDI

During the wedding ceremony, the groom's family and friends apply the paste made by the bride's mother to the groom, while the bride's relatives and friends apply Haldi made by the groom's mother on the bride. This ritual is performed by married women.

Dhritdhaari & Matripooja

Seeking the blessings of elders, ancestors.

This ritual is performed by the bride and groom's parents to seek blessings from their departed ancestors and elders. To ask for forgiveness from the ancestors, parents (both sides) offer money or clothes called Paun-pooji on this auspicious day. In addition to the elders of the family, Paun-pooji (clothes for elders or any cash) is offered to them.

Silpoha and Imli Ghutai

Rice grinding ritual - Silpoha ceremony is otherwise known as the rice grinding ritual that is done as soon as the sun comes out on the marriage day. An elderly married woman or the groom's mother grinds rice wrapped in a shawl (chunni) on a flat stone (Silbatta) to obtain blessings from the gods and elders for a trouble-free wedding at the dawn of the wedding day. In this rice grinding process called silpoha, she is also accompanied by other female relatives.

Bihari Wedding
Day Rituals and Ceremonies

Mor-Mukat Ritual

On the day of the wedding, this ceremony is performed by the husband of the sister. Mor-Mukat is placed on the groom. Thereafter, a gift or money is given to the brother-in-law. Groom takes blessings from God and elders and sits in the car to leave with baraat.

Imli Ghutai

Warding off evil eyes

To ward off the evil eye or Buri Nazar, Imli Ghutai is performed. Imli Ghutai is a ritual performed to ward off bad omen performed by the groom's maternal uncle (or aunt). During the Bihari wedding ritual, the groom's maternal uncle or mama advises him to refrain from common vices and habits. He then gives the groom a betel nut, which he holds with his teeth, and his mother removes it, only to eat it herself in a symbolic gesture that she will put up with any aspersions directed at her son. As a token of appreciation, the groom's uncle or aunt presents him with clothes.

BARAAT PRASTHAN

On the day of the Bihari wedding, the mother of the groom performs Paricchavan or aarti. The whole ritual is conducted before the Baratis leave for the wedding. During aarti, the mother also applies tilak on the groom's forehead. And prays for a happy married life for the couple. The mother blesses her son for a great beginning of a married life and this ritual is called Paricchavan.

DECORATED CARAVAN

The groom is taken around in a well-decorated car, usually accompanied by his younger brother (the sahwala).

In Baraat Prasthan, the groom and his family leave for the wedding venue. The groom's car is decorated elaborately with flowers. The car with the groom and his younger brother leaves first and is followed by the rest of his family and relatives.

Once the Baraat (groom and his family) reaches the venue, they are welcomed by the bride's parents and family with garlands. In the meantime, the priest applies tilak to the groom seated in the car and guides him out. In addition, the bride's father/brother escorts the groom to the wedding venue.

JAIMALA & GALSEDI

After the groom and bride have arrived at the wedding venue, they both perform aarti for each other and exchange garlands, known as Jaimala, to the cheers and applause of the large crowd.

Once the garlands are exchanged, a Galsedi ritual is conducted by the bride's mother and other 5-7 married women for 5 times using left hands. The women heat up the betel leaves in a lamp and burn it to ashes. This ash is then smeared on the groom's face. Then, cow dung is thrown behind the groom. This is done in a sequence.

The groom is usually escorted to the altar by his brother (or brother-in-law), while the bride wears a yellow silk saree without jewelry.

The priest ties bracelets made of mango leaves, cotton thread, turmeric, colored rice, and money on the couple's right hand for four days. As part of this elaborate ritual called Kangna bandhana, the barber cuts the couple's fingernails and toenails.

A bride donation ceremony involves the bride's father, mother, groom, and bride placing their right hands palm to palm. In addition, the bride will hold a conch.

Kangnabandhana and Kanyadaan

As soon as the ceremony is over, Kanyadaan occurs, which is the ceremony of the bride's parents giving her over to the groom.

Bhaisur Nirakshan, Kuldevta Puja & Pheras

Bhaisur nirakshan is the ritual of gifting saris, jewelry, and lehengas to the bride by her husband's elder brother or bhaisur. During this ceremony, the bride receives the family jewelry.

In a ritual called Bhaisur Nirakshan, the duo (brother-in-law or father-in-law) bless the bride, give her saris and lehengas while wearing handkerchiefs or big caps. In the end, she receives all the family jewelry given by her mother-in-law.

During the Kuldevta puja, the bride and groom attend pujas on family deities wearing a new saree and jewelry.

Circumambulation of sacred fire: In a soop (), the bride throws lava (roasted husked rice) l) into the sacred fire as they circle it. The soop is periodically refilled by her brother. This ritual is called pheras.

As soon as this ritual has been completed, ghee is applied on the bride's maang and the groom applies sindoor to the bride's forehead, starting at the topmost point of her nose and moving down to the parting of her hair. While performing this act, the bride closes her eyes five times.

To conclude the wedding rituals, the groom ties the Mangal sutra (also known as taagpaag or dholna patwasi) around the bride's neck, and they retire to their decorated bridal chamber.

POST BIHARI WEDDING CEREMONY

Kohwar Parikshan, Salami & Vidaai

Next morning, the couple bathes early and dresses up for Kohwar Parikshan. The married ladies of the family check whether the couple has solemnized their marriage. Post meal, salami is offered to the groom by the elders either in cash or in kind. To bring his wife to his house, the groom seeks permission from his wife.

A bedecked car accompanies the newlyweds as they say farewell to the bride's brother. As part of the Vidaai ritual, family members and relatives shower them with flowers and colored rice.

Before leaving for the groom's house, the car moves forward and backward thrice to ward off evil eyes.

As per Hindu rituals, Vidaai marks the completion of the wedding. Hindu weddings include this emotional event. After marriage, the bride steps out of the house with teary eyes in Vidaai. The bride keeps throwing a handful of rice over her head as she moves towards the house's gate. Rice is thrown five times. Rice thrown backwards signifies wealth and prosperity even after the departure of Goddess Laxmi (girls are considered Goddess Laxmi in Hinduism).

As a result of this ritual, the girl also pays back what she took from her parents all these years ago. Her brothers and cousins push the bride's car as she leaves in a car/vehicle, symbolizing their support as she begins a new life with her partner. To ward off evil spirits, people throw money on the road after starting the car. Different parts of the state refer to this event by different names. Despite this, it is a very important ceremony everywhere in the country.

WELCOMING BRIDE

Swagratri, Mooh Dikhai and Chauthari

Placing paan patta, Diya, sindoor, and performing parchan in a thalli is essential.

The newlyweds are welcomed home by the womenfolk of the groom's family with an aarti (Swagat aarti) and flowers (Akshat).

Dwar Rokai

At the entrance, there is a copper vessel filled with rice, an Alta plate, and two cane baskets. By pushing this with her right foot, the bride then steps on the Alta plate and then places her feet in the cane baskets.

When the bride enters her new home with her husband, the Dwar Rokai ceremony takes place. It is a fun ceremony in which the bride's sister-in-law prevents the bride and her brother from entering the house. In this way, they can ask for a gift. Whether it is cash or ornaments, the present could be anything. In essence, the groom must present his sisters with a gift, such as cash or a precious item, for the bride and groom to be allowed entry into the house.

She receives a pair of gold bangles, money, and other gifts from her in-laws in mooh dikhai.

Dahi Badi ritual: When she reaches the main door of the house, she ties dhaga on her wrist with dahi ka chuka. Dahi ka chuka is held by the groom.

Having sought God's blessings. Dahi badi ritual takes place. A coin is placed in the Dahi chuka. The bride gives the coin to her elder brother-in-law and he places it back in the pot. After this is done 5 times, Brother-in-law must take the coin and stick it to the roof wall with the help of a stick.

As soon as they complete the grih pravesh ritual, they proceed directly to the mandav.

The bride and groom are welcomed by placing warmed betel leaves on newly weds cheeks 5 times on both sides(parchaned) and later the pachisi game is played. Chumona(ritual where bride and groom are made to sit and with white rice and turmeric and money are rotated on them 5 times. It starts with touching their feets, knee, shoulder, and head) and is done by all adults. The money collected is kept by the newly wed. its customary for the bride to eat 5 types of vegetables, kheer, dalpuri, dahi, and rice for dinner.

The bride and groom are sent to their bedroom and the doors are closed.

Chauthari

To thank God for a successful Bihari wedding, Chauthari or Satyanarayana puja is performed after Mooh Dikhai. She has now been accepted into their family as an integral member.

To mark the culmination of marriage proceedings, a thanksgiving puja with a Satyanarayana Katha is performed.

Chauka Chulai

Chauka Chulai. is the last wedding ritual in the Bihari community. As part of this ceremony, the bride receives the house keys. It marks the passing of responsibility from her mother-in-law to her.

Additionally, the bride must prepare five dishes. After the meal, the elders shower the bride with gifts or shagun. Bihari weddings are generally considered to be elaborate affairs. It is a period of colorful rituals steeped in tradition and culture.

Pag Phera

The term "Pag Phere" literally means "return of the foot," which symbolizes the bride returning to her parental home. It strengthens both the bonds between the bride and her family, as well as those between the two families involved in the marriage.

Post-wedding rituals such as Pag Phere are prevalent in Hindu culture, especially in North India. During this ritual, the bride returns to her parents' home for a short visit after her wedding. She can spend quality time with her family and reconnect with them. It is symbolic of the bride's continuing relationship with her natal family after she moves to her husband's house. In Pag Phere, the bride's parents perform a special puja (prayer ceremony) to ensure their happiness and prosperity. There may be festive celebrations with family and friends, as well as gifts and blessings exchanged.

ANTYESHTI – FUNERAL

Hindu's last sanskara is Antyeshti, which is performed by their relatives after one die. Human souls take rebirth after leaving the old body, according to Hindu scriptures and the Bhagavad Gita. Brahmin priests perform the final rituals meticulously. On the eleventh day after mourning for ten days, a purification ceremony is conducted. It is customary to hold a feast on the thirteenth day of the year to indicate that the soul has crossed over and has finally reached its final resting place.

When any death happens in the family. Below are the rituals which need to be followed. The Dead person needs to be placed on the floor. Head should be placed north and Ganga jal is placed on the floor in rotation. Place Dhoop near that person.

Death of any female family member

13 days rituals take place

First day: Person who cremates can take rice and milk

Second day: Person who lit fire on the dead family members would eat only fruits on the day and only sweet food needs to be taken. No salt intake. This is done until the 9th day.

Seventh day: Whole house cleaning is done, and all family members take shower

Before tenth day Oil, haldi or no food with sizzling is done. No hair cutting or nail cutting to be done.

On the tenth day: Hair cutting done by all male family members. Food with haldi and oil are allowed. Start the food with kala Channa and sharbat. Khasedi saag is eaten by all in the evening. Food should be served to any barber and dhobi and then to all.

On the eleventh day: Fasting food during the day. Pind Daan is also done on this day.

On twelfth day: Garur Purana is read, and food is offered to Pandit Ji. After 3 days do Pind Daan.

Pitrapaksha Mela

In September, Gaya hosts this mela every year. As part of the Shraddha ritual, people from all over the country attend this fair to worship their ancestors. Shraddha is performed by the gayalis(descendants of the Magga Brahmans). In Hinduism, this ritual is mandatory to bring salvation to the departed. The tradition dates to Buddha, who performed the first pindan here.

Cremation rituals such as Pind Daan follow the cremation of an individual. After the death of a loved one, Hindus believe that Pind Daan is a must. Among the followers of Hinduism, it is the most significant, the most vital, and the most mandatory ritual of the entire life cycle. This ritual has a lot of importance, so let's discuss it.

Importance of Pind Daan

To guide a departed soul to salvation, this ritual is performed. If this activity is performed, the soul will not have to suffer the tortures of hell nor fall into the cycle of rebirth. Being the soul of a person who had materialistic inclinations makes it difficult for him to leave the earth, his relatives, and his possessions. Trying to achieve feelings that aren't possible for his form, the soul dwells around unsatisfied and unhappy. In this way, Pind Daan will show enlightenment to the soul and lead him to Moksha, which is freedom from the eternal cycle of life, death and rebirth. In Hindu culture, Pind Daan is performed in a holy river. Based on their capacities and beliefs, people choose the location for this ritual. Gaya is the most prominent place where this activity gives the best results. For pind daan, the Pitru paksha period is also considered auspicious.

Why is Gaya considered to be most sacred?

In mythology, God Rama Chandra performed Pind Daan for his father Dasharatha at Gaya. Gaya asur, the demon who was granted the wish by God Vishnu to be known as the origin of the most sacred place, is also well known. Vishnupad temple is the most sacred Vishnu temple in Gaya, making it the most sacred place for Pind Daan. People who worship Vishnu's footprint present in the temple and sacrifice the ash of their ancestors in Gaya are given the power to attain salvation, according to the Purana.

PIND DAAN

The Vedas and religious Granthas outline three major categories of Rin that must be fulfilled.

- PitraRin
- DevRin
- Rishi Rin

There are certain procedures which are conducted to complete these Rin rituals.

For PitraRin

- Antyeshti Sanskar or the Funeral Ceremony:
- Its root word means "Last", and its root word means "Sacrifice". Funeral rites are performed for the dead. In most cases, it is called "Antim Sanskar". By following certain Vedic rituals, the body of the dead is burned.
- Asthi Visarjan or the Flowing of ashes of the funeral in Holy Ganges
- In a copper vessel, the ash collected during the Antyeshti ceremony is stored. The ash is allowed to flow in the river Ganga according to the appropriate time and date.

- Sradha or the Feasting ceremony for the remembrance of the deceased person:
- Food offerings and prayers for peace are invited for those who know the deceased. Priests are invited for food and Dakshina offerings from the Brahmins, who are the caretakers of God.
- Vedic Karma Kanda
- Rudrabhishek
- Yagya

For Rishi Rin

- Seva Satkar
- Daan

In contrast, Rishi Rin and DevRin can be integrated into your daily routine, but PitraRin requires a separate time commitment and attention.

Appropriate day for performing Pind Daan

A Pind Daan ritual is performed on the banks of Gaya throughout the year, but there is a specific time that is the most auspicious. Amavasya is most significant during the months when there is Krishna Paksh during the auspicious Pitru-Paksha Mela held for 18 days. These rites are performed here by large numbers of people.

Following are the rituals as part of the Shradh or PindDaan rite performed in Gaya Ji that includes: -

- Snana and Sankalpa: Before performing Pind Daan, take a bath in the holy Ganges River.

- PindDaan: Worship of departed souls and ancestors.

- Tarpan:

- During this act, the closest relatives make a sacred offering to God so that the soul may enter Swarga. Tarpan is also known as Arghya, in which an offering is made to all 5 Devas and Navagraha. Tila Tarpan is performed using water and sesame seeds during Pitru Paksha.

There are various sets of rites which are supposed to be performed depending on the type of death.

Ekodrishti Gaya Shradh

This is performed in a day. For Ekodrishti Shradh you need to cover only three important vedis i.e., Falgu River, Vishnupad Temple, and the Akshavata.

If the death is unnatural then you need to visit Pretshila, Gayakup, and Dharmaranya.

Vrihada Gaya Shradh

This requires more time, and one needs to visit 54 Vedis or locations.

Poonpooncharan Puja, Falgu River, Vishnupada, Brahma Kunda, Pretshilla, Ram shilla, Ram Kund, Kartikpada, Mat Gowapi, MundaPristha, Jiwha Loll, Kagbali, Ganeshpada, Ram Gaya, DhudTarpan, Uttarmanas, Amarasichen, Sandyanagnipada,

Sitakund, Baitarni, Udichi, Rudrapada, Yagnipada, Souvagyadan, Akshoybata, Kankhal, Brahmapada, Dadhisthipada, Gayasir, GayatriGhat, DakhinManas, Kannapada, Gayakup, Kopada, Agasthapada, Indarapada, kashyapapada, Gajakaran, Dadhigagni, Ahabaniagni, suryapada, saraswati , gajhadarji, dharmaranya, brahmasarover, amrasichen, akshoybata, gayatrighat, dhodpada, adhigaya, Mundaprishta, udichi, kannapada.

13

BHOOMI –
LAND POOJA RITUALS

Bhoomi pooja is performed in honor of Goddess Bhoomi and Vaastu Purush (deity of directions). The word bhoomi means mother earth. Therefore, this pooja eliminates Vats Doshas from the land. By beginning before the construction of any structure, the construction process will be smoother.

A Bhoomi Pooja is always performed in the north-east corner of a construction site or on a farm to ensure good harvests.

It is dedicated to Vaastu Purusha, Goddess Bhoomi, and the Pancha Boothas (the five elements of nature). In accordance with Vaastu Shastra, this pooja is performed. Additionally, Vaastu doshas and ill effects are eradicated by honoring the deity of directions

Do's and Don'ts after the purchase of Bhoomi or land

A compound wall must be built before a house can be constructed. In comparison with the other walls of the house, the southwest wall should be taller. Walls on east and north sides should be 21 inches shorter than those on the south and west sides. Plants must be grown on the land after selecting the construction site. The land becomes even more auspicious if a calf or cow is kept on it. It is very beneficial to consult a priest with experience to perform Bhoomi Pooja. In addition, it contributes to an individual's happiness and prosperity.

Here's who should perform Bhoomi Pooja

The head of the family and his wife should perform this pooja. The ritual of honoring Mother Earth must also be performed by a priest proficient in this practice. You will be provided with all the details for a Shubh Muhurat by a proficient priest. Furthermore, he can assist in carrying out the task correctly.

Benefits of doing Bhoomi Pooja

Prior to constructing a building or using land for cultivation, it is imperative to seek the blessings of Mother Earth. By performing this ritualistic pooja, the land is cleansed from all evils and negativities. In addition, Bhoomi Pooja ensures that work is completed smoothly and without any obstacles. As well as ensuring the well-being of those who will occupy the property, it also ensures their happiness. It is beneficial to have better yields when land is used for agricultural purposes. During Bhoomi Pooja, the Vaastu Purusha grants the worshiper his blessings. The purpose of this pooja is to purify the construction site of all negativities. Building a house with it helps to pacify every corner.

When should one perform Bhoomi Pooja?

Ideally, Bhoomi pooja should take place during the months of Shravan, Margshirsh, Paush, and Kartik. The date for Bhoomi puja is determined by Vaastu time. There are times when it falls twice in a month. Mondays and Thursdays are suitable weekdays for this pooja. This pooja is very auspicious on these two days. Additionally, this pooja should not be performed on Saturdays, Sundays, or Tuesdays. Such auspicious activities should be avoided during Divaskarma, Hadpaksha, and Shradh paksha. For this pooja, it is not recommended to use the fourth, ninth, and fourteenth teeth. When a female member of the household is more than seven months pregnant, do not begin the construction work.

How does Lunar Constellations impact Bhoomi Pooja?

To begin construction work, it is necessary to calculate the number of lunar constellations on the very first day. At that time the day for performing the pooja is inauspicious if the number is between 1 and 7 or 19 to 28. If the resulting number is between 8 and 18, that day is very auspicious.

Here's how to do Bhoomi Pooja

Cleaning the site is the first step in performing the pooja. The area must also be cleaned of dirt and trash holes. The construction site must also be dug in a northeasterly direction. It is necessary that the milk should spill over this pooja when the lady of the house boils the milk after the puja. Thirdly, the worshiper should face east at the time of this puja. Ensure that the idols of Ganesha and Goddess Lakshmi are placed on a clean platform. Any auspicious work in Hinduism begins with the Ganesh pooja. After that, a havan is performed. As part of the pooja, coconuts are covered with red cloth and placed in the ground. The ground is also adorned with silver idols of Naag and Nagin. The other major rituals are Devi pooja, taking a Sankalpa, shatkarma, pran pratishtha and Manglik dravya sthapana.

Requirements for Bhoomi Pooja

Here's a list of articles required for Bhoomi Pooja – Kumkum (red sindoor), Turmeric powder, Camphor /Karpuram, Sandalwood powder, Incense (agarbatti) sticks, Fruits, Beetle nuts, Beetle leaves, Coconuts, Rice, Flowers

Other requirements for this pooja are –

- 1 set of Navaratnas (9 types of gems), a packet of dry dates, 5 Lemon (green limes), a set of Pancha Lohas (5 metals), 2 packets of Navodaya (9 types of seeds).
- Coins- Quarters 40, a 1/2-meter-long white cloth, a matchbox, lamp, cotton wicks, oil, 10 panchpatras, udharini.
- A plate, a kalash, 5 bricks, a bell, a bedsheet, 4 plastic plates, a god's picture and 5 foam cups etc.

Stages related to construction of home

As per the ancient scriptures, home-related muhurtas are divided into the following stages –

As a form of honoring the mother earth, Bhoomi Pooja is performed. Hinduism has an offertory ritual known as Balidaana. The leveling of the site will take place at Hala Karshaana next. Afterwards, Ankuraa-Roopana seeds are sown. Shilaanyaasa, the laying of the foundation stone, follows. The next step is to dig a well or source of water. After that, the door frames are fixed. Finally, is the entry into the new house.

14

Grih Pravesh –
Entry into new home

W hen it comes to buying a new home, it's the beginning of a new chapter in life, and who wouldn't want to start it on a positive note? When a house is purchased, this tradition is followed.

The tradition of housewarming has been celebrated in Hindu families for decades. India and other parts of the world are not new to this. In Hindu families, such things are normal if you have experienced Indian culture. The first thing any Indian family does after buying a new house is Grih Pravesh (housewarming).

This pooja is performed before entering the house and ideally before moving the old furniture. To ensure happiness and prosperity in the new home, this pooja is performed.

It is called Grih Pravesh in Hindi, GruhaPravesam in Telugu, a housewarming in English, and Grihoprobesh in Bengali.

A ceremony like this should be performed on an auspicious day and before entering a new home; it is one of the important things to remember when performing Grih Pravesh.

The most important part of the Griha Pravesh puja is moving into the new house once the construction is completed. Ensure that all major fixtures like doors, windows, wall paint and electrical fittings are in place before deciding the date for pooja. It is also recommended that you sleep in your new home with your family on the night of the pooja day.

Before the ceremony, decorate the main door. Main doors and home entrances serve not only as entry points for people but also as gateways to good health and prosperity. It is therefore one of the most important parts in the house and should be decorated with flowers since it represents Vaastu Purush and is called Simha Dwar. A rangoli at the entrance and religious symbols like a swastika or

Goddess Lakshmi's feet can make your main entrance welcoming and attractive.

To get the blessings of the deities and planets, a mandala should be drawn during the housewarming ceremony.

When entering a house, break a coconut at the entrance to sanctify the home and remove any obstacles in your path.

It is important to clean the house thoroughly before the Griha Pravesh puja so that the deity and their blessings can enter the house. Using salt water to clean the floor will remove all the negative energy and purify the house before pooja.

For prosperity and good fortune, you must enter the house on the right foot. When you first walk into the house on the day of Griha Pravesh Muhurat puja, keep this simple tip in mind.

During Griha Pravesh pooja, a string made of mango leaves and lemons is hung on the entrance gate. It is believed that mango leaves have the power to absorb negative energy, which is why they are used.

Griha Pravesh puja day is the best day to build a temple at home. In Vaastu, the temple should be in the northeast corner of the house, and the images and idols of Gods must face east.

When performing pooja rituals, a Shankh should be blown enthusiastically as it is known to spread distressing vibrations.

To purify the energy of the room and fill the house with positive vibes, you should perform a havan before settling into a new home, followed by Ganesh puja, Vaastu Dosh puja, and Navagraha Shanti puja. Havan smoke contains healing ingredients that eliminate any evil energy in the rooms, which is carried in the havan Kunda or vessel used for the havan.

On the day of the housewarming ceremony, boiling milk is another important Griha Pravesh ritual. On puja day, boiling milk brings prosperity to the house. Milk must be boiled in the new house's kitchen using a new utensil. When this boiling milk is ready, rice is added to make sweet rice prasad, which is offered during the pooja rituals and distributed to everyone.

Housewarming Ceremony: Griha Pravesh Pooja Don'ts

During Holi, do not move into the house.

It is not advisable to leave the house locked at night on the Griha Pravesh pooja day. To attract divine protection, you must light a lamp.

Following the Griha Pravesh puja, make sure that the house is filled with all the essential items.

A housewarming ceremony should not be held if there are pregnant women in the family or if there is a death in the family or if a close relative is mourning.

The priest should be fed well after the Griha Pravesh pooja, and he should be asked for his blessings. Food should be served to everyone, and good wishes should be taken.

15

Festival celebration in Bihari Society

Makar Sankranti

Sakraat or Khichdi are also names used for this festival in Bihar. Throughout the country, the 14th of January welcomes a wave of festive cheer. The country celebrates Makar Sankranti, Festival, and colorful kites fill the sky.

Makar Sankranti is celebrated on January 14th. It is a Hindu festival that is celebrated on the first day of the sun's transit into Capricorn.

What Is Makar Sankranti & Why Is It Celebrated?

Sankranti represents the moving of the Sun from one of the rashi (constellations of the zodiac) to the next in the Vedas. In a year, there are 12 Sankranti. In the Hindu calendar, Makar Sankranti, also known as Poush Sankranti, is one of the few festivals aligned with the solar year. In addition to its religious significance, Makar Sankranti has a lot of cultural significance as well. Moreover, the festival also marks the beginning of harvest season, when new crops are worshipped and shared. From this day, the Sun begins its journey from Dakshinayana (South) to Uttarayana (North), marking the official end of Winter. Besides being a religious occasion and seasonal observance, it also marks the sun's transit into Makar Rashi (the Capricorn zodiac sign).

How to celebrate?

Makar Sankranti is a day of auspicious beginnings, as it is recommended to wake up before sunrise and take a bath before the sun rises on this day. Adding Til or Sesame Seeds to your bath water is also recommended. The Gayatri Mantra must be chanted after bathing, and water must be offered to the Sun in Arghya, a form of prayer. Kite-flying rituals are also believed to be associated with good health. Early morning sun exposure and Vitamin D ingestion were the intended benefits.

Food to eat

The traditional breakfast for the occasion is chuda-dahi (beaten rice and yogurt) and gur (jaggery). Makar Sankranti is celebrated with a special dish called tilkut, a combination of jaggery and sesame seeds. As part of the meal, Khichdi is often served with 'chaar yaar' (four companions) - chokha (roasted potatoes), ghee, papad, and achaar (pickles).

Do And Don'ts on Makar Sankranti

During Makar Sankranti, people often fly kites, take baths, donate clothes and food, indulge in festivities, exchange gifts, etc.

Makar Sankranti begins with ritualistic baths and prayers to the rising Sun before dawn.

Aside from providing food, clothing, and cash to Purohits, it entails promising to provide them with shelter, clothing, and food.

Female relatives, such as married daughters, sisters, and daughters-in-law, as well as their families, receive generous gifts of food, clothing, jewelry, and cash.

Yogurt, sesame seeds, jaggery, chiura, and chiura are eaten after the prayers.

After this, Khichdi is the next meal of the day.

Story

Legend has it that Sankranti, after whom the holiday is named, killed an evil force called Sankara Sur. The day after Makar Sankranti is called Karidin or Kinkrant. On this day, Devi killed

Kinkarasur. Panchang offers a glimpse of Makar Sankranti and information about it. Sankranti's age, structure, attire, movement, and development are described in the Hindu Panchang. According to the Mahabharata epic, people back then also considered the day auspicious. Despite suffering injuries during the Mahabharata War, Bhishma Pitamah persisted until Uttarayana arrived so that he could enter a heavenly abode during auspicious times. Moksha, or salvation, is believed to be granted to those who die on this day.

BASANT PANCHAMI

On the fifth day of the Hindu month of Magha (January-February in the Western calendar), Vasant Panchami marks the beginning of the end of winter and the beginning of spring. A new endeavor, such as getting married, buying a house, or starting a job, is considered auspicious during this time. The mustard crop blooms yellow flowers in spring, a color that symbolizes knowledge, light, prosperity, and peace in India, and is also known as the "king of all seasons.".

Goddess Saraswati is worshipped on this day

A celebration of Vasant Panchami commemorates the time when the great Sanskrit poet Kalidasa, who is believed to have lived somewhere between the 4th and 5th century CE, was blessed by the goddess Saraswati (goddess of wisdom, knowledge, learning, and art).

How to celebrate Vasant Panchami

The devotee's focus of worship determines how Vasant Panchami is celebrated. In honor of Goddess Saraswati, many wake up early and dress in yellow (her favorite color), eat yellow sweets and snacks, and perform puja. Students who wish to succeed in their studies also pray to Saraswati because she is the goddess of learning and wisdom. Some honor Shiva and Parvati with mango flowers and ears of wheat, while others commemorate Surya. As worship is not restricted to any one deity, it is possible to appreciate all deities associated with Vasant Panchami. The celebrations typically include family and friends gathering for feasting, dancing, and singing, like any Hindu seasonal holiday.

In Vasant Panchami, yellow is associated with harvesting the mustard crop, which has yellow blooms, which is the color of Goddess Saraswati. Saraswati's followers wear yellow clothing. For the festival, traditional dishes are prepared in yellow and saffron colors. Hindu culture attaches great significance to Basant Panchami. As such, it is considered a very auspicious day for starting a new business, getting married or performing a housewarming ceremony (Griha pravesh).

Do And Don'ts on Vasant Panchami?

Dos

- ◆ Start your day early (preferably two hours before sunrise at Brahma Mahurat)
- ◆ Wear clean clothes and take a bath.
- ◆ The occasion calls for yellow-colored dresses.

- Put your heart into the ritual (do Sankalpa).
- Offer yellow-colored food preparations to Goddess Saraswati.
- The yellow color can be obtained naturally by using turmeric or saffron.
- Perform the Puja of Goddess Saraswati.
- While performing puja, you may also keep a book, a notebook, a slate, a whiteboard, pencils, markers, musical instruments, etc. at the Goddess' feet.
- Get together with friends and family to fly kites and share sweets and delicacies.
- Provide underprivileged children with books and learning kits.
- Be respectful of elders, teachers, and mentors.

Don'ts

- Foods containing onion, garlic, or meat should not be consumed.
- Tobacco and alcohol should be avoided.
- When you observe a Vrat, you should avoid rice, wheat, and pulses.

Story

According to legend, Vidyottama was an extraordinarily intelligent princess who defeated many prominent scholars in debate. As soon it was time for her to get married, she declared she would only marry someone smarter than her. After finding her to be overly arrogant, a group of pandits decided that they would teach her a lesson, by tricking her into marrying a fool. During their journey, they came across a man named Kalidasa cutting the same branch he was sitting on from a tree. The men presented Kalidasa to the princess as a highly learned sage, persuading her to marry him. Having been deceived by the pandits, she agreed to a swift marriage with Kalidasa.

Vidyottama threw Kalidasa out of the palace when she discovered he wasn't the knowledgeable man she thought he was. Kalidasa was dejected and ashamed, so he tried to end his life, but Goddess Saraswati intervened and directed him to take a dip in the nearby river instead. He submerged himself in the water after she instructed him to do so. He was no longer the Kalidasa he used to be when he came out. As a poet, he became extremely renowned for his intelligence and wisdom. While Kalidasa's transformation is always similar, there are varying accounts of the story. On Vasant Panchami, devotees pray to Saraswati, hoping to receive her wisdom and intelligence.

Second story:

During Vasant Panchami, Kamadeva, the god of love, attempted to wake Shiva from his meditation. As described in the Matsya Purana, Shaiva Purana, and other numerous retellings, Parvati, a manifestation of the feminine Divine, desired Shiva as her husband. Since Shiva had gone into deep meditation after his wife, Sati, had died, nothing Parvati tried could get his attention. The god of love, Kamadeva, was eventually asked to break Shiva meditation and arouse his desire for Parvati, who had previously been Sati. To help Shiva, Kamadeva created a congenial springtime atmosphere and fired five desire-inducing arrows. Shiva was furious at Kamadeva's interruption of his meditation and immediately burned him to ashes with his third eye. Kamadeva's wife, Rati, approached God Shiva and begged him to revive her husband after learning what had transpired. Shiva resuscitated Kamadeva, but only Rati could see him physically. Others would see him as a disembodied spirit of love and desire.

Vasant Panchami is therefore regarded as both the day when Kamadeva was asked to stir Shiva's desire for Parvati, as well as the time of year when Kamadeva stimulates both the earth and its people with blossoms. On Vasant Panchami, many also celebrate the founding of the Sun Temple (a shrine dedicated to the Sun God Surya in Bihar). With Surya, winter comes to an end, bringing the sunlight needed for trees to grow and bloom. It is Surya's warmth that inspires people out of reclusion after months of cold and short days, inspiring them to take on new challenges and make fruitful plans. Surya is therefore honored in Bihar through song and dance, as well as by cleaning the statues at the Deo-Sun Temple.

MAHA SHIVRATRI

❦

According to legend, it is on this night that God Shiva performs his heavenly dance or 'tandav', which is called the Maha Shivratri, which literally means 'the great night of Shiva'.

What you must do on Maha Shivratri

Observe fasting on the day of Maha Shivratri. Through fasting, the body is detoxified, and a restless mind is curbed. Meditation comes easily to a mind that is not restless. Fasting on Maha Shivratri detoxifies the body and aids meditation. Fruits and easily digestible foods are recommended during a fast. Maha Shivratri is considered an auspicious time for meditation because of the constellations' position. On Shivaratri, people should keep awake and meditate. Traditionally, people used to say, 'If you cannot meditate every day, keep awake and meditate on Shivratri day at least once a year'.

Do not sleep throughout the night on Shivratri and spend the night contemplating spirituality if possible.

Sing songs, chant mantras, and meditate while listening to stories about God Shiva.

In most Shiva temples, prayers are performed throughout the night.

Praying and pujas can also be performed at home if possible. On Shivratri, start the puja after sunset and continue it until sunrise.

Offering Bilva leaves, white flowers, Ganges water, sacred ash, and milk to Shiva. The day is considered auspicious.

Donate food, clothes, and other items to the poor at the end of Shivratri puja.

What you must not do on Maha Shivratri

Shivratri is not a festival for feasting and making merry. Consider God, visit temples, perform Shiv puja at home, and spend time in spiritual pursuits.

If you are observing a complete fast during Shivratri, do not sleep. Chant the mantras of the God throughout the night and sing the divine praises.

Shivratri is not the time to watch movies or play video games. Avoid all indulgences. During this time, focus your attention and devotion on worshiping God.

It is never a good idea to use falsehoods and quarrels. Avoid eating non-vegetarian food. Avoid alcohol and other addictive substances.

After the Abhishek ritual, Shiva Linga is adorned with a garland made of Bilva leaves. It is believed that Bilva leaves cool down God Shiva.

After that bhasm is applied to the Shiva Linga which is followed by lighting lamps and Dhupa. The other items are used to adorn God Shiva.

The mantra to chant during Puja duration is ॐ नमः शिवाय – Om Namah Shivaya.

Story

First story

According to one story, a poisonous pot emerged from the ocean during Samudra Manthan.

The gods and demons were terrified that this would destroy the entire world, so they ran to Shiva for help. Shiva held the poison in his throat instead of swallowing it to protect the entire world from the evil effects. This causes his throat to turn blue, which is why he is also known as Neel-kantha. Shiva saved the world through Shivratri, which is celebrated every year.

Second Story

As described in the Shiv Purana, once upon a time Brahma and Vishnu fought among themselves to determine who was superior. Other Gods were terrified, so they turned to God Shiva for help. Shiva took the form of a massive fire that spread across the length of the universe to make them realize their fight was futile. After seeing the magnitude, both Gods decided to establish supremacy over the other by finding one end each. For this reason, Brahma assumed the form of a swan and went upward, while Vishnu assumed the form of Varaha and went downward. Despite their efforts, they couldn't find an end to the fire, which had no limit. Brahma encountered a Ketaki flower on his journey upwards. Asked where she had come from, Ketaki replied that she had been placed at the top of the fiery column as an offering. When Brahma could not find an upper limit, he took the flower as a witness and came. Shiva then revealed his true form and became angry. Brahma was unable to find the uppermost limit and told a lie. For telling a lie, Shiva punished him by cursing that no one would pray for him. Ketaki flowers were also prohibited as offerings for worship. Maha Shivratri is celebrated since Shiva first manifested himself as a Linga on the 14th day of the dark half month of Phalguna. It is believed that worshipping Shiva on this day will bring one happiness and prosperity.

Third Story

Shiva granted Goddess Parvati, an avatar of Adi-Shakti, and wished to marry her because of her devotion, according to another popular legend. After their marriage, the goddess observed a fast for his health on a moonless night. Indian women still follow this ritual today to pray for the long life of their husbands.

Forth Story

Another legend says God Shiva caught Goddess Ganga in his matted locks as she descended from heaven and released her on Earth as several streams. As a result, Earth was spared destruction.

On this auspicious night, the Shivalinga is bathed as a tribute to Him. At midnight, the formless God Sadashiv appeared as a Lingodhbhav Moorthi. Therefore, people stay awake all night praying to God.

HOLI

oli Festival celebrates the arrival of spring season and marks a new beginning where people can let all their inhibitions go and start fresh.

Do you know why Holi is celebrated?

Originally, Holi Festival was a ceremony for married women to spread prosperity and goodwill to their new families. There have been many changes to the festival since then. The Holi Festival focuses on celebrating the victory of good over evil as one of its main focuses.

When is it celebrated?

Holi is celebrated on the last full moon day of (Phalguna), which is usually around the end of March. Depending on the year, Holi may fall on a different date.

How is it celebrated

Day before Holi

Before Holika Dahan, take a bath and then proceed to the Holika's location with the appropriate offerings. Holika dahan can be created at temples or other locations. As the idols are assembled inside the pyre, firewood and other combustible items are piled around them. At Holika Dahan, do pooja and pray to God Narasimha seven times. Offerings include flowers, cotton, jaggery, moong, turmeric, coconut, gulal, batasha, seven different varieties of cereals, and other crops as you circle the flames. Pray for your loved ones, your friends, and everyone on earth. Holika Dahan melodies are sung and danced around the pyre.

In common belief, your prayers during this time would be answered if you sacrificed your bad traits symbolically at the Holika Dahan fire.

On Day of Holi

Start your day by taking a bath, changing into clean clothes, and visiting your home temple.

Put a red cloth on the blooms of the Radha Krishna idol while facing east.

The altar should be set up and Radha Krishna's lotus feet covered with gulal for pooja.

Incense sticks, earthen lamps, and tulsi are offered to the gods and goddesses after applying sandalwood paste.

Give out sweets next, followed by Gangajal.

When you have given the offerings to the god, join your hands and move in a circle.

As a blessing and a token of gratitude, everyone should be sprinkled with Gangajal, apply gulal to their faces, and receive Prasad.

Story

In Hinduism, good triumphs over evil in the story of Hiranyakashipu (Sanskrit: हिरण्यकशिपु, romanized: Hiraṇyakaśipu), also known as Hiranyakashyap. The ancient king claimed to be immortal and demanded to be worshipped as a god. Prahalad, Hiranyakashipu's son, worshipped the Hindu deity Vishnu over him, and Hiranyakashipu was furious. The story goes that the God Vishnu appeared as a half-lion, half-man, and killed Hiranyakashipu because of his appearance as a half-lion, half-man. Thus, good triumphed over evil.

Second Story

The Holi Festival is also associated with the story of Radha and Krishna. Many consider Krishna to be the supreme god since he is the eighth incarnation of the Hindu god Vishnu. As legend has it, Krishna drank poisonous milk from a demon Putana when he was a baby, which caused his blue skin. Because of his blue skin, Krishna feared Radha would not love him - but Radha dyed her skin with color, making them a true couple. Holi is celebrated by applying color to each other's skin to honor Krishna and Radha.

VAT SAVITRI

❧

Vat Purnima Vrat is observed by married women for their husband's well-being and long life. A sacred thread is tied around a trunk of the banyan tree by women in Vat Savitri Vrat, and they fast and listen to the priest's Savitri-Satyavan Katha. A banyan tree is the main idol of this festival, which represents God Brahma, God Vishnu, and God Shiva. Traditionally, the root of the plant represents God Brahma, the stem represents God Vishnu, and the upper portion represents God Shiva. Fasting for Vat Savitri Vrat begins on Trayodashi day of Jyeshta month and ends on Purnima day.

In honor of this auspicious day, women take holy baths early in the morning, wear new colorful clothes, wear bright bangles, and apply vermillion to their foreheads. One banyan leaf is added to the hair.

Goddess Savitri is also offered 9 types of fruits and flowers. The day is observed with the Savitri Vrat Katha and Bhog (offerings) of wet pulses, rice, mangoes, jackfruits, palm fruits, kendu, bananas, and several other fruits are offered. Following the fast, they consume prasad and take blessings from their husbands and elders. Vat Savitri Vrat is believed to transform even the worst of fortunes into good ones.

Story

Markandeya Rushigalu told this story to Yudhishthira in his "Vana Parva" of Mahabharata. Madra's king was Aswapathi. He had no children. Savitranamaka Soorya prayed for a child. As a result, he was blessed with a female child, who was named after him as "Savitri". Devotion and asceticism are traits Savitri practiced herself. When Savitri reached marriageable age, her father looked for a groom for her. Satyavan, son of blind king Dyumatsena, was suggested by Narad.

As a forest dweller, he was living a very simple life. Satyavan and Savitri were happy together.

Satyavan had a short life. According to the Vrata, Savitri must upavasa/fast for 3 days. Satyavan's death was foreseen, and Savitri performed the vrata with utmost care. Satyavan's death day arrived. Satyavan also led Savitri to the forest. Satyavan died thereafter, being attacked by a severe headache. Satyavan was pulled by Yamraj (God of death). Yamraj was followed as well by Savitri. No one could stop her because of her devotion to her husband. Also, she followed Yamraj to Yamaloka. Having been pleased with her, Yamraj granted her a boon that her father-in-law would regain his sight and be given the kingdom back. In response to her request for 100 children from Satyavan, Yamraj advised her to ask for another boon. As a result, Yamraj blessed Satyavan with 104 years of "Ayau". It is on this day that Savitri completed her Vrata, which was completed on this day. It is for this reason that this Vrata is called Vat Savitri.

RAKHI: A SACRED THREAD OF LOVE AND PROTECTION

❧

What is it

Rakhi, also known as Raksha Bandhan, is a significant Hindu festival celebrated in India and worldwide. Culturally and emotionally, this festival symbolizes the bond of love and protection between siblings. A Rakhi is the bracelet of red or yellow strings tied by a sister round the wrist of a brother on a Hindu festival to set up brotherly relations.

When to celebrate:

Rakhi has been practiced since ancient times. According to legend, the festival originated during medieval period when Rajput queens would send sacred threads to neighboring rulers to seek their protection. The tradition evolved over time to include siblings' bonds. Rakhi, or the sacred thread, is at the heart of the Rakhi festival. In addition to symbolizing love, protection, and duty, this thread holds immense importance. Rakhis are traditionally made from colored threads embellished with beads, sequins, and decorative elements, making them cherished symbols of affection.

Day changes per calendar

Rakhi is usually celebrated on the full moon day of the Hindu month of Shravan.

How to do it

Sisters tie Rakhi threads on their brothers' wrists on this day, praying for their well-being and protection. A Rakhi ceremony is usually held in the presence of family members, who witness and bless the bond between siblings. Rakhi is not just a festival of sibling love; it is also a celebration of family unity. Sisters often prepare delicious sweets and traditional delicacies for their brothers during Rakhi. As part of their cultural activities, families sing traditional songs, perform rituals, and exchange heartfelt wishes.

Rituals prep work

- All family members should only do pooja after they have taken shower and wore clean clothes
- Have Rakhi thali prepared beforehand
- Rakhi thalli can be decorated as per choice.

Each thalli should contain:

- Rakhi
- Roli/Akshat
- Diya

♦ Sweets

Tying the Rakhi thread

♦ Have brother sit facing the east direction. Place tilak on brother's forehead

♦ Tie the Rakhi on brother's right-hand wrist

♦ Place Akshat on his head and do aarti 2 times clockwise

♦ Give him sweets. Followed by meals.

♦ Brother's give sister gifts

Story

Several stories surround the origins of Raksha Bandhan, including those associated with mythology and history:

♦ Ganesh and Mansa: During Raksha Bandhan, Devi Manasa visited Ganesh. She tied a Rakhi around Ganesh's wrist. Ganesh's sons, Shubh, and Labh were taken by this beautiful tradition, but angry that they had no sister. To participate in Raksha Bandhan, they begged their father for a sister. Ganesh agrees after much persuasion. As a result, Santoshi Maa is created, and every year thereafter, the three siblings celebrate Raksha Bandhan together.

♦ Krishna and Draupadi: Raksha Bandhan is often associated with Krishna and Draupadi, two characters from the Mahabharata. To stop the bleeding, Draupadi tore a piece of her sari and tied it around Krishna's finger. As a result of her gesture, Krishna promised to protect her forever. When Draupadi was in distress during the infamous "cheer-haran" (disrobing) episode in the Mahabharata, she prayed to Krishna, who miraculously extended her sari to save her honor.

HARTALIKA TEEJ

❧

Hindu women fast for the longevity, prosperity, and health of their husbands. Hartalika Teej is one of the festivals celebrated by married women. This festival is in honor of Goddess Parvathi over a three-day period. Unmarried girls can also observe fasts to find a good life partner along with married women. For the marital bliss of their husbands, married women observe the Hartalika Teej fast, while unmarried women observe in search of a good husband. During the monsoon season, all the women gather to sing, dance, and celebrate.

Women celebrate Teej as the union of God Shiva and Goddess Parvati. Hartalika Teej is mostly held in north Indian states. Teej is celebrated in three forms in India: Hariyali Teej, Kajari Teej, and Hartalika Teej.

When to celebrate

Shukla Paksha Tritiya was observed by Hartalika Teej in Bhadra month. Day changes per calendar

How to do it

Fasting is observed by married women for the whole day. No drinking or eating after the previous night. Based on health, fasting can be observed with or without water and fruits. No grains, garlic, nonveg, onions, alcohols are consumed.

Hartalika teej should be done in the same manner as it is started. Hartalika teej vrat recommends avoiding grains and water. First Teej if you want to start without water or any food, you could do that. However, due to health or any other reason, you can't do nirjala (without water), this fast can be done with eating fruits and or water too. After vrat, you can drink water or the next day as well.

Besides wearing green clothing, green bangles, and golden bindis, women apply henna (mehndi) to their hands.

They pray to God Shiva and Goddess Parvati, also known as Teej Mata, while keeping the Nirjala fast.

When they return home from the temple or pooja at home, they touch their spouses' feet to seek their blessings.

Before sunset, the women dress as newlywed brides and take another bath.

Clay or sand Shiva and Parvati statues are made for Hartalika Teej Puja rituals.

Bilva leaves, flowers, incense, and burning Diya are offered to the gods.

The Hindi song Hartalika Teej Vrat Katha tells the well-known Hindu myth about God Shiva telling Parvati that she is the daughter of the Himalayas, Goddess Shailaputri.

Hartalika Teej Vrat ends the following morning when the fast is broken and rituals of devotion are performed.

- This pooja vidhi/ritual is done at night. If possible, make clay God Shiv, Parvati, and full family else, pray with pictures.
- Worship the God by doing jal Arpan, tilak, Akshat, flowers, fruits, and food offerings
- Place kala chana, cucumbers, corns, and banana as fruit
- After doing aarti, all offerings are kept overnight
- Next day, early morning take shower and wear clean clothes (new if possible) and then do aarti
- Post that woman open their fasts. Husband makes lemonade for their wives and make them drink
- Bihari chana jhor and rice are eaten as lunch
- Husband then gives blessings to his wife

Rituals prep work

- All family members should only do pooja after they have taken shower and wore clean clothes
- Have teej thalli prepared beforehand
- Teej thalli can be decorated as per choice.

Each thalli should contain:

- Bilav leaves, Kala chana, Roli/Akshat, Diya, Sweets (thekua, gujiya and any other mithai of choice), Corn, Cucumber, fruits (5 types), flowers (red, if possible)

Next day:

- Morning pooja can be done early in the morning.
- Wear new or clean clothes after taking bath
- Do the daily pooja rituals and worship
- Tie the offered cloth from Goddess Parvati onto chunri/saree pallu and add the new sindoor into our sindhur
- Take corn, cucumber, banana, kala chana and any offered prasad onto saree pallu/chunri
- Seek Spouse blessings. Spouse makes lemonade and offer to his wife
- Wife can then open her fast with lemonade, cucumber or prasad

Story

Hartalika Teej 2023 celebrates God Shiva and Goddess Parvati's reconciliation. Goddess Parvati underwent austerity to marry God Shiva. In the Himalayas, Goddess Parvati practiced strict abstinence along Ganga's banks. Her father Himalaya became dejected after seeing the Goddess in such a state. Maharishi Narad appeared one day with a marriage proposal on behalf of God Vishnu. However, Goddess Parvati didn't weep until she learned about it. It is for the purpose of marrying God Shiva that she is undergoing this asceticism. Goddess Parvati then went to the jungle on the advice of her companion, where she immersed herself in Shiva's adoration. During this time, on the third day of Shukla Paksha in the Bhadrapada month, Goddess Parvati created a Shivalinga out of sand and then immersed herself in worshiping God Shiva. Seeing Goddess Parvati's strict austerity, God Shiva appeared before her in his heavenly form and proposed marriage. As a result, both married and single women have followed Hartalika Teej Vrat in hopes of finding a suitable husband and keeping their husbands healthy. Through this Vrat, people also seek the blessings of God Shiva and Goddess Parvati.

JITIYA

❧

There is a significant aspect of Jitiya related to the fast, which is observed by women for the sake of their children's well-being and longevity. Fasting usually lasts 24 hours, starting at sunrise, and ending at sunrise the following day.

When to celebrate

Jitiya is performed in the Krishna Paksh of the Ashwin maas (month) on Ashtami tithi (eighth day) as per the Indian calendar guided by the moon. The day is also celebrated as Lakshmi Parv (worship of Goddess Lakshmi). Fasting is observed by mothers for the whole day. No drinking or eating after the previous night. Based on health, fasting can be observed with or without water and fruits. On this day, Hindu women observe Nirjala fasts (without water) and break them on Ashtami the following day. When Ashtami begins in the afternoon, women may have to fast for two days. As practically nothing, even a drop of water, is placed in the mouth, the rapid is also known as Khar Jitiya. A mother who is blessed with a son prays Jimutvahana on the ashtami of Krishna Paksha. Women who pray to Lord Jimutvahana in the pradosh kaal are blessed with sons.

No grains, garlic, nonveg, onions, alcohols are consumed one day before fast.

The paaran of the fast is finished after the dawn (sunrise) of the Navami.

Rituals prep work

All family members should only do pooja after they have taken shower and wore clean clothes

How to do it

- Worship sun God by doing jal Arpan, tilak, Akshat, flowers, fruits, and food offerings
- As part of the worship of Jimutvahan, agarbatti, dhoop, rice, flowers, etc., are offered.
- Eagles and siyarin's idols are made of cow dung and red sindoor is applied to their foreheads.
- On the following day, the fast is usually broken early in the morning. Prior to consuming food or water, mothers offer prayers to the rising sun after taking a ritualistic bath.
- Post that woman open their fasts.
- Bihari traditional foods are made as next day meals. The dishes which are cooked for Paaran are also fixed. Women break their fast with saag (edible herbs) like Noni saag, Poi saag and so on. and Roti created from the

flour of Mahua which is a neighborhood crop. This observance is based mostly on legendary mythology and stays unaffected by modern culture.

Jitiya fasts were originated by Syavan Kumar and Queen Karnawati, who were narrated by women. Observing this fast is believed to protect children from untimely deaths. A puja called Jivit Putrika Puja is performed after the story has been narrated. During this process, parents pray to deities and seek blessings for their children.

Story: Jitiya vrata Katha

When Kali Yuga started, mothers had been worried about the fate of their young children. According to Hinduism, Kali Yuga, or the age of vice, occurs just before the annihilation of all creation.. So, mothers wanted to know what they can do to defend their children from evil and death. To find an answer on how to conserve their youngsters from the effects of Kali Yuga's, mothers approached the wonderful sage Gautam. The saint agreed to uncover a remedy and narrated a story that happened during the Mahabharata era.

Pandavas had been quite unhappy following the end of the 18-day Mahabharat war as all their sons had been killed. Draupadi, the mother of the young children, approached a discovered Brahmin named Dhaumya for a solution to alleviate their unhappiness.

Dhaumya mentioned an incident that took place in the Satya Yuga.

There lived a renowned king in Satya Yuga named Jimutvahan. The King was renowned for his honesty and excellent rule. He also was prepared to go to any extent to shield his citizens. Once, although the King was at the property of his wife's mothers and fathers, he heard the cry of an old female. Jimutavahan soon approached the woman and found out that she was crying as her son was killed and eaten by Garuda who was the Vahana of Lord Vishnu. Jimutavahan promised the woman that he will get back her son. (In some versions of the story – The previous woman was a Snake and had lost her son who was a Snake. Garuda had killed and eaten the Nag.)

Soon Jimutavahan approached Garuda on a mountain. The king noticed skeletons of human beings lying in a big pit. The bones were of all the folks that Garuda had killed and eaten. Garuda soon observed Jimutavahan and wished to know why he was there? The King demanded that he return the son of the woman and rather he could consume him. Garuda agreed and began to eat Jimutavahan. But quickly Garuda stopped and needed to know why he was sacrificing himself for an ordinary man or woman. Jimutavahan replied that no little one is ordinary for a mother. I am sacrificing myself so that a previous mom will get back her only youngster. No mom can bear the loss of her child and there is no greater grief than shedding a youngster.

Garuda soon realized that the man just before him was no ordinary person and wished to know his identity. Jimutavahan launched himself and said not to appear standing. Asked Garuda to kill and consume him so that the outdated lady will get back her son.

Soon Garuda stopped eating Jimutavahan and was pleased by the generosity and empathy displayed by the King and presented him with a boon.

As boon – the king asked for the daily life of all the folks that Garuda had killed and had eaten. Garuda agreed to carry all those he had killed and eaten back to daily life. He brought Amrit (elixir) and sprinkled on the skeletons in the pit and all the individuals came back to lifestyle. According to Garuda, mothers who fast during the Krishna Paksha of Ashwin month and practice rituals with Kusha grass won't lose their children. (In several versions this boon is offered to King Jimutavahan by Lord Shiva and Goddess Parvati, who were pleased by the dedication and selflessness of the King and his willingness to aid a mother get back her kid. Draupadi was content to understand about the Vrat and she performed it. Mothers who hear about the story of Jivitputrika Vrat from Sage Gautama performed it in Kali Yuga to save their young children from all the dangers. Mothers still do it for the welfare of their youngsters.

KRISHNA JANMASHTAMI

✧

Krishna Janmashtami, also known as Janmashtami, marks the birth of the Hindu God Krishna who is the eighth incarnation of God Vishnu. As part of this holiday, prayers are offered, night vigils are observed, fasting is observed, and dance-drama reenactments of Krishna's life are performed. As part of this festival, cultural events and competitions are held, the most interesting of which is Dahi Handi, where yogurt pots are strung up high from buildings and people form a human pyramid to break them open.

During the Dahi Handi celebration, people form a human pyramid to break open clay pots strung high from buildings.

At many Krishna temples in Mathura, watch rasa Lila, a dance-drama performance portraying Krishna's life.

The Krishna temples are decorated with idols and colorful lights.

Sweets made with milk, paneer, and dried fruits such as rasmalai are perfect for the season.

Young boys dress up as Krishna.

When is Janmashtami?

According to the Hindu lunar calendar, Janmashtami occurs on the eighth day of the waning moon phase in the month of Bhadrapada. Late August or early September is usually the time when this occurs.

How Janmashtami is Celebrated

Devotees fast until midnight the day when God Krishna is believed to have been born. Traditional prayers are offered at midnight. During Janmashtami, God Krishna's idols are washed and adorned with new clothes and ornaments. To symbolize his birth, the idol is placed in a cradle. In honor of God Krishna's journey into their homes, women draw tiny footprints walking towards their houses. On the second day of the festival, there is an event called Dahi Handi that is especially fun to watch in Mumbai. People form a human pyramid to reach and break open clay pots filled with yogurt strung high from buildings during the event. The celebration represents Krishna's love of food, especially yogurt, which he enjoyed most. According to legend, Krishna was quite mischievous and would steal yogurt from village homes. It was hung up high out of his reach by the housewives to stop him. To reach it, he gathered his friends and climbed up. Dahi Handi is performed today as a tribute to Krishna and to liven up the celebrations with a competitive atmosphere. Dahi Handi competitions are part of the big celebrations during the festive season.

We begin the day by cleaning our home-temple. This includes washing all the idols and cleaning the temple corners.

The idols are rearranged by placing Laddu Gopal (little Krishna idol) in his Jhula at the center of the temple once it is clean.

Following the daily puja, the temple is decorated. The temple is decorated with fairy lights, glitter threads, shiny balls, and other items.

There is a different muhurat for Janmashtami puja/aarti every year. Janmashtami has two types of Puja. People who perform the birth ceremony of Krishna fast all day and then perform the puja. Others simply do aarti during the puja muhurat.

Krishna Janmashtami Puja at Home?

Preparation: (What all to include in Krishna Janmashtami puja samagri?

- Tulsi leaves
- fresh flowers
- Incense sticks and Diya
- New clothes and ornaments for krishna
- As krishna loves butter, prepare home-made butter (white butter) to offer him
- Krishna loves milk as well, to prepare or bring Milk-based sweets
- Fruits and sweets

- A Jhula or cradle for God Krishna
- An idol of God Krishna
- A flute
- Kumkum
- Decorative pooja thali
- Panchamrit
- Makhan mishri
- Chandan
- Gangajal (holy water)
- Coconut
- Mango leaves Toran (door hanging)
- Kalash

How to do Krishna Janmashtami puja at home?

Given below are the steps that you need to follow for performing Krishna puja at home:

Take a bath and apply Gopi Chandan (mud of Vrindavan) or ashwagandha (sandalwood) to your forehead before doing the puja.

Spread a white/yellow cotton cloth on a clean surface. In a large, deep container, place a painting or image of God Krishna in the middle of the altar. Put together a puja thali with flowers, an incense burner, an aarti lamp, kumkum powder, and sandalwood paste. The second plate of sattvic meals and fruit, along with some water, should be added. A diya (light) made of ghee, also known as clarified butter or sesame oil, should be placed there.

Deity needs to take a bath with milk, ghee, orange juice, flowers, and plain water. Set the bowl aside and dry the murti. Place the food, flowers, water, and ghee diya near him after the abhisheka (the bath). Sandalwood's or tilak should be applied on God Krishna's statue forehead.

Start the prayer by lighting the diya. Afterward, apply a tilak to your forehead and give the remaining kumkum as prasad to other devotees. Since the provided kumkum has been accepted and blessed by God Krishna, it acts as a conduit for his blessings. A conch shell should be blown to conclude the worship ritual and to seek pardon for any errors or omissions made during the Archana. You can leave the fruits, water, Naivedya, flowers, and rice offerings for God to enjoy for a while and then consume them as prasad, submerge them in running water, or give them away. Now you can pray to God.

In the aftermath of the puja, you can perform a Jaap meditation while chanting "Hare Krishna" or "Om Namo Bhagavate Vasudeva".

Janmashtami Legends and History

Hindu mythology holds that Kansa the evil king married his sister Devki to the Yadav King Vasudeva, to extend his empire. Kansa's death was predicted to be caused by Devaki's eighth child. Angered by this, Kansa sent his sister and Vasudev to the dungeons and promised to kill all their children. Devaki and Vasudev's six newborn babies were killed by Kansa, but the seventh child was miraculously saved by Rohini, Vasudev's another wife, when the child was magically transferred from Devaki's womb to Rohini's. The child was then called Balram and was Krishna's elder brother. Krishna was born on the eighth day of the dark fortnight in the Bhadrapada month. After the birth of the child, all the dungeon guards fell asleep, and the gates flew open. Taking advantage of this opportunity, Vasudev smuggled the child to Gokul with his friend Nanda. Krishna was raised believing he was the son of Nanda. He killed his uncle Kansa when he grew up and freed all the people of Mathura

DURGA POOJA

ndia celebrates many auspicious religious festivals, and Navratri is one of the most popular. There is a great deal of enthusiasm and energy surrounding the celebration. Indians perform Navratri pujas with devotion all over the country. The nine auspicious nights of Navratri are celebrated to honor and pray to Goddess Durga. In Kolkata, Navratri is also known as Durga Puja and is celebrated for four days with great enthusiasm. During these puja days, people observe fasts and perform spiritual rituals. Following the right methods makes it easy for During Navratri Puja, it is considered auspicious to chant the prayers and invoke Durga Maa, who will visit your home and bless you and your family. Performing Navratri puja at home requires knowledge of the customs, rituals, and Navratri Puja Samagri. These are the essentials you'll need: -

- ♦ Goddess **Durga idol** or picture
- ♦ Saree or a red dupatta to offer to Goddess Durga
- ♦ *Panjika*, or the sacred Hindu book

167

- Coconut
- Sandalwood
- Fresh mango leaves, wash them before using
- Paan
- Supari
- Ganga water
- Roli, the red holy powder which is used to put tilak
- Cardamom
- Incense sticks
- Cloves
- Fruits
- Sweets
- Incense sticks
- Fresh flower to offer to Maa Durga
- Gulal
- Vermilion
- Raw rice
- Moli, a red sacred thread
- Grass

7 Easy Steps to do Navratri Pooja at home?

Step 1: To place the deity (Ghata Sthapana)

In the first place, you must place the idol of Maa Durga on a chowki and plant barley on a clay plot near it.

Step 2: Establish the Kalash

Next, you must pour holy water (Gangajal) over it and place flowers, mango leaves, and coins on it. Place raw rice on top, then cover it with a lid. Place a coconut that is wrapped in a roll (the red clothing) on top of the coconut.

Step 3: Worship of Goddess Durga

To worship Durga, a Diya is lit in front of her. Panchopchar can be used to worship Kalash or Ghat. Naivedya, incense stick, deepak, and incense stick are the five items used in panchopchar to worship the deity.

Step 4: Chowki Sthapana

This process involves invoking Goddess Durga. On the chowki, spread the roli and tie mouli around it. On the chowki, place the idol of Goddess Durga.

Step 5: Navratri Puja

During Navratri Puja, it is considered auspicious to chant the prayers and invoke Durga Maa, who will visit your home and bless you and your family. To perform the ritual of Navratri puja, you must offer flowers, bhog(sweets), diya, fruits, etc.

Step 6: Aarti

During aarti, decorate a thali with all the Navratri decorations. Carry the thali in one hand and a bell in the other. Jingle the bells and sing the aarti song to seek Maa Durga's blessings

Step 7: Inviting and Feeding Goddesses

Invite nine girls aged 5 to 12 on the last day or ninth day of Navratri and prepare food for them. The ritual process is called Kanya puja, and they are referred to as Goddesses. Follow these steps to perform Navratri puja at home and bring peace and blessings to your family and home.

Story

The story associated with Navratri is the battle that occurred between Goddess Durga and the demon Mahishasura. Mahishasura had been granted immortality by Lord Brahma and had been told that he could only be defeated by a woman. He attacked Trilok (Earth, Heaven and Hell), and the Gods were not able to defeat him. Finally, Lord Brahma, Lord Vishnu and Lord Shiva together created Goddess Durga, who finally defeated Mahishasura. She fought with him for 15 days, and the demon kept changing his form. Mahishasura would take various forms to confuse Goddess Durga.

Finally, when he turned into a buffalo is when Goddess Durga killed him with her trishul. It is on the day of Mahalaya that Mahishasura was killed. Each day of Navratri has a separate color attached to it.

The word Navratri is derived from Sanskrit, meaning nine nights - nava (nine) ratri (night). On each day a different form of Goddess Durga is worshipped. They are Goddess Shailputri (Day 1), Goddess Brahmacharini (Day 2), Goddess Chandraghanta (Day 3), Goddess Kushmanda (Day 4), Goddess Skandamata (Day

5), Goddess Katyayani (Day 6), Goddess Kaalratri (Day 7), Goddess Mahagauri (Day 8) and Goddess Siddhidatri (Day 9).

Navratri is celebrated as Durga Puja, where the festival symbolizes the victory of Goddess Durga over demon Mahishasura, signifying the victory of good over evil.

DUSSEHRA

A Hindi word called Dussehra is composed of two words, 'Dus' and 'Hara', where 'Dus' means ten and 'Hara' means annihilated. These two words can be combined to form the word 'Dussehra', which represents the day when the ten evil faces are destroyed.

In India, Dussehra is celebrated between September and October on the 10th day of the Hindu autumn lunar month of Ashvin. Throughout the Indian subcontinent, the festival is observed and celebrated differently for different reasons. The occasion is celebrated with enthusiasm and zeal in all parts of the country. As the harvest season begins in India, 'mother earth' is invoked to reactivate the soil's vigor and fertility. Vijayadashami is celebrated by performing rituals and religious activities. As a result of rituals and customs, soil is rejuvenated by cosmic forces. This festival is commonly known as Dasha-hara, Dussehra, and Durgotsav. The festival marks the victory of good over evil.

Hindus celebrate Dussehra as one of their most important festivals. Hindu religion is very important to the people. There is great religious and cultural significance to this festival. This festival is celebrated with great enthusiasm and belief by the people. During this festival, goodness triumphs over badness, which means truth triumphs over evil power. A lot of rituals and pooja ceremonies are performed during this festival. Devotees and religious people keep fasts throughout the day. While some people fast only the first and last day (9th day), others fast for all nine days, worshiping Goddess Durga for getting blessings. The tenth day is celebrated as a celebration of Rama's victory over Ravana, the demon king. The day commemorates God Rama's victory over Ravana when he killed the ten-headed demon Ravana and handed over the throne of his kingdom Lanka to his brother Vibhishana.

On this day, people celebrate Durga Puja, which commemorates Durga's victory over Mahishasura, the buffalo demon, to restore Dharma. The celebration of Navratri culminates with Dussehra on the tenth day, when the idol of goddess Durga is immersed in a river or lake. Festivals like Dussehra are unique in their perception and significance. This day symbolizes not only Ram's victory, but also the victory of humanity. People who believe that whenever there will be chaos in society and evil will try to take over humanity, God will appear in the form of a savior to save his devotees are held in high regard on this day. Hindu religious festivals are celebrated throughout India and Nepal. The celebrations are usually concluded with processions to a river or

173

seaside to immerse clay statues of Saraswati, Lakshmi, Ganesha, and Durga.

During Sindoor Khel, married women apply sindoor to Durga and to each other, and smear it on each other's faces. The ritual symbolizes the married women's prayers for a happy and prosperous marriage. In addition, it celebrates womanhood and the special bond that exists between married women.

By immersing idols, devotees seek forgiveness of sins and blessings from the gods. During Dussehra celebrations, enormous effigies of Ravana are usually burned along with those of his brothers Meghanada and Kumbhakarna, symbolizing Ram's victory over the Sri Lankan king, Ravan. It also marks the beginning of preparations for Diwali, which occurs twenty days after Dussehra. During Ramlila celebrations, people enact the life and glory of the righteous God Ram through short plays. Every evening for a month in cities like Varanasi, artists act out Ram's entire life.

Story

Sri Lankan king Ravana was a devotee of God Shiva. Although he was highly intelligent, he was cruel and arrogant. Having ten heads signifies Ravana's extensive knowledge of the four Vedas and six Upanishads, which made him as powerful as ten scholars. The ten heads can be interpreted as ten Indriyas [five Gyan (sensory) Indriyas and five Karm (instruments of bodily action) Indriyas}. His powers were used for evil. Ravana represents a worldly personality who lusts for power, women, and greed. Ravan could not stay happy despite his high stature and gold-plated kingdom.

Whenever there is only knowledge without love and compassion in life, one becomes egoistic.

As for Rama, the king of Ayodhya, he was known as Maryada Purushottam, literally the Perfect Man or the God of Virtue. Rama's life was marked by perfect adherence to dharma despite harsh tests throughout his life. Despite his father's promise, Rama abandoned his claim to the throne and lived in exile for fourteen years. Love, Peace & Bliss are personified by Rama as our spiritual personality. Hindus have celebrated this festival every year since God Rama killed the demon king Ravana on the 10th day of Ashwayuja month of Hindu calendar. Ravana was killed by Rama because he had kidnapped Mata Seeta and refused to return her to him. With the help of his younger brother Lakshman and Vanara soldiers of Hanuman, Rama had won the war with Ravana. By knowing Ravana's killing secret on the 10th day of the war, God Rama gained victory. His wife Seeta was safely retained after he killed Ravana.

The victory of Rama over Ravana [good over evil] is the replacement of ego and negativity with divine knowledge, love, and happiness.

There is only Light (Eternal Happiness) when Rama wins.

Second story:

As a result of Mahishasura' s death on the tenth day of Dussehra, the festival is also known as Durga Utsav. The battle between Durga and Mahishasura lasted nine days and nine nights. On the tenth day, Durga killed Mahishasura. Each year, different manifestations of goddess Durga are worshipped during the nine-day long Navratri festival. The tenth day is dedicated to Durga as Vijayadashami. Navratri celebrates the feminine power and worships it.

AYUDHA PUJA

The very names of Dasara, Dussehra, and Navaratri evoke a sense of resplendence. The mind fills itself with all the vibrancy of a festive occasion when one thinks of this grand Indian festival. Traditionally, Ayudha Puja is celebrated on the ninth day of Dasara by worshiping implements, arms and ammunition, tools, and vehicles, mostly in the southern parts of the country. Ayudha Puja is a worship of whatever implements one uses for his or her livelihood. Traditionally, these implements are placed on an altar to the Divine the evening before. To see one's work as an offering to God, one must make a conscious effort to see the divine in the tools and objects one uses every day. Keeping the divine in mind will also help one maintain constant remembrance.

Traditionally, one prostrates before one's tools before starting one's work in India; it is an expression of gratitude to God for assisting one in fulfilling one's duties. Despite being observed in different places for different reasons, Ayudha Puja is about worshiping tools and implements.

Ayudha puja was performed on the day before Goddess Chaudhari's war on demon Mahishasura and all her weapons were worshipped before she left for the battle. Afterwards, she celebrates her victory over the demon Vijayadashami, which indicates her victory over evil. In addition, Ayudha Puja may be important on this occasion because Arjuna, one of the Pandavas brothers, took back his arsenals that he had hidden in a Vani tree on Vijayadashami. To live in disguise for the promised exile period, he returned the weapons. Nowadays, Ayudha Puja has become Vahana Puja when people worship their vehicles such as cars, scooters, and motorbikes. During Vahana Puja, all types of vehicles are decorated with vermilion, garlands, mango leaves, and banana saplings. To get rid of all evils, a white pumpkin is decorated with vermilion and turmeric and smashed in front of a vehicle during Vahana Puja.

9 DAYS AND IT'S CONSECUTIVE COLORS

Sarees are worn by women during Navratri in a variety of colors and styles. Each of these colors has its own meaning. These nine colors are believed to represent nine moods of goddesses, each different and beautiful. There is a specific color assigned to each of the nine days. Wearing these different colors is believed to bestow Divine Mother's divine qualities on the wearer. Wearing nine colors consecutively on nine days is considered auspicious because of this.

Traditionally, on the first day of the festival, women wear yellow sarees in honor of the goddess for her divine qualities of happiness and cheerfulness. Yellow color energizes the festival.

Green is the color associated with the second day. Green symbolizes nature, growth, and energy. Healing properties are also associated with green color.

Third day's color is grey, which symbolizes intellect and compromise. This is the color of diplomacy that mediates and negotiates the distance between black and white.

Orange represents the brightness and luminosity of the sun. Passion and creativity are also created by orange. On the fourth day of Navratri, it is worn.

White is the color associated with the fifth day. The white color symbolizes peace, purity, innocence, and clarity.

Red is the color of the sixth day. Symbolizing action, passion, and vigor.

On the seventh day, Royal blue is worn, which combines the shades of blue and violet. As a symbol of clairvoyance and intersensory perception, this color is associated with Divine Mother's fierce form. According to legend, this color can help people see beyond illusions.

The eighth day is dedicated to pink. Symbolizing love and compassion. A sense of hope and a fresh perspective.

Purple is a color that symbolizes ambition, nobility, and power when blue and red are combined. It's the color of the ninth day.

Dussehra Puja Process

Image of Dussehra

Cow dung

Roli

Chawal

Wheat Flour

Flowers

Jaggery

1-1/4 kg Rice

Prasada

Fruits

Bananas

Money for offering

Vidhi / Steps for performing the Puja

Draw the Dussehra image with wheat flour

Make 2 katori of cow dung (in absence/or can be replaced with wheat flour) with a lid.

In one katori, keep the coins and in the other keep a little roli, chawal and fruits.

Do the puja with water, roli, chawal and flowers.

Offer Banana, jaggery, 1-1/4 kg.

Light the dhoop and the Deepak, then do the parikrama.

Puja is offered with flowers, Jhawar, roli and chawal.

After the puja is done, money from the cow dung box is taken out and placed in a safe place.

Finally, food and Dakshina are offered to the Brahmins.

On this auspicious occasion, expert priests perform pujas. During the puja, mantras and slokas are chanted. During pujas, people seek the blessings of the almighty for happiness, health, wealth, and prosperity. During the Puja of Dussehra, people are offered sweets as 'prasad'. The puja can be performed by both men and women, but they must know the basic rituals and procedures. Each region of the country has its own Dussehra puja rituals.

It is an age-old tradition to perform Dussehra puja. People believe that if you perform the puja dedicatedly, you will receive the blessings of Almighty God.

VAHANA PUJA

Vahana Puja is a Hindu ritual dedicated to worshiping vehicles. To ensure safety and protection during journeys, Hindus believe that vehicles, especially those used for religious or spiritual purposes, should be blessed and respected. In preparation, the vehicle is cleaned and decorated with flowers, garlands, and traditional ornaments. Vermilion and turmeric paste can be applied to the vehicle as a sign of auspiciousness and protection. A lit lamp and incense sticks are placed in front of the vehicle. In aarti, a lit lamp is waved in front of the deity as part of the ritual. Priests or persons performing pujas may offer blessings for the vehicle's well-being and safety. At the end of the ceremony, Prasad (blessed offerings) is distributed to the attendees.

This puja is most beneficial with Maha Mrityunjaya mantra, which provides protection to everyone:

ॐ त्र्यम्बकं यजामहे सुगन्धिं पुष्टिवर्धनम्

उर्वारुकमिव बन्धनान् मृत्योर्मुक्षीय मामृतात्

Om Tryambhakam Yajamahe Sugandhim Pushtivardhanam

Urvarukamiva Bandhanan Mrityor Mukshiya Maamritat

The meaning of the above mantra is

Om - We worship the three-eyed one (God Siva), who is fragrant and who nourishes all beings well. May He save us from death as a cucumber is freed from its creeper bonds.

APRAJITA PUJA

It is often used in Hinduism to refer to deities or divine forms that are considered unconquerable. The Sanskrit term Aprajita means "undefeated" or "invincible." In Hinduism, there isn't a specific "Aprajita Puja.". There may, however, be some localized or specialized rituals or pujas associated with deities or forms that are considered Aprajita in some regional traditions.

Story

On Vijayadashami, God Rama worships Devi Aprajita a day before beginning his journey for Lanka to bring back Sita. On Dussehra, Aprajita Puja is also held during the Aparahna Muhurat. Throughout history, Goddess Aprajita has been worshipped for safe and successful journeys.

The following mantra is chanted during Aprajita Puja:

इमां पूजां मयां देवि यथाशक्ति निवेदिताम्।

रक्षार्थं तु समादाय व्रजस्व स्थानमुत्तमम्॥

हारेण तु विचित्रेण भास्वत्कनकमेखला।

अपराजिता भद्ररता करोतु विजयं मम॥

SHAMI TREE PUJA

Shami Tree Puja, also known as Banni Tree Puja, is an important Hindu ritual, especially on Vijaya Dashami or Dussehra. There is a connection between this ceremony and the epic Mahabharata.

Story

After twelve years in exile, the Pandavas, along with their mother Kunti, spent a year incognito hiding their weapons in a Shami tree (Prosopis cineraria) to avoid detection by the Kauravas. It was Vijaya Dashami when they returned to retrieve their weapons, marking their victory over adversity. On Vijaya Dashami, people perform the Shami Tree Puja to remember this event. Shami Tree Puja symbolizes victory over challenges and the triumph of righteousness. In addition, it emphasizes the importance of nature and how it plays a role in our lives.

During the puja, mantras are chanted, and the deities associated with the ritual are invoked.

शमी शमयते पापं शमी लोहितकण्टका ।
धारिण्यर्जुनबाणानां रामस्य प्रियवादिनी ।।
करिष्यमाणयात्रायां यथाकाल सुखं मया ।
तत्रनिर्विघ्नकर्त्रीत्वंभवश्रीरामपूजिते ।।

Shami Shamayate papam shami lokhitkantaka

Dharinyarjunbananam Ramasya priyavadini

Karishmanyatraya yathakal such mya

Tatra nirvighanktri twam bhav Sree Rampujite

This mantra means: O Shami, God Rama has worshipped you. My journey to victory begins now. I wish you a pleasant and obstacle-free journey.

DIWALI

〜

'Diwali' means "rows of lighted lamps" in Sanskrit. Across India, households decorate their spaces with colorful lights and small lamps called diyas. During Diwali, the festival of lights, millions of Hindus, Sikhs, and Jains around the world celebrate the triumph of good over evil with beautiful rituals like festive lights, fireworks, sweet delicacies, and family gatherings.

To help you take part in the magical festivities of Diwali, we explore its story, history, and traditions.

Why Diwali is celebrated

There is a different story and historical event associated with each religion's Diwali celebration. Based on the Hindu lunisolar calendar, Diwali's dates change each year. Mid-October to mid-November is the typical time for the festival.

What food to eat?

There are dishes that are popular in each region. It is not customary to fast on Diwali, and there is no set dinner menu. Some homes don't serve non-vegetarian food. There are several savory snacks you can prepare: samosas, bhajis, potato patties (aloo tiki) and spiced chickpeas (channa bhatura). Gujarat is famous for its crunchy snacks, known as 'farssan'. Keep some room for the main course, which may include curries, such as our next-level tikka masala, or vegetarian dishes, such as dals and pulses.

How to celebrate

The five days of Diwali are as follows:

Dhanteras: On the first day of Diwali, people perform rituals called pujas or poojas and place tea lights around their balconies and entryways, as well as purchase kitchen utensils, gold, and silver, which are believed to bring good luck.

Narak Chaturdashi: On Narak Chaturdashi, people will spend time at home and exchange sweets with friends and family. Rangolis, which are intricate patterns made from colored powder, rice, and flowers, can also be used to decorate the floors of a home.

Lakshmi Puja: It is considered the most auspicious day to worship the goddess Lakshmi on Lakshmi Puja. In addition to a prayer to honor her, families usually gather for a feast, fireworks display, and more festivities. Unmarried girls do 'chuka-bharna' tradition in which they fill a small katori(bowl) and worship in their doll house, representing their future house wellbeing.

Govardhan Puja: Known as Govardhan Puja, this day celebrates the new year of Gujarat and God Krishna. For Puja, a mountain of food offerings is prepared.

Bhaiya Dooj: This day is dedicated to celebrating the sibling bond. In tradition, brothers will visit their sisters and bring gifts, which are then honored with special rituals and sweets.

Process

Diwali puja rituals vary from family to family and region to region. The following items are indicative of what you will need:

- Pot/Kalash
- Aam Patta/Mango leaves
- Idol or picture of Goddess Lakshmi
- Milk and curd
- Honey
- Ghee
- Puffed rice
- Sweets/Mithaai
- Coriander seeds
- Cumin seeds

Muhurat time for this puja is usually in the evening between 6 p.m. and 8 p.m.

Laxmi and Ganesh Puja Vidhi for Diwali

As with the method of Diwali puja, the method varies largely based on the region and the rituals observed by individual households. One may follow the following basic methodology.

Prepare a bed of rice on a clean cloth where you want to perform the puja. Place the kalash on top of the rice.

Pour water into the kalash. Arrange the aam patta around the opening and place the betel nut, flowers, a coin, and rice inside. On the kalash, place a thali (plate). Goddess Lakshmi will sit here.

The thali can be decorated by painting a lotus with rangoli colors/turmeric powder and placing coins on it.

The God Ganesha usually sits on the right side of the kalash. It is also possible to place the idols of Saraswathi alongside Lakshmi, Saraswathi, and Durga, thus completing the three forms of Adi-Shakti.

All items should be sprinkled with Gangajal (or clean water). Keeping the atmosphere clean and well-lit is essential.

It is now possible to recite the mantras for invoking Goddess Lakshmi. Depending on your native language, you can find these in puja books or online.

At the puja, offer flowers, rice, garlands of marigolds, coconut, fruits, sweets, betel nuts, sandalwood, Kumkum, and incense sticks.

After the puja, recite the Diwali puja aarti with the entire family and post that we distribute the prasad.

Diwali is also a day of worship for God Kuber, or the treasurer of the Gods, in addition to Laxmi and Ganesh. At home, worship the locker or safe where you keep your gold and cash for Kuber puja.

Girls also make houses from clay or cardboard and decorate it. They perform pooja at the same night on the ghar. Girls eat the prasad thereafter.

Why do we clean our house on Diwali?

Diwali is popularly known as the festival of lights. It is one of the most important & favorite festivals among all Hinduism. And it's not only about Hinduism, but people also all over India celebrate this festival with great enthusiasm. Festival season is the one where you have lots and lots of preparation to be done. From clothing to sweets and from cleaning to doing preparation for puja, there is quite a lot of work which must be done.

But the most important part of every festival is cleaning. And especially Diwali is that festival which itself has a great significance regarding cleaning as the objective of this festival is to welcome god Lakshmi as a symbol of peace, prosperity & wealth. As it is always said, Cleanliness is next to godliness. So here are some of the major factors which perfectly describe the significance of cleanliness during Diwali.

Story

According to Hindu mythology, Diwali is the day God Rama, his wife Sita Devi, and brother Lakshmana return to their homeland after 14 years in exile. Rama had defeated Ravana when the villagers lit a path for him. In some regions, this story is reenacted as part of celebrations.

Diwali also commemorates God Krishna's victory over Narakasura, the demon who ruled his kingdom, in Hindu mythology. God Krishna declared it a day of celebration after slaying the demon. People often burn effigies of the demon kings as part of the celebration in some parts of India.

During Diwali, Hindus also celebrate Lakshmi. According to the romantic Diwali story, she chose God Vishnu, one of Hinduism's most important deities, as her husband. Diwali coincides with harvest and new year celebrations in other cultures. Whatever Diwali story you celebrate, it's always a day of new beginnings and light over darkness.

BHAIDHUJ

hai Dooj is celebrated by several communities in India on the second day after Diwali. It is a celebration of brother-sister love. In different states, it's known as Bhai Teeka, Bhau Beej, or Bhai Phota. Traditionally, brothers and sisters celebrate their bond by applying Teeka to their foreheads. Bihar, however, celebrates the festival in a rather unique way. Bhai Dooj is also known as Godhan Puja in Bihar. Yama Dwitiya is another name for this festival.

When to celebrate: A Day after Diwali morning or evening

How to do it

Traditional Way

- This festival is celebrated by women in a community gathering early in the morning.
- Women of one area gather in the courtyard or open space of one house and make a large rectangle out of cow dung in the courtyard or open space of that house.
- The women sit around this structure. There are two idols of Yama, the God of Death, and of his sister Yami (also known as the river Yamuna) in the center. There are also idols of snakes and scorpions.
- Folk songs are sung after the legends behind the festival are read.

New Way

- Girls take shower and get ready
- On an open area on the floor, they place a thali/paper. They create same structures as above with the help of wheat flour (earlier days it was done by cow dung)
- Have a clay Diya and wooden stick with nails at the very end of the stick
- Put Jal on all followed by roli, Kumkum (if married) on all
- Place kala chana, batasa (sugar candy) and place the diya on the center

- Break the clay Diya with the help of wooden stick
- Make thread rakhis with cotton balls and (haldi plus water) solution
- Pick up the left-over kala chana on the plate

Tying the Bhai Dooj thread

- Have brother sit facing the east direction. Place tilak on brother's forehead
- Tie the thread (cotton thread Rakhi or red thread molli) on brother's hand
- Give him 5-7 kala chana to swallow with or without water
- Offer him sweets. Followed by meals.
- Brother's give sister gifts

Story

According to legend, Yama takes away anyone who is too good and has never been cursed. On this day, sisters curse their brothers in the hope that Yama won't venture near them, and they'll live a long life.

When I was a child, I would burst into tears when I was told to say, "I wish my brother died". Even if I had fought with them moments earlier, this would happen year after year. Another tradition follows the curses by the women piercing their tongues with a regni kaanta (rose thorn can be used) as an expression of regret. There are other legends surrounding this festival. There is a story that King Prithu invites his married daughter to her brother's wedding. She hears a potter saying that the prince will die during the baraat (wedding procession) since his sister has never cursed him. Upon reaching the wedding, she begins cursing her brother, much to the guests' shock. Afterwards, she insists on joining the procession and leading the baraat. As she travels, she kills poisonous snakes, scorpions and also hides them within the folds of her saree. Yamraj appears when the baraat reaches its destination. After seeing their love for each other, he decides to go back empty-handed. Afterwards, the sister proceeds to demonstrate to everyone the ways in which she protected her brother from a great number of venomous creatures.

CHITRA GUPT POOJA

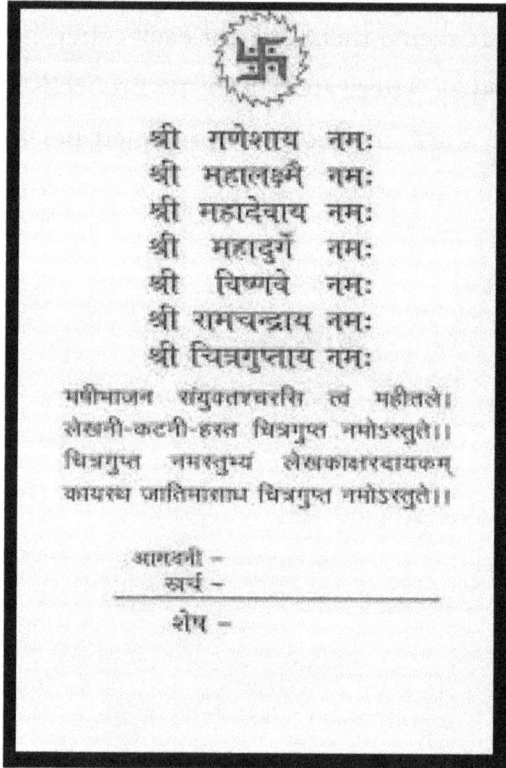

श्री गणेशाय नमः
श्री महालक्ष्मी नमः
श्री महादेवाय नमः
श्री महादुर्गे नमः
श्री विष्णवे नमः
श्री रामचन्द्राय नमः
श्री चित्रगुप्ताय नमः

मषीभाजन संयुक्तश्चरसि त्वं महीतले।
लेखनी-कटनी-हस्त चित्रगुप्त नमोऽस्तुते।।
चित्रगुप्त नमस्तुभ्यं लेखकाक्षरदायकम्
कायस्थ जातिमाश्रय चित्रगुप्त नमोऽस्तुते।।

आमदनी –
खर्च –
शेष –

With a new pen, write the names of five or seven gods & goddesses on a plain new paper by drawing swastikas with roli-ghee. Afterward, write a "MANTRA (Given above)" and write your name, address (permanent & present), date (Hindi date), your income & expenditure. Fold the paper and present it to Chittragupt Ji.

Hindu Dharam is based on a life cycle involving reincarnation. According to Hindu beliefs, those who do not attain a balance between their good and bad deeds will have to reincarnate into any living form.

Shree Chitraguptjee's primary task is to create a record of all living beings, to judge their lives based on their good deeds and misdeeds, and to decide, upon death, whether one will attain Nirvana - complete their life cycle and be free from all worldly troubles - or if they will be punished in another life form for their misdeeds.

Twelve Sons of Chitragupta Ji Maharaj

Shrivastava, Mathur, Gaur, Nigam, Asthana, Kulshrestha, Suryadwaja, Bhatnagar, Ambastha, Saxena, Karana and Valmik.

Puja Items

Sandalwood Paste, Til, Camphor/Kapoor, Paan, Sugar, Paper, Pen, Ink, Ganga Water, Unbroken Rice, Cotton, Honey, Yellow Mustard, Plate Made of Leaves, Puja Platform, Dhoop, Yoghurt, Sweets, Puja Cloths, Milk, Seasonal fruits, Panchpatras, Gulal (Color powder), Brass Katora, Tulsi leaves, Roli, kesar, Betel nut, Match box, Frankincense and Deep.

Puja Process

After cleaning the puja room, wash Chittragupt Ji's idol or photo first with water, and then with panchamrit/rose water, then with water again. Put the Deepak (Lamp) of ghee in front of Chittragupt Ji. Using milk, curd, ghee (clarified butter), sugar, and honey, make a Panchamrit. As a prasad, place a few mithais, snacks, and fruits. Offer flowers, Abir (red), Sindoor (vermillion), and Haldi (turmeric). Agarbatti (incense sticks) and lamps filled with ghee should be lit. Chitragupta puja's holy book should be read. Chitragupta puja's holy book should be read. With a new pen, write the names of five gods & goddesses on plain new paper. Write a "MANTRA (Given Below)" and write your name, address (permanent & current), income, and expenses. Present the folded paper to Chitragupt Ji.

Chitragupta Puja and Dawat Puja

It is performed by the Kayastha Parivar, which believes in peace, justice, knowledge, and literacy, the four virtues symbolized by Shree Chitraguptjee's form. During this puja, books and pens are worshipped, symbolizing the significance of study in the life of a Kayastha. Earning members of the household also give an account of their earnings at Chitragupta Puja, writing to Chitragupt Maharaj the additional amount required to run the household next year.

CHHATH POOJA

orship of Sun God. Chhath Puja has a Vedic or yogic
history. In the past, rishis used this method to survive
without any external food intake and to obtain energy
from the sun. Chhath Puja rituals were used to accomplish this.

What is Chhath Puja?

Chhath Puja's origin is unclear and ambiguous. According to
legend, it originated from the Vedas, Mahabharata, and Ramayana.
The legend also states that the King Priyabrat and his wife Malini
were blessed with a beautiful baby boy and started worshiping
Chahthi Maiya and celebrating Chhath Puja.

The Rituals of Chhath Puja

The goddess worshipped in this Puja is Chahthi Maiya, also
known as Usha. There are several rituals involved in the Chhath
festival that are considerably harsher than other Hindu festivals. A
person may also take a dip in rivers or water bodies, practice strict
fasting (one cannot even drink water during the entire fast), stand

and offer prayers in water, face the sun for long periods of time, or offer prasad to the sun at sunset and sunrise.

Nahay Khay

Devotees are required to take a dip in the holy river on the first day of the Puja and cook a proper meal for themselves. On this day, Kadu Bhaat is cooked with Chana Dal using mud or bronze utensils and mango wood over a mud stove. On this day, women who observe the fast can eat only one meal.

Lohanda and Kharna

On the second day, devotees observe fast for the entire day, which they can break after sunset. Parvaitins prepare the whole Prasad themselves, including kheer and chapatis, and break their fast with this Prasad, after which they fast without water for 36 hours.

Sandhya Arghya

During the third day, the entire household of the Vratins prepares the Prasad at home and then makes offerings to the setting sun on the riverbank in the evening. When making offerings, females usually wear turmeric yellow sarees. Folk songs enhance the evenings even more.

Usha Arghya

All devotees go to the riverbank before sunrise on the final day to make offerings to the rising sun. At the end of the festival, the

Vratins break their 36-hour fast (called Paaran) and their relatives come over to enjoy Prasad.

Story of Chhath

The celebrations last for the four days thanking the Sun God, the source of all powers. Devotees of the Sun God observe a fast called Vrati. Chhath Puja occurs twice a year - once during summer and once during winter.

Karthik Chhath is performed on the sixth day of the Karthik month known as Kartika Shukla Shashti. This day falls during October or November every year as per the Hindu Calendar. In the summer, it is celebrated a few days after Holi, and is known as Chait Chhath.

The rituals surrounding Chhath Puja are supposedly harsher when compared to other Hindu festivals. They involve strict fasting (without water), taking a dip in rivers/water bodies, standing in water, and offering prayers, facing the sun for a prolonged period, and offering 'prasad' to the Sun during sunrise and sunset. Any food prepared during the festival will have no salt, onion, or garlic.

Chhath Puja Story- King Priyabrat

This is the story of a king named Priyabrat and his wife Malini. Despite living happily, neither of them has a child. Maharishi Kashyap helped them decide on Maha Yagya. Malini, the wife of the king, became pregnant and delivered a dead child. After losing hope of giving his life, the Manas Kanya (Devsena) suddenly appeared and said, "I am Goddess Khashti, and I am the sixth part of the universe.".After worshiping me with pure mind and soul for six days, you will definitely be blessed with a child." The King and Queen agreed to worship and then they were blessed with a beautiful son.It is believed that the costume originated from ancient Vedas, namely the Rigveda, which contains hymns for worshiping the sun, describes the ritual, and exemplifies similar attire. It describes the frugality and abstinence rituals associated with the worship of God Sun. Chhaiti Maiya is also worshiped and known as USHA in the Vedas and is believed to be Surya's younger wife.

Chhath Puja Story- Mahabharat story

According to the Sanskrit Epic poem, Draupadi observed a similar ritual to today's Chhath Puja. Draupadi started crying during the Pandavas' exile in the forest. Yudhishthira went to Sage Dhaumya to get a solution to their misery. "The Food grain is the form of the Sun god that helps maintain life on earth," Sage Dhoumya explained. Thus, the Sun god is their father. In Kartik Mas on the sixth and seventh days of Shukla Paksha, people who worship the sun god and chant the 108 names of God Surya will be blessed with sons, gems, wealth, and wisdom. Yudhishthira began worshiping God Sun after being enlightened and recommended by Sage Dhaumya. As a result of Yudhishthira's devotion, God Sun appeared before him and presented him with a magical copper vessel. Until Draupadi, the wife of the five Pandavas, took her meal, this vessel would cook four types of food for them. As a result, Pandavas came out of their troubles and helped regain their kingdoms. By worshiping Bhagwan Surya during Chhath Puja, one can fulfill all their desires and be free of pain and suffering.

Mahabharat also mentions Karan, the son of Kunti and God Surya, doing daily worship of his father - Sun and special puja in Shukla Paksha during the month of Kartik. In Bihar, Karan is also a king of Aang (now known as Bhagalpur). In that part of Bihar, people also worship the Sun.

Chhath Puja Story- Ramayana Story

It is believed in Ramayana that after completing Banwas (Exile) of 14 years, God Rama & Mata Sita fasted together and offered puja to Surya (The Sun God) in Kartik (between October and December). As a result, Chhath Puja became the most important and traditional festival in Hinduism.

Hindu Fastings Based on Moon/Lunar Phases

❧

Pooranmasi

urnima divides the month into two equal lunar fortnights. Many Hindu devotees observe fast on this day to celebrate Purnima Vrat and Shree Satyanarayana Puja with deep faith. This brings prosperity, health, and happiness to one's life and their entire family.

On Purnima, the full moon day, devotees observe a fast to pay homage to Chandra Deva and receive the divine blessing through the brightest light of the Moon. This fast controls the acid content of the body and cleanses the digestive system.

As per the Hindu lunar calendar, there are 12 full moon nights in a year and many Hindus celebrate Purnima vrat on this auspicious day.

The day of Purnima or Full Moon holds great significance in Hindu mythology. Reciting the mantras of Mahamrityunjaya and Chandra Gayatri on this auspicious day is extremely significant to receive divine blessings from God.

India celebrates Guru Purnima to honor the teachings and efforts made by our gurus/teachers. Hindus celebrate Arshad Purnima as Guru Purnima to pay homage to God Shiva, who taught myths about the creation of the earth, gods, and humans.

A mythological plot describes a yogi who appeared in the upper regions of the Himalayas, sat among them, and did nothing. Seven people hung on, and after 84 years of meditation, God Shiva decided to become their guru and revealed the divine knowledge to them on the day of Guru Purnima.

Hindu devotees observe Purnima Vrat and keep fast on this auspicious day, which brings them positive energy and tranquilizes the mind and emotions. It also helps them to achieve spiritual, physical, and economic upliftment beyond expectations.

Mantra for this vrat: The day of Purnima also as Full Moon holds a great significance, as per the Hindu mythology. Our very own Upanishads and Puranas explain that reciting the Mantras of Mahamrityunjaya and Chandra Gayatri on this auspicious day is extremely significant to receive divine blessings from the God.

Mahamrityunjaya Mantra

Om Tryambakam yajaamahe

sugandhim pushtivardhanam |

Urvaarukamiva bandhanaan-

mrityormuksheeya maamritaat ||

Mantra meaning: We worship the three-eyed One, who is fragrant and who nourishes all life forms. Like the fruit falls from the bondage of the stem, may we also be liberated from the cycle of death, from mortality.

Chandra Gayatri Mantra

Om Padmadwajaya Vidhmahe |

Hema Roopaya Dheemahe

Tanno Chandra Prachodayat' ||

Mantra meaning: Om let me meditate on God Chandra who has the flag of lotus.

His shrines are in the brilliant color of gold. Let God Chandra illuminate my mind.

Below is the complete list of Purnima Vrat-

1. Chaitra Purnima – April
2. Vaishakh Purnima – May
3. Jyeshta Purnima – June
4. Ashadh Purnima –July
5. Shravan Purnima – August

6. Bhadrapad Purnima – September
7. Ashvin Purnima- October
8. Kartik Poornima -November
9. Margasirsha Purnima – December
10. Pushya Purnima – January
11. Magha Purnima – February
12. Phalguna Purnima – March

My mother has been doing Purnima vrat since I was a child. Every twelve years you do vrat udyappan and restart the fast or take a break before starting the fast.

EKADASHI

Ekadashi is an auspicious day in Hindu culture. It is the eleventh lunar day (tithi) of each of the two moon phases – the period of the rising moon (Shukla Paksha) and the period of the fading moon (Krishna Paksa).

According to Hindu mythology, the origin of Ekadashi fasting is related to a fight between God Vishnu and a brutal demon called Mura. God Vishnu changed his strategy with a hoax, and he hid in a cave near the Himalayas.

When Mura saw that God was sleeping inside the cave, he wanted to kill Him, but a gorgeous & luminous young girl appeared from within the God and slew Mura with a roar. God was pleased and blessed the young girl with boons.

Ekadashi fasting is an important Upvasa for Hindus as it helps them to control their fluctuating mind, gain the right peace of mind to think of Omnipresent God, and purifies their mind, body, and soul without any doubt.

Hindus celebrate 24 types of Ekadashi in a year, each associated with a different incarnation of Supreme Brahman (God Vishnu). Each Ekadashi accompanies certain food rules during fast.

Hindus celebrate 24 types of Ekadashi in a year, all of which are associated with various incarnations of Supreme Brahman (God Vishnu).

On Ekadashi, a devotee is supposed to fast and take 1000 baths in the holy river Ganga to get rid of all sins accumulated during this lifetime and past life.

During fast, each of them accompanies certain food rules, which must be followed to develop a sattvic mind.

Below are a few Ekadashi, the month in which they fall, the deity to whom they are dedicated, and the permitted foods to eat during a complete fast.

A devotee who is unable to observe the complete fast may eat permitted foods and refrain from rice, pulses, beans, peas, garlic, onions and other tamasic foods.

It is the highest form of love and faith towards God to fast on Ekadashi and bring peace and serenity into one's own life.

1. Chaitra (March-April) - **Papavimchini Ekadashi** (Kishna Paksha) - **Kamada Ekadashi** (Shukla Paksha) -

What to eat - Milk, fruits, and juice can be taken on this day, however, any form of vegetables (raw or cooked) is prohibited.

2. Vaisakha (April-May) - **Varuthini Ekadashi** (Kishna Paksha) - **Mohini Ekadashi** (Shukla Paksha)

What to eat - one meal in the afternoon without any onion or garlic. The fast gets over the next morning. It is okay to have fruits or milk.

3. Jyeshta (May-June) - **Apara Ekadashi** (Kishna Paksha) - **Nirjala Ekadashi** (Shukla Paksha)

What to eat - Waterless fasting is the best on this auspicious day. The devotees can take just water and it's before sunset.

4. Ashaad (June-July) - **Yogini Ekadashi** (Kishna Paksha) - **Shayani Ekadashi** (Shukla Paksha)

What to eat - Only saltless vegetarian foods (without onion/garlic) on this day.

5. Shraavana (July-August) - **Kamika Ekadashi** (Kishna Paksha) - **Shravana Putrada Ekadashi** (Shukla Paksha)

What to eat - one meal in the afternoon, without rice, grains or any beans.

6. Bhadrapada (August-September) - **Annada Ekadashi** (Kishna Paksha) - **Parsva Ekadashi** (Shukla Paksha)

What to eat - Only fruits, dairy products, and dry fruits after the evening prayer.

7. Ashvin (September-October) - **Indira Ekadashi** (Kishna Paksha) - Paashunkushaa **Ekadashi** (Shukla Paksha)

What to eat - Only water throughout the day

8. Kartik (October-November) - **Rama Ekadashi** (Kishna Paksha) - **Prabodhini Ekadashi** (Shukla Paksha)

What to eat - fruits and dairy products

9. Margashirsha (November - December) - **Utpanna Ekadashi** (Kishna Paksha) - **Mokshada Ekadashi / Vaikunta Ekadashi** (Shukla Paksha)

What to eat - sabudana, milk, water, fruits, and sweets

10. Pausha (December- January) - **Saphala Ekadashi** (Kishna Paksha) - **Pausha Putrada Ekadashi / Vaikunta Ekadashi** (Shukla Paksha)

What to eat - Milk and fruits

11. Maagha (January-February) - **Shat Tila Ekadashi** (Kishna Paksha) - **Jaya Ekadashi** (Shukla Paksha)

What to eat - Different types of fruits

12. Phalguna (February-March) - **Vijaya Ekadashi** (Kishna Paksha) - **Amalaki Ekadashi** (Shukla Paksha)

What to eat - Potatoes, nuts, milk, fruits, black pepper, and rock salt.

13. Adhika month (once in 3 years) - **Padmini Visuddha Ekadashi** (Kishna Paksha) - **Paramaa Shuddha Ekadashi** (Shukla Paksha)

What to eat - Fruits and dairy products

My grandmother used to do Ekadashi fast. She lived a very happy and content life and passed away on Ekadashi day.

AMAVASYA

❦

As per the Hindu calendar, there are two fortnights (Shukla and Krishna) and begins with the new moon, (Amavasya). The moon completes one full cycle around the earth within a duration of 29.5 days.

Hindu tradition believes that it is during Amavasya, that the negative forces and evil powers are strong and roam free, affecting the subconscious mind.

Hindu scriptures consider every Amavasya auspicious to perform rituals for the forefathers, but no positive things like marriages, thread ceremonies, a new job, or new business are started on this day.

An Amavasya which falls on Mondays features a special importance, as it is believed to keep off widowhood in women and ensure the bearing of progeny. Hindus offer shraddha to their forefathers to receive blessings from them.

Hindu devotees worship Chandra Dev (Moon God) on this day to seek blessings for success and for good fortune. A story from mythology beautifully explains the reason behind it, where Chandra Dev was cursed to slowly lose his beauty and radiance.

According to spiritual science, Amavasya tithi(date) creates adverse conditions for the human body , mind due to certain positions of the stars, moon, and sun.

During Amavasya, devotees should wake up early in the morning, worship God Shiva or God Vishnu, visit a temple, light a lamp with ghee and chant mantras to praise God Vishnu, the creator, and operator of this Universe, and observe fast or have light food at night.

Since antiquity, the Hindu calendar has been based on the lunar cycle. The day of Amavasya begins in the morning of the Amavasya tithi and completes when the moon is sighted on Pratipada day.

Hindus consider Amavasya as an inauspicious day and do not formalize auspicious functions such as weddings or house-warming ceremonies.

Dos and don'ts during Amavasya

As per the philosophy of Yoga, the human mind is closely connected to the Sun and the Moon. When the moon is full, our mind remains powerful and pure, but when the moon is dark, our mind becomes weak with negative thoughts, and when Amavasya approaches, our mind rises to its peak.

♦ Before sunrise, devotees should take a bath and worship God Shiva or God Vishnu.

211

- Visit a temple to keep our mind calm and clear
- Light a diya with ghee and chant mantras to praise God Vishnu, the creator, and operator of this Universe.
- Narada Purana describes that Anna daan or giving food to the hungry is very significant on this day.
- Our mental state and physical state are quite unbalanced on his day. Observing fast or having light food at night.is good for our health
- According to Hindu beliefs, plucking basil (Tulsi) leaves from the plant is prohibited on this day.
- Non vegetarian and onion/garlic foods must be avoided

Hindu calendars have calculated time based on the fortnightly cycle of the moon since antiquity. Different moon positions in the waxing and waning half of a month mark different occasions, festivals, and celebrations. New moon is known as Amavasya. Amavasya starts early in the morning of the Amavasya tithi and lasts until the moon is sighted on the first day of the waxing phase (Pratipada day).According to Hindu belief, Amavasya is an inauspicious day, except on the day of Diwali when it occurs on Kartik Amavasya. Additionally, during the Amavasya period, auspicious ceremonies such as weddings and housewarmings are not formalized. During Amavasya, customary rituals are performed for the deceased ancestors. Most people fast or do pooja (Sadhana) and also perform havan for their ancestors. It is also the day to offer donations and foods to the needy ones and also to the Brahmans.

PRADOSH

The Hindu festival of Pradosh is observed on the thirteenth day (tithi) of the lunar month and is the most powerful vrat (fast). It is aimed at seeking good health, peace, and liberation (Moksha).

God Shiva saved the universe by drinking poison that emerged from the ocean when the demigods and Asuras churned the cosmic ocean to obtain ambrosia and consume it to become immortal. This poison was so venomous that neither the Devatas nor the Assur came forward to claim it.

The Skanda Purana beautifully describes the importance of Pradosh fasting: - By just visiting a Shiva temple and lighting a single diya during the Pradosh Kaal pleases Mahadev (Supreme among deities) and provides contentment, health, and wealth.

The Shiva Chalise explains the significance of keeping a fast on Pradosh vrat as per their fall on weekdays and lists the benefits of keeping a fast on each day.

On Pradosh fast, devotees worship God Shiva and Goddess Parvati by chanting the Maha Mrityunjaya mantra for 108 times and lighting a Diya (lamp) with clarified butter/ghee.

As per the Hindu calendar and beliefs, there are two ways of fasting on this holy day. One way involves taking a bath in the morning and fasting from sunrise till the next sunrise, while the other involves fasting from sunrise to sunset.

Hindu devotees do not eat food during Pradosh fasting, but a few can have a restrictive and light diet after the evening puja. Fruit salads, Aloo Raita, Kuttu Puri, and Mango Lassi are some great food ideas.

Hindus celebrate the day of Pradosh with joy and devotion, and keep a fast, pray, and chant mantras during the evening hour (sandhyakaal). God Shiva and Goddess Parvati fulfill all wishes of a devotee on this day.

Hindu Fastings based on Days

❦

Shravan Somvar Vrat (Monday Fasting)

Hindus maintain austerity, observe strict fasts, and pray to God Shiva. Fasting in this holy month of Shravan fulfills all desires and wishes with divine blessings.

Shravan Somvar Vrat Vidhi / Monday Fast procedure

Take a holy bath, fast from sunrise to sunset, light a Diya of ghee and incense sticks, offer milk and water to the Shivling, chant the mantra "OM Namah Shivaya", recite the Shravan Vrat Katha, and distribute prasad among family members.

Hindus observe a sattvic lifestyle during the month of Shravan, which includes eating saltless chips, fruits, dhokla, Shrikhand, and sago stew. One who observes fast during the Shravan month is blessed with spiritual bliss, and a woman who observes fast on Shravan Mondays (Somvar) is bestowed with a suitable life partner.

Chanting of Shiva mantras and fasting on this day improves physical and mental health.

Why is it done?

Hindu mythology says that during the churning of the sea between the devas and the demons, the deadliest poison emerged from the ocean and God Shiva drank it to save the creation. However, Goddess Parvati placed her hand on Shiva's Throat, so that the poison wouldn't go down further. Hindu Devotees observe Shravan Somvar Vrat to thank Mahadev for stopping the massive destruction of the universe. They perform Abhishek on Shravan Somvar every Monday. Shravan Maas is a holy month dedicated to God Shiva and believed to be the most auspicious and beneficiary month. On the first Monday of Shravan Maas, devotees of God Shiva observe a fast to please him.

What to eat during the fast

Any food or beverages of sattvic nature or vegetarian form.

- ◆ Fruits
- ◆ Sago Stew (Sabudana Khichdi)
- ◆ Curd, buttermilk

Mantra to chant on Shravan Somvar:

Shiv Mantra (Panchakshari): *Om Namah Shivaya*

Shravan Somvar Vrat Katha (Story)

According to Hindu mythology, the sea was churned, to take out amrit, was done in this period. *Samudra Manthan-* is the Mount

Mandara as the churning rod, Vasuki, the biggest snake as the churning rope. The devas and the demons were on both sides holding the snake. During this churning process, numerous jewels and *Airavat* (divine elephant of God Indra) came out from the ocean of Milk (*Kshirsagar*). One such thing that came during this process was the *Halahala* (deadliest poison) from the ocean. It is well written in various sacred texts that this poison was so deadly, that it could have destroyed the entire universe. It is then, the merciful God Shiva decided to drink it to save the universe and life forms. Goddess Parvati saw God Shiva taking poison, she at once held Shiva's throat so that the deadliest venom, wouldn't go down his throat. As a result, this turned Shiva's throat blue, and this is when Shiva was called **Neelkanth**.

Hindu devotees observe Shravan Somvar Vrat with devotion to express their gratitude to Mahadev for his great sacrifices and to stop the massive destruction of the universe. Also, many devotees do the Kanwar-yatra. During which they collect water from the different holy rivers and thereafter, they perform Abhishek on Shiva. Keeping fast every Monday of this month brings fruitful results and devotees live a happy life.

Devotees of God Shiva celebrate this auspicious day throughout the month, with a fast which is commonly known as Shravan Somvar Vrat. Devotees observe a full day fast on Monday. They visit Shiva's temple to offer water from a holy river or gangajal and bel leaves to receive Shiva's graceful blessings. Married women(For long life for their husband) and unmarried women (seeking a perfect partner) observe fast on this day to appease God Shiva and to receive His blessings.

MANGALVAR VRAT
(TUESDAY FASTING)

❧

India is a multicultural country and Hinduism celebrates many festivals and rituals in a year. Every Monday, worshippers chant to God Shiva and keep fast, and every Tuesday, devotees celebrate the birthday of God Hanuman.

Astrologically, Mangal, the planet Mars, is the deity of Mangalwar Vrat and it brings good luck and success to one's life.

When to start fasting?

A devotee can start Mangalwar or Tuesday fast/vrat from the first Tuesday of the rising half of the lunar month and continue for 21 weeks.

Tuesday Fast Vidhi (Procedure)

Tuesday Fast is considered auspicious to reduce the Mangal Dosha (Manglik) with the grace of God Hanuman, and to improve the metabolic rate and vitality.

Children should observe the Tuesday fast to increase stamina, courage, peace of mind, memory power, health, and enhance positive energy

Tuesday represents the powerful planet Mars and is dedicated to God Hanuman. Worshiping the monkey God Hanuman fulfills all desires and develops strength and virility.

The procedure starts early in the morning and ends in the evening. As per Hindu mythology, observing fast for full 21 consecutive Tuesdays bless positive results to the devotee

- After waking up before sunrise and taking a bath. Wear clean, washed clothes- red color is preferred
- Purify the pooja area with Ganga jal. Place the idol of God Hanuman in a suitable place
- Light a diya with cow ghee. Offer sindoor (red vermillion), Paan (betel) leaf garland, garland or single red flower, and small red new cloth to Lord Hanuman.
- Offer besan (gram flour) ladoos and any kinds of fruits as offering
- Sit comfortably in front of the idol. Thereafter, begin the puja, worshiping God Ganesh followed by God Hanuman and Mangalvar Vrat Katha.

- God Hanuman is the greatest devotee of God Rama, and it is believed that prayer to God Rama or reading the Sundarakanda chapter of Ramayana is the simplest way to please God Hanuman. Receive Hanuman's blessings
- To conclude the puja, do aarti.

After completion of this pooja, distribute the Prasad (whatever offering- bhog/prasad) to all family members

- If devotees cannot keep a full day fast, then they can eat food made of wheat and jaggery (cane sugar). This day avoid adding any salt to the food
- Donating food to hungry and clothes to needy is symbolic and helps in spiritual growth

Mantra to chant during Mangalvar Vrat:

Om Hanumate Namah ॥

BUDHVAR VRAT

(WEDNESDAY FASTING)

Hindu mythology describes every planet of our solar system as a celestial body. Each day of a week is dedicated to a particular deity. Wednesday is dedicated to the planet Mercury (God Budhdev). This is beneficial for anyone with weak or malefic Mercury in their birth chart

When to start fasting?

The ideal day to start the Budhvar Vrat is on the first Wednesday of the Shukla Paksha of any lunar month.

Procedure for fasting.

Devotees observing Budhvar Vrat should wake up before sunrise and take bath. They must then purify the puja room by sprinkling Gangajal or water from any other holy river. Offer fruits, colorful flowers, garlands, bel leaves, incense sticks, and light a diya of ghee.

Why is this fasting done?

Wednesday fasting is beneficial for increasing intelligence, wisdom, thinking process, career growth, business growth, happiness, and worshiping God Ganesha.

Keeping fast and celebrating this Vrat with devotion increases reasoning power and analytic ability and helps to overcome the ill-effects of the planet Mercury. It also develops qualities like love, kindness, forgiveness, etc.

Story

Keshav went to his parents-in-law's house to bring his wife, but her parents refused to bid farewell to her on Wednesday. Keshav forced his wife to sit under a tree and drink water but was surprised to see a man exactly like him sitting next to his wife. Keshav asked a man if he was sitting with his wife, the man replied that he was, but Keshav started shouting and saying that the man must leave the place or else he will call the nearby soldier and get you caught. Keshav prayed to God Budhdev and the merciful God Budhdev pardoned him. Immediately, Keshav's duplicate vanished. Thereafter, Keshav and his wife happily started their journey towards Varanasi.

Procedure for Budhvar Vrat:

♦ Devotees observing this fast should wake up before sunrise and take a bath. Green colored clothes are preferred to be worn on this day as the cosmic color of the planet Mercury is green or light green.

- The devotee should purify the puja room by sprinkling Gangajal or water from any other holy river.
- Place an idol or pictures of God Budhdev and God Ganesh in the North-East direction of the house
- Offer variety of fruits, colorful flowers, garlands, bel leaves, incense sticks, and light a ghee diya to start with the puja
- Reciting the Budh (Mercury Mantra) for 108 times
- Reading the Budhvar Vrat Katha is significant. It is not recommended to get up or leave pooja place in the middle
- To conclude the puja, aarti and flowers are offered
- A devotee must eat the prasad after distributing it to all family members
- The devotee of this fast can eat fruits or drink water. Avoid salt

Mantras for Budhvar Vrat:

Om Budhaaye Namaha

GURUVAR VRAT
(THURSDAY FASTING)

The Hindu religion observes a fast on Thursday to please God Brihaspati, an incarnation of God Vishnu.

When to start?

A devotee can start the Thursday fast from the very first Thursday falling in the Shukla Paksha of a lunar month.

A devotee must finish his/her morning routine before sunrise, and avoid washing their hair, clothes and do not shave on this holy day, should wear yellow-colored clothes, and use yellow-colored foods and flowers. One should light a diya with cow ghee and incense sticks in front of the deities.

Why is it observed?

Observing Thursday Fast helps to develop knowledge and wisdom with the blessing of God Brihaspati, who is an incarnation of God Vishnu. It also destroys all accumulated sins of a devotee.

Story

A rich man called Dayavan used to observe fast every Thursday and offer worship, but his wife Natasha detested it and forbade her husband also from doing so. One day a saint asked Natasha to give alms, but Natasha refused and said she didn't want to give any money.

Natasha cooks her food without cleansing her kitchen, eats meat and wine during meals, and gives her clothes to the washerman for washing. Within 7 consecutive Thursdays all her wealth was destroyed. Natasha realized and followed 16 Thursday vrat with utmost clean mind, regaining her wealth and prestige back. Hindus worship God Brihaspati and God Vishnu on Thursday and observe Guruvar Vrat to have the divine blessing of God Brihaspati.

Procedure for Thursday fast:

♦ The Thursday fast (Vrat), starts from sunrise. The devotee must finish his/her morning routine before the sunrise. As per sacred books, devotees should not wash their hair-head, clothes and one should avoid shaving/plucking hair on this day

- Wearing yellow-colored clothes. Yellow-colored foods and flowers are considered auspicious, as the yellow color is connected with the planet Jupiter.
- Place the idol or pictures of God Vishnu and God Brihaspati in a clean place
- Offer some yellow-colored flowers or garlands

Food items like banana and sweets like Laddu as offerings to the deities

- Light a Diya with cow ghee(preferred) and incense sticks in front of the Idols.
- Applying yellow Tilak on the forehead is considered auspicious.
- Sit in a meditative position and chant Guru mantras. Recite Guruvar Vrat Katha
- Perform the aarti and prayer to conclude puja
- The observer of this Vrat may choose either for a complete fast or can have one meal after completion of the puja or can have some yellow-colored fruits. Foods made of gram dal or gram flour can be consumed. The food-eatables should not have salt.
- Donation of any yellow items like foods, clothes, and turmeric in the temple or to the poor is of high importance.

Mantras to recite:

- *"Om Brim Brhaspataye Namah"*

- *"Om Gram Grim Graum Sah Gurave Namah"*

Significance of observing Thursday Fast:

- Observing Guruvar Vrat helps to gain knowledge and wisdom with the blessing of God Brihaspati as he is the epicenter of wisdom and Guru of all gods.

- Hindu sacred books describe that God Brihaspati is an incarnation of God Vishnu, so, observing this fast with pure heart fulfills the desires of a devotee

- Per the Vedic literature and ancient Hindu texts celebrating Guruvar Vrat and offering prayers to planet Jupiter, destroys all sins of a devotee. Also, it tranquilizes one's greed and brings wisdom and peace.

SHUKRAVAR VRAT (FRIDAY FASTING)

According to Hindu, they believe in the powers of devotion and worship; hence, they perform different rituals, observe vrat (fast) to receive divine blessings of their favorite God or Goddess. Observing fast on Friday/Shukravar Vrat is one such auspicious ritual. In this, Hindu women observe Vrat to please Goddess Santoshi and to seek Her blessings.

When is it Observed?

Hindu devotees observe a fast on Fridays to pay tribute to Santoshi Mata. They can begin the fast at any time.

What is the procedure?

On this day, nobody in the house should eat or touch anything sour.

They should take a bath, wear clean clothes, use Ganga Jal (water) in the temple area, light a ghee diya and incense stick, and

229

offer Kumkum, Haldi, flowers, chuniri (a piece of red cloth), coconut, and bananas.

Regular reciting Jai Santoshi Mata aarti or 108 names gives peace of mind, wealth and happiness and it also helps to develop the confidence to battle evil.

Observing fast and chanting a mantra increases wealth, attracts life partners, and bestows joyful life.

Story

An old woman who had seven sons served the leftovers of his brother's meals to her youngest son, who was an irresponsible person. Her husband felt sorry for himself and left the house overnight to seek his fortune, but forgot about his wife, who completed 16 Friday fasts. People of his village started observing Shukravar Vrat with full faith and devotion, knowing the power of Maa Santoshi.

Significance

Santoshi Maa is considered as the Goddess of satisfaction and a manifestation of Goddess Durga. Her devotees observe the Shukravar Vrat of Santoshi maa fast.

Shanivar Vrat
(Saturday Fasting)

⁓⁓

This is the easiest way to receive divine blessings from the mightiest God Shanidev and enjoy a blissful life with good health, prosperity, and respect.

When is this fast observed?

Hindus worship the powerful God Shanidev (Saturn) on Saturday and observe fast on this day to please Shani Dev.

How is this fast observed?

Devotees offer black flowers, black sesame seeds, and black clothes to the deity.

Most devotees follow this procedure to observe a Saturday Vrat: wake-up before sunrise, take a bath, arrange all essentials for the puja, visit a temple of Shanidev, offer panchamrit and mustard oil to Shanidev.

Also, offer black color clothes, a garland, any color flowers, black sesame, incense, oil lamp in front of the idol.

Significance of this fast?

Saturday fasting is auspicious because it reduces the negative effects of the planet Saturn, helps to receive divine blessings of God Shanidev. It reduces the adverse effects of Sade Sati, the seven-and-a-half-year period of Saturn.

Story

Raavan the mighty King of Lanka had control over all nine planets and kept them under the staircase of his central hall where his throne was situated. Shanidev told the demigods that he might help them to get freedom and Ravana imprisoned Shani in a dark room. Hanuman freed Shani from a dark room but became the victim of Shani's gaze towards himself. Therefore, Hindu devotees worship God Hanuman along with God Shanidev to receive His graceful blessings.

The planet Saturn is also called Jeevan Karaka and gives people results according to their deeds. Observing Saturday fast is believed to please God Shanidev and help a devotee to overcome various difficulties of life.

Procedure of this vrat?

Most of the devotees follows this procedures to observe a Saturday Vrat:

- ◆ Wake-up before sunrise and take a bath

- After arranging items for the puja such as mustard oil, black flowers, flower garlands, sesame seeds (til), fruits, an oil lamp (Diya), an incense stick, and a black cloth, then visit Shanidev temple
- For doing Shanigraha Puja at home take priests help
- Offering water to a *Peepal* tree on Saturday, is believed to be most auspicious
- At the beginning of the puja, they offer mustard oil on Shanidev.
- Offer all the pooja items, black clothes, garlands, flowers, black sesame, incense, oil diya in front of Shani Dev idol
- Sit comfortably inside the temple and chant mantras, ten divine names of God Shani Dev, followed by Shanivar Vrat katha
- Offer aarti and prayer to the God to conclude the pooja
- At the end, Invite Brahmins (as per your ability) and donate food, money. Also, donate items made of iron to poor people.

Mantra for Shanivar Vrat:

- Chant 10 names of God Shanidev –

Babhru, Konastha, Krishna, Manda, Pippala, Pingalo, Rodrutko, Sauri, Shanasture, Yama

- Beej Mantra: Om Aim Hreem Shanecharaya Namah
- Ekashari mantra: Om Sham Shaneicharaya Namah

233

♦ Maha Mantra:

"Om Nilanjana Sama Bhasam, Ravi Putram Yamagrajam

Cahaya Martanda Samhubhutam, Tama namami Shanescharam".

Significance of Saturday Fasting

♦ According to Astrology experts, Shanivar Vrat has a great potential in reducing and or completely removing the negative or ill effects of the planet Saturn

♦ Shani gratefulness to Hanuman for his great help and hence praying to God Hanuman on this day helps to receive divine blessings of God

♦ Donations on this auspicious day brings good fortune in life as, Saturn is the planet of service and represents servants and people who does good

♦ Donation of food to the needy and performing yajna (ritual done in front of sacred fire) on this day, hence, reduces the adverse effects of Sade Sati. The seven-and-a-half-year period of Saturn which is a difficult time.

♦ Observing Shanivar fast with full faith and devotion can also reduce the effects of an ill placed Saturn in horoscope.

Ravivar Vrat
(Sunday Fasting)

The Hindu origin people of India have been praying to the Sun since time immemorial and Ravivar Vrat is an important festival.

Hindu devotees observe a fast to please God Sun, who is the primary source of all energy to the world. Sun is called by many names, including Ravi, and the day of the Ravi is known as Ravivar.

Procedure for the fast?

The procedure for Ravivar Vrat is to wake up early in the morning, complete a bath and other household activities before the sunrise, offer water to the Sun, place an idol of Sun God in your puja room. Offer sandalwood paste, wheat grain, Kumkum, red flowers, diya as well as dishes specially prepared for this Vrat.

Mantra for the vrat?

Mantra to chant while offering water to God Sun:
"Nama Suryaya Santaya Sarvaroga Nivarine,
Ayu Rarogya Maisvairyam Dehi Devah Jagatpate"

Significance of the vrat?

Observing fast on Sunday helps to stay healthy and happy, and helps people with weak Sun in their horoscope to overcome problems related to heart, blood circulation, issues in childbirth, downfall in career or fame, etc.

Hindu devotees worship the sun god to receive blessings and to cure many critical diseases.

Story

An old lady used to clean her house with cow dung and offer food to the Sun God on every Sunday. One day, her neighbor tethered her cow inside her house and the old lady could not clean her house with cow dung. Later, the old lady was surprised to see a beautiful cow and calf in her courtyard. Her neighbor got more jealous than before and replaced the gold dung with ordinary dung, until the merciful God Sun caused a storm. The neighbor of the old lady went to see the king of the city to inform him about the divine cow. The king, thereafter, ordered his soldiers to bring the divine cow to his palace, and the neighbor was punished for her wickedness and the state was filled with health and wealth.

16

Major Hindu
Temples of India

❧

India is home to numerous Hindu temples, each with its own history, architecture, and religious significance. The temples each have their own unique significance and attract devotees from all over the country. In addition to these temples, India has many others of great religious and cultural importance.

WHY CHAR DHAMS

Among the lofty peaks of the Himalayas, Uttarakhand is home to the Chota/Laghu Char Dhams, the four most sacred Hindu pilgrimages. This Hindu pilgrimage consists of four sites: Yamunotri, Gangotri, Kedarnath, and Badrinath. Hinduism considers all these locations to be highly sacred. Hindus strive to attain salvation (Moksha) by visiting the holy shrines at least once in their lifetime.

The main Char Dhams include **Badrinath, Dwarka, Jagannath and Rameswaram**. It is recommended that every Hindu should visit the Char Dhams during one's lifetime.

Why should one do Sacred Pilgrimage Yatras?

The pilgrimage tirthayatra (Teertha Yatra) is one of the five duties of every Hindu. Along with following Dharma, Worship, Sanskaras, and Observing religious festivals. Devotees often travel to difficult locations on pilgrimages, leaving their problems at the feet of the Deity and forgetting everything but God during their pilgrimage. The pilgrimage is an intimate experience, a direct connection between the seeker and the sacred. Devotees go on pilgrimage to worship at holy shrines, and to see Deities residing in ancient sanctuaries. A pilgrim journeys to see God to experience life-changing, bliss-engendering, and karma-eradicating encounters with him.

SIDDHIVINAYAK TEMPLE

ぐ∕⌐∽

Location: Shree Siddhivinayak temple which is located at Prabhadevi is very famous and favorite as Desire Fulfilling Shrine of Greater Mumbai. This ancient shrine is a place of worship for finding solace for its devotees and the pilgrims all over the globe.

Significance: God of solidarity, success, and learning, Ganesh is one of the most respected Hindu divine beings. He is likewise called Siddhivinayak, as he will fulfill everyone's wishes and grant you lots of success and good health in one's life.

Main attractions: Kanheri Caves, The Gateway of India, Global Vipassana Pagoda, Shree **Siddhivinayak Temple**, Girgaon Chowpatty

AYODHYA

Location: On the bank of the Sarayu River, Ayodhya is approximately 6 km away from Faizabad.

Significance: Ayodhya is the land of God Ram's birth. God Vishnu is said to have manifested him as the seventh incarnation. As the holiest city in India, it has been a prominent part of Uttar Pradesh's economic, political, and historical background for thousands of years.

As the capital of Raja Dashrath's prosperous kingdom, this city is believed to be 9000 years old. Among the most sacred cities in India, this auspicious city has more than 700 temples.

Main attractions: In Ayodhya, some of the top places to visit include Ram Janam Bhumi, Kanak Bhawan, Sita ki Rasoi, Hanumangarhi, Gular Bari, Dashrath Bhawan, Nageswara Temple, Treta ka Thakur, and Dashrath Bhawan.

VARANASI

Location: Varanasi, also called Benares, Banaras, or Kashi, is a city in northern India, in the state of Uttar Pradesh. One of the seven sacred cities of Hinduism, it is located on the left bank of the Ganges (Ganga) River.

Significance:

Varanasi is prominently known as Shiv ki Nagari and said to be the oldest city of India. There are almost 20, 000 temples in the city that you can find at every corner of the street. It is said that God Shiva created the holy city of Kashi with his hands and that's why it is said to be the spiritual capital of India. There is a popular belief that if you die in this city, you will attain Moksha (salvation). Varanasi is all about the sacred Ghats which will give utmost peace to your soul with the most scenic and tranquil views of holy River Ganga.

Main attractions:

Manikarnika Ghat, Dashashwamedha Ghat, Pancha-Ganga Ghat, Asi Sangam Ghat, Varana Sangam Ghat, Kashi Vishwanath temple, Bindhu Madhava, Adi Keshava temple, Durga temple, and Sankat Mochan temple.

MATHURA

Location: The city of Mathura, formerly Muttra, is located in western Uttar Pradesh state, in northern India. Located on the Yamuna River about 25 miles (40 km) northwest of Agra, it lies in the Ganges-Yamuna Doab and is situated near to the city of Vrindavan and Govardhan hill in Uttar Pradesh.

Significance: Mathura is the birthplace of God Krishna. God Krishna is also believed to be the incarnation of God Vishnu who came to protect the earth from evil and powerful King Kansa.

Called as the heart of Indian culture, Mathura is full of multi-hued temples. The best time to explore this holy city is the time of Krishna Janmashtami when the entire city is in full swing, and every person is excited to welcome Krishna on his birthday. Other than being important for Hindus, Mathura is also known for magnificent Buddhist Art which is preserved from the golden era of Indian culture.

Main attraction: Mathura and Vrindavan offer hundreds of places to see. However, the following are must-see places: Seven Goswami Temples in Vrindavan, Nidhivan, Seva Kunj

Rangji Mandir, Prem Mandir, Vrindavan Parikrama, Boat ride in Yamuna, Govardhana Parikrama, Radha Kunda and Shyam Kunda on Govardhan parikrama route, Mathura Janmabhumi, Vishram Ghat in Mathura, Gokul, Raval, Nandagaon

HARIDWAR

Location: Located in North India's Uttarakhand state, Haridwar is an ancient Hindu pilgrimage site where the river Ganges exits the Himalayan foothills. The Haridwar district is in the southwestern part of Uttarakhand state. It covers a total area of 2,360 km2 (910 sq mi).

Significance: Haridwar literally means Hari ka Dwar (gateway of God Vishnu). It is the place where Hindus come before going on Char Dham Yatra (Four Abodes of Hindu Religion) for the ritualistic bath in holy water of River Ganga. According to Hindu Religious Books, Bhagirath prayed to God Shiva and succeeded in bringing Ganga on Earth for the welfare of humanity. A nightly Ganga Aarti (river worshipping ceremony) takes place at Har Ki Pauri, one of several sacred ghats (bathing steps). Har ki Pauri is said to be the place where Ganga landed first. Festivals such as the Kanwar Mela draw large crowds to the city.

Main attraction: Some prominent temples in Haridwar are Mansa Devi Temple, Bharat Mata Temple, Maya Devi Temple, and Chaandi Devi Temple etc. Renowned Kumbh Mela is organized every 12 years in this holy city of India.

KANCHIPURAM

Location: Located on the bank of River Vegavathi, Kanchi is also called the City of Thousand Temples and the City of Gold. Kanchipuram is just 75 km away from the capital city of Tamil Nadu state – Chennai.

Significance: Kanchipuram is one of the seven sacred cities of India because of its divine temples. Great Hindu Philosopher, Adi Shankar disseminated Advaita philosophy in this city. Therefore, it turns out to be one of the most visited holy cities of India.

Main attraction: There are around 108 Shiva temples and 18 Vaishnava temples in Kanchipuram. Ekambareswarar Temple,

Varadharaja Perumal Temple, Kailasnathar Temple and Kamakshi Temple are some of the famous temples in Kanchipuram.

UJJAIN

Location: In the central Indian state of Madhya Pradesh, Ujjain is an ancient city located along the Kshipra River. Known for its centuries old Mahakaleshwar Temple, a towering structure with a distinctively ornate roof, it's an important Hindu pilgrimage destination. The nearby Bade Ganesh Temple has a colorful statue of the elephant-headed Hindu deity Ganesh. A pair of tall dark pillars are studded with lamps at Harsiddhi Temple.

Significance: Ujjain is one of the SaptaPuri - seven sacred cities of India. It is believed that this holy city emerged during the time of Samudra Manthan. Out of 12 Jyotirlinga, Mahakaleshwar Jyotirlinga is situated here. Ujjain has deep-rooted connection with God Krishna as it is said that Krishna along with his elder brother Balram came to Ujjain to get their education by Muni Sandipani.

Main attraction: There is a Gopal Temple in Ujjain, which has silver statutes of God Krishna, Balram and Muni Sandipani

DWARKA

Location: The city is located on the right bank of the Gomti river at the mouth of the Gulf of Kutch, facing the Arabian Sea on the western shore of the Okhamandal Peninsula.

Significance: Dwarka which is said to be the place where God Krishna spent his life after the assassination of King Kansa. It is another sacred destination in India to visit for mental peace. Dwarka depicts the tale of Krishna's life when he shifted the capital of Yaduvansh Kingdom and how it eventually submerged in the Arabian Sea after the death of Krishna. Poetess Mirabai was also from this divine city who taught the world power of Krishna Bhakti.

Main attraction: Here are some of the top tourist attractions in Dwarka:

1. Dwarkadhish Temple: This temple is dedicated to Lord Krishna and is one of the most important pilgrimage sites for Hindus. The temple is believed to have been built over 2,500 years ago and is an important example of Hindu architecture.

2. Rukmini Devi Temple: This temple is located about 2 km from the Dwarkadhish Temple and is dedicated to Lord Krishna's wife, Rukmini Devi. The temple is known for its beautiful architecture and intricate carvings.

3. Nageshwar Jyotirlinga Temple: This temple is located about 17 km from Dwarka and is one of the 12 Jyotirlingas (or sacred shrines of Lord Shiva) in India. The temple is known for its beautiful architecture and is a popular pilgrimage site for Hindus.

4. Bet Dwarka: This is an island located about 30 km from Dwarka and is believed to be the place where Lord Krishna lived with his family. The island is accessible by ferry and is known for its beautiful beaches and temples.

5. Gomti Ghat: This is a famous bathing ghat located in Dwarka and is believed to be the place where the river Gomti meets the Arabian Sea. The ghat is known for its beautiful architecture and is a popular spot for devotees to take a holy dip.

6. Beit Dwarka Beach: This is a beautiful beach located on the island of Bet Dwarka and is known for its clear waters and beautiful scenery.

7. Ohka: This is a small town located about 30 km from Dwarka and is known for its beautiful beaches and temples. The town is also the starting point for the ferry to Bet Dwarka.

TIRUPATI

Location: The Tirumala Venkateswara Temple is situated on the last hill of the Seshachalam range in Tirupati, Andhra Pradesh.

The Sri Venkateswara Temple stands atop one of the seven peaks of Tirumala Hills, attracting thousands of Hindu pilgrims every year.

Significance: Tirupati is known as the abode of the Hindu god Venkateshwara, God of the Seven Hills. Like many temples in south India, this holy temple is known for its exquisite architecture. It is also amongst the most visited Hindu temples in India that attracts over 60,000 pilgrims each day.

Main attraction: Sri Venkateswara National Park, home to the temple, also has a zoological park with lions and primates. Sri Kapileswara Swamy Temple, dedicated to Lord Shiva, is located near a sacred waterfall and cave.

SHIRDI

Location: The town of Shirdi is in Maharashtra, in western India. It's located about 250 kilometers (143 miles) northeast of Mumbai, and 90 kilometers (56 miles) southeast of Nashik, in Maharashtra.

Significance: Also known as the Land of Sai, Shirdi is famous for Shirdi Sai Baba's shrine, the city's main attraction. Shirdi is a treasure trove of divine vibrations due to its strong association with the renowned Saint Shri Sai Baba. The three main festivals celebrated here are Ramanavami (March/April), Guru Purnima (July), and Vijayadashami (September). These festivals are celebrated with great devotion and enthusiasm, and zeal for two to four days each.

A major pilgrimage site, it is the former home of revered spiritual leader Sai Baba. Sai Baba Temple devotees gather daily to honor his legacy. A marble statue of Sai Baba stands beside his tomb at the Samadhi Mandir shrine.

Main Attractions: Dwarkamai, a mosque where Sai Baba once lived, and Lendi Garden are nearby. Within the state of Maharashtra there 3 Jyotirlingas i.e., Trimbakeshwar (Nasik) Grishneshwar (Aurangabad) & Bhima Shankar (Pune).

Somnath Temple

Location: Located in Prabhas Patan, Veraval in Gujarat, India, the Somnath temple is also known as the Samantha temple or Deo Patan. By Road The temple city lies 82 km from Junagadh, 270 km from Bhavnagar and 120 km from Porbandar. Ahmedabad is just 400 km away from Somnath.

Significance: Among Shiva's twelve jyotirlinga shrines, it is one of the most sacred pilgrimage sites for Hindus. A timeline of the ancient temple can be traced back to 649 BC but it is believed that the temple is much older than that. Somnath Temple is a specimen of fine architecture of one of the 12 Jyotirlingas Shrines of Shiva. This legendary temple has been vandalized numerous times in history, but with the help of some Hindu Kings, the temple was reshaped each time. It is believed that worshiping in Somnath destroys all the sins and misdeeds of the devotees.

Main attraction: Some good places to visit in Somnath include:

- Triveni Ghat: This is a sacred bathing spot located on the banks of the Somnath River, where visitors can take a dip and purify themselves.
- Panch Pandav Gufa: This is a group of five caves said to have been used by the five Pandava brothers during their exile, as described in the Indian epic, the Mahabharata.
- Bhalka Tirth: This is the spot where Lord Krishna is said to have been accidentally shot with an arrow, leading to his death.
- Sita Gufa: This is a cave where Sita, the wife of Lord Rama, is said to have stayed during her exile.
- Somnath Beach: This is a beautiful beach with a long shoreline and a lighthouse, visitors can enjoy the scenic view of the sea and the sunset.
- Prabhas Patan Museum: This is a museum that exhibits the history and culture of Somnath.
- Shree Somnath Science Centre: This Science Centre is a perfect place for science lover and educational visit to learn and explore the scientific facts and theories in an interactive

Golden Temple

Location: The Golden Temple is a gurdwara located in **the city of Amritsar, Punjab, India**. It is the preeminent spiritual site of Sikhism.

Significance: The unparalleled reflection of the pious golden tower on the ambrosial nectar (lake) and the horde of pilgrims loitering in the shrine complex urge one to visit this popular religious place in India. Built by the fourth Sikh Guru- Ramdas Sahib Ji, the Golden Temple is the most important Sikh pilgrimage site to visit in India. The temple is surrounded by a pool of clear water that is sacred to Sikhs. The holy water is believed to have healing powers.

Main Attractions: Jallianwala Bagh – War Memorial, Wagah Border – Beating Retreat, Durgiana Temple – Explore Inner Peace, Akal Takht – Historical Significance, Tarn Taran – Holy Pilgrimage, Harike Wetland – Scenic Beauty, Maharaja Ranjit Singh Museum – Brush Up Your History, Bathinda Fort – Heritage Site, Jama Masjid Khairuddin – Architectural Marvel, Pul Kanjari – Historic Belief, Ram Tirith – Sacred Place, Goindwal Sahib – Find Belief, Faridkot Fort – About History And Architecture, ISKCON Temple – Where Prayers Are Answered, Partition Museum – A Glimpse Into The History

VAISHNO DEVI TEMPLE

Location: It is in Katra, Reasi on the slopes of Trikuta Hills within the union territory of Jammu & Kashmir in India. Distance between vaishno devi and uttrakhand(Haridwar as a reference) is about 590 kms.

Significance: Vaishno Devi (also called Mata Rani, Trikuta, Ambe, and Vaishnavi) is a manifestation of Durga or Adi Adi-Shakti[1]. She is revered as a combined avatar of Mahakali, Mahalakshmi, and Mahasaraswati. In addition, she is the Kaliyugi Avatar of Kalika. In addition, she is seen as a potency or manifestation of Vishnu or Hari. Known for being one of India's most famous ancient shrines, the Vaishno Devi Temple is believed to be Goddess Durga's dwelling place. Devotees choose different ways, like walking bare feet and crawling all the way up to seek Goddess's blessing and pay gratitude.

Main attraction: If you want to explore the many places around Vaishno Devi in Jammu, you will need a week to do so, for example, Patnitop, Sanasar, Mansar, Surinsar, Devi Pindi, Udhampur Krimchi Temple, etc. In Uttrakhand, there are numerous places, such as Haridwar, Rishikesh, Srinagar (Uttrakhand), Badrinath, Kedarnath, Yamunotri, and Gangotri.

Rameswaram

Location: In the southeast Indian state of Tamil Nadu, Rameswaram is a town on Pamban Island. Known for its Ramanathaswamy Temple, a Hindu pilgrimage site with ornate corridors and huge pillars. Off the beach east of the temple, devotees bathe in the waters of Agni Theertham. There is a view of the islands from Gandamadana Parvatham. It is believed that the feet of Lord Rama are imprinted on this chakra (wheel).

Significance: In Hinduism, Rameswaram is considered an integral part of a pilgrimage to Varanasi. Along with Badrinath, Puri, and Dwarka, Ramanathaswamy temple is one of the holiest Hindu Char Dhams (four divine sites).

Main attraction: The seaside town of Rameshwaram is home to the Ramanathaswamy Temple, renowned for being a part of one of the twelve Jyotirlingas (Lingam of light) of God Shiva in India. Taking a dip in the 23 theerthams(holy water bodies) in and around Ramanathaswamy Temple is an integral part of washing away sins. The temple is dedicated to the Hindu god Shiva and is closely associated with Rama. The temple and the town are considered a holy pilgrimage site for Shivas and Vaishnavas.

RISHIKESH

Location: Rishikesh, also known as Hrishikesh, is a city in Uttarakhand's Dehradun district near Dehradun.

Significance: Located on the right bank of the Ganges River, it is a pilgrimage town for Hindus where ancient sages and saints meditated in search of higher knowledge.Many temples and ashrams line its banks. The Tehri Dam is located 86 km (53 mi) away from Rishikesh. Uttarkashi, a popular yoga destination, is 170 km (110 mi) uphill on the way to Gangotri.

Main attraction: The emerald Ganga, innumerable Hindu temples, and the heavy settlement of yoga centers in Rishikesh redefine spirituality. Preserving the ancient Hindu practice called Yoga, Rishikesh opens the door to a different level of spirituality in India. At Rishikesh, one can praise nature in its most authentic forms and take a chance to lose himself in it. Rishikesh is the starting point for traveling to the four Chota Char Dham pilgrimage places: Badrinath, Kedarnath, Gangotri, and Yamunotri. It is also a starting point for Himalayan tourist destinations such as Harsil, Chopta, Auli, as well as summer and winter trekking destinations like Doidital, Dayara Bugyal, Kedarkantha and Har Ki Dun.

JAGANNATH TEMPLE

Location: Jaganath Puri is a coastal city and municipality in Odisha, eastern India. Located on the Bay of Bengal, 60 kilometers (37 miles) south of Bhubaneswar, Puri is the district headquarters of Puri district. As one of the original Char Dham pilgrimage sites for Hindus, it is also known as Sri Jagannatha Dhama.

Significance: An important Hindu temple, the Jagannath Temple is dedicated to Jagannath, a form of Vishnu, one of the three supreme divinities in Hinduism. On the eastern coast of India, Puri is in the state of Odisha. The main temple of Jagannath at Puri was built by King Indradyumna of Avanti. It is said that to kill Krishna and Balram, Kansa, their maternal uncle, sent them an invitation to visit Mathura. And honoring this invitation, Krishna and Balram left for Mathura sitting on the chariot that was sent by their uncle. It is this day of departure that the devotees celebrate as Rath Yatra. There are also stories that devotees celebrated the day when Krishna took Subhadra, his sister, to show the city's beauty and splendor on a chariot.

Main attraction: The Jagannath temple is of utmost importance to the Hindu devotees as it is one of the Char-Dham Pilgrimages. It also serves as a mighty historical structure built about millennia ago, in the year 1078. Millions of people visit Odisha to gain God Jagannath's blessings. The temple is also well-known for the annual chariot festival or Rath Yatra.

SUN TEMPLE

Location: Odisha's temple is situated in an eponymous village (now NAC Area) about 35 kilometers (18 mi) northeast of Puri and 65 kilometers (40 mi) southeast of Bhubaneswar on the Bay of Bengal coastline.

Significance: During the reign of Narasimha Deva I (AD 1238-1264), the Sun Temple is a physical testament to the 13th-century Hindu Kingdom of Orissa. This monument represents the strength and stability of the Ganga Empire, as well as the values of the historical period.

Main attraction: Sun Temple is a masterpiece of Indian architecture and an epitome of exquisite architecture and unmatched spirituality. Situated in Konark, Odisha, the Sun Temple boasts massive size and is an incredible example of genius. The Sun God sitting on a majestic chariot depicts the victory of King Narsimhadeva.

KEDARNATH

Location: Kedarnath is a town and a Nagar Panchayat in Rudraprayag district of Uttarakhand, India, best known for its Kedarnath Temple. Rudraprayag, the district headquarters, is approximately 86 kilometers away. Of the four Chhota Char Dham pilgrimage sites, Kedarnath is the most remote.

Significance: Originally built by the Pandavas, the temple is one of the twelve Jyotirlingas, the holiest Hindu shrines to Shiva. By doing penance in Kedarnath, the Pandavas were supposed to have pleased Shiva.

Main attraction: When you can get your eyes off the scenic beauty of Kedarnath, the temple is what you must visit. Situated on the banks of the Mandakini River, the temple is one of the trendy religious places all over India. But it is only open between April and November.

BADRINATH

Location: The temple is in Garhwal hill tracks in Chamoli district along the banks of Alaknanda River. In the state of Uttarakhand, India, Badrinath is the name of a hill town and a nagar panchayat in Chamoli district, in the town of Chamoli. As part of India's Char Dham pilgrimage, it is a Hindu holy place. As part of India's Chota Char Dham pilgrimage circuit, it gets its name from the Badrinath Temple.

Significance: In India, the Badrinath Temple is one of the most important pilgrimage sites dedicated to Lord Vishnu. Hindus revere it as one of the four holy places or char Dham. In order to reach this holy shrine, devotees travel through the mighty Himalayas.

Main attraction: Nestled in the pristine Himalayas, Badrinath in Uttarakhand is a door to unmatched spirituality. It is the place where everything is cuddled by divinity. Badrinath is believed to be the home of God Vishnu or Badrinath, who had come here to meditate after being rebuked by Narad for being too indulgent in worldly affairs. Thus, today Badrinath offers confinement from the materialistic world and takes you a step closer to the Supreme Power.

NASHIK

Location: Nashik is located **about 165 km northeast of the state capital Mumbai,** and about 210 km north from Pune. Nashik is an ancient holy city in Maharashtra, a western Indian state.

Significance: "Ramayana" is associated with it. Panchavati is a temple complex on the Godavari River. Nearby, Hindu devotees worship the Ram Kund water tank, where Lord Rama is believed to have bathed. Sita Gufaa caves are said to have been where Rama and Sita worshipped, while Shri Kalaram Sansthan Mandir is an ancient shrine to Rama. Nashik is a historically, mythologically, socially, and culturally significant city in the northern part of the state of Maharashtra in India. It is known for the temples on the Godavari banks, and it has historically been one of the holy sites of the Hindu religion. Nasik is well known for being one of the Hindu pilgrimage sites of the Kumbh Mela, held every 12 years in the Trimbakeshwar Shiva Temple.

Main attraction: Other places to visit in Nashik include Ramshej Fort, where Lord Rama used to rest, and Tringalwadi Fort with its Hanuman temple and Trigalwadi Lake. Nashik's Coin Museum and Nandur Madhmeshwar Bird Sanctuary, home to many migratory birds, are also must-see attractions. There are several things to do in Nashik, including a visit to the Sula wine yard.

MEENAKSHI TEMPLE

Location: Meenakshi Temple is an ancient Hindu temple which is in the temple town of Madurai, Tamil Nadu. It is situated on the southern bank of the Vaigai River.

Significance: South India is famous for its number of temples. One of the most popular is Meenakshi Amman Temple which is beautifully designed by architects and is located on the banks of River Vaigai. It attracts around 15,000 people every day who pray to the Almighty here. Dedicated to Lord Shiva and Goddess Meenakshi, this temple has become a major tourist spot over the years and is often referred to as the 'Mathura of South'.

Main attraction:

1. **Thirumalai Nayakkar Palace:** A magnificent 17th-century palace known for its Indo-Saracenic architecture, impressive pillars, and light & sound show depicting the history of Madurai.

2. **Gandhi Memorial Museum:** This museum houses artifacts related to Mahatma Gandhi, showcasing his life and India's struggle for independence.

3. **Vandiyur Mariamman Teppakulam:** An ancient temple tank with a beautiful mandapam in the center. During the Teppam festival, colorful floats are displayed on the tank.

4. **Goripalayam Dargah:** A significant Islamic site, housing the tomb of Hazrat Sulthan Sikandhar Badhusha Shaheed Radiyallah Ta'al anhu.

5. **St. Mary's Cathedral Church:** An elegant church with Gothic-style architecture, featuring stunning stained-glass windows.

6. **Koodal Azhagar Temple:** Dedicated to Lord Vishnu, this temple boasts intricate carvings and a peaceful ambiance.

7. **Samanar Hills:** A site with ancient Jain caves and inscriptions, perfect for history and nature enthusiasts.

KANCHIPURAM

Location: Kanchipuram also known as Conjeevaram, is a city in the Indian state of Tamil Nadu in the Tondaimandalam region, 72 km (45 mi) from Chennai.

Significance: Kanchipuram, also known as Kanchi, is an ancient city in Tamil Nadu, southern India. Hindus consider it a holy pilgrimage site, with many temples. Kailasanathar Temple is an 8th-century temple dedicated to Lord Shiva with intricate sandstone carvings. A huge statue of Lord Vishnu can be found at Ulagalanda Perumal Temple. It is believed that a mango tree in the courtyard of the Ekambareswarar Temple is sacred.

Main attraction: Kanchipuram, in the state of Tamil Nadu, is one of the most sacred cities in southern India and the second holiest after Varanasi. Also known as "The City of Thousand Temples," Kanchipuram is an important religious pilgrimage for Hindus. People travel from far and wide to admire the magnificent stone carvings, chariot processions, and shrines.

KHAJURAHO

Location: The Khajuraho monuments are in the Indian state of Madhya Pradesh, in Chhatarpur district, about 620 kilometers (385 mi) southeast of New Delhi.

Significance: The Khajuraho Group of Monuments are a group of Hindu and Jain temples in Chhatarpur district, Madhya Pradesh, India. Khajuraho is famous for its artistic temples built by the Chandela rulers between the 10th and 12th Centuries. The Khajuraho Temples are a group of shrines dedicated to both Hinduism and Jainism, located in Madhya Pradesh, India. Known for its breathtaking sculptures and aesthetics, the Khajuraho group of monuments is one of India's UNESCO World Heritage sites.

Main attraction: Near Khajuraho:

- Panna National Park/Tiger reserve
- Pandava falls (part of panna)
- Raneh falls and ghariyal point

SABARIMALA

Location: The Sabarimala Sree Ayyappan Temple is a Hindu temple complex located on the Sabarimala hill inside the Periyar Tiger Reserve, Ranni-Perunad Village, Ranni Taluk, Pathanamthitta district, Kerala, India.

Significance: Sabarimala in Kerala, also known as God's Own Country, is the home to the holy and temple of God Ayyappa on the magnificent Western Ghats of the region. It is surrounded by thick, lush green forests and almost 18 hills. Around 40 to 50 million devotees visit this temple every year, especially during the annual festival of Makaravilakku.

Shravanabelagola. Sabarimala is believed to be the place where Lord Ayyappa meditated after killing the powerful demoness, Mahishi. Sabarimala is a popular pilgrim center in India. Located towards the east of Pathanamthitta district in Kerala, the Sabari hills are part of the world famous Periyar Tiger Reserve.

Main attraction: The temples included in the circuit are the Sastha temples at Pandalam, Kulathupuzha, Aryankavu, Achankovil and Erumeli. "These shrines have a mythological link with the life of Lord Ayyappa.

SHRAVANABELAGOLA

Location: Shravanabelagola is a town located near Channarayapatna of Hassan district in the Indian state of Karnataka and is 144 km (89 mi) from Bengaluru.

Significance: Shravanabelagola is an important Jain pilgrimage Centre in South Karnataka. Shravanabelagola is home to the 18 m high statue of Lord Gometeshwara; considered to be one of the world's tallest free-standing monolithic statues. The Shravanabelagola temple is a holy place for the Jains and is world-renowned for the majesty of God Gomatheeswara towering over everything around. It is one of the most religious sites for the Jain community attracting millions of devotees annually. The Shravanabelagola Gomatheeswara statue is the largest monolithic idol in the world. It spans centuries with different ruling dynasties and kings adding their contributions and living historical evidence of the last millennia.

Main attraction: 6 places to visit in Shravanabelagola.

- Chandragupta Basadi
- Gommateshwara Statue
- Chandragiri Hill
- Akkana Basadi
- Bhadrabahu Cave
- Kambadahalli

VRINDAVAN

Location: Vrindavan, also called Vrindaban or Brindaban, town in western Uttar Pradesh state, northern India. It is situated on the west bank of the Yamuna River, just north of Mathura.

Significance: Vrindavan is a holy town in Uttar Pradesh, northern India. The Hindu deity Krishna is said to have spent his childhood here. It's home to temples, many dedicated to Krishna and his lover, the deity Radha. At Banke Bihari Temple, the curtain in front of Krishna's statue is opened and closed every few minutes. At Radha Raman Temple, a gold plate beside Krishna signifies Radha. Prem Mandir is a huge white marble temple. Vrindavan is the holy town of Uttar Pradesh, northern India. The Hindu deity Krishna is said to have spent his childhood here. It's home to temples, many dedicated to Krishna and his lover, the deity Radha.

The city is most vibrant and beautiful during the holy Hindu festivals of God Krishna's birthday known as Janmashtami and Holi—the festival of colors.

Main attraction: Banke Bihari temple, Prem Mandir, Sri Sri Krishna Balram Temple, Shree Rang Nath Ji Temple, Seva Kunj, Keshi Ghat, Sri Ashta Sakhi Temple, Sri Jugal Kishore Ji temple, Sri Giridhar Dham Ashram, Priyakant Ju Mandir, Madan Mohan temple and Mata Vaishno Devi Dham.

Srisailam

Location: Srisailam is a census town in Nandyal district of the Indian state of Andhra Pradesh. It is the mandal headquarters of Srisailam mandal in Atmakur revenue division. It is located on the Nallamala Hills.

Significance: Sri Mallikarjuna Swamy Temple is the most popular attraction in Srisailam. The temple at Srisailam is an ancient and sacred place of South India. The presiding deity of the place is Brahmaramba Mallikarjuna Swamy, in natural stone formations in the shape of Lingam. It is listed as one of the twelve Jyotirlingas existing in the country. In many ancient Hindu texts, this temple has been mentioned as one of the 12 jyotirlingas. The main deity in this temple is Lord Shiva in the form of Sri Mallikarjuna Swamy. This ancient temple is visited by devotees from all over the world who come to seek Lord Blessings.

One of the unique aspects of this temple is that devotees can even enter the sanctum sanctorum of the temple and offer prayers. Another aspect that is worth noticing is the architecture of this temple. The main temple is built in the center of a square shaped courtyard. The main shrine is surrounded by various small shrines. It consists of around 116 inscriptions. Stone pillars, exquisitely carved sculptures, and the Mukha mandapam make this temple even more alluring.

Main attraction: Mallikarjuna Jyotirlinga enshrines Lord Mallikarjuna and is an ancient temple built in a Dravidian style with specimens showcasing the Vijayanagara architecture. Sakshi Ganapati Temple- Sakshi Ganapathi temple is located 2 km east of the main temple. Akka Mahadevi Caves, Pathalaganga, Srikanteshwara Temple are few other attractions in this place. Siddi Ramappa Kolanu waterfalls located at Srisailam Half Kilo Meter Distance from Main Temple.

MURUDESHWAR

Location: Murdeshwar Temple was built on the Kanduka Hill which is surrounded on three sides by the waters of the Arabian Sea.

Significance: The temple is dedicated to Lord Shiva. In fact, Murudeshwar is one of the forms of the great Hindu deity Shiva who is revered by devotees across the globe. What the Murudeshwar temple is most famous for is the massive Shiva statue it houses. The Murudeshwar temple is built on the Kanduka hill in the quaint town of Murudeshwar which lies in the Bhatkal Taluk of the north Kannada district. As a result, it is surrounded by beautiful views of the Arabian Sea, which falls on three sides of the temple.

Main attraction:

♦ Lord Shiva Statue: Feel The Divine Presence. ...

♦ Gopuram: Gaze The Beauty. ...

♦ Mirjan Fort: Walk Amidst History. ...

♦ Netrani Island: Explore The Biodiversity. ...

♦ Statue Park: Capture The Gigantic Beauty. ...

♦ Yana Hike: Taste The Adventure. ...

♦ Murudeshwar Beach: Soak In The Tranquility.

AMARNATH

Location: The Amarnath Temple is a Hindu shrine located in the Pahalgam tehsil of the Anantnag district of Jammu and Kashmir, India.

Significance: Amarnath is famed for the Linga that is created naturally by ice here every year. The Amarnath Yatra is an annual event in which pilgrims are allowed to trek to the cave temple. The holy Amarnath Cave is situated in the beautiful state of Jammu and Kashmir and can only be reached after a rigorous trekking expedition. The cave holds importance as one of the ancient pilgrimages in India.

Main attraction: Srinagar, Sheshnag Lake, Pahalgam, Sonmarg, Patni Top, Gulmarg

ALLAHABAD (PRAYAGRAJ)

Location: Prayagraj; formerly Allahabad, also known as Ilahabad or Prayag, is a metropolis in the Indian state of Uttar Pradesh. Located in **southern Uttar Pradesh**, the city covers 365 km² (141 sq mi).

Significance: Prayagraj is believed to be the most important pilgrimage center for Hindus. Traditionally river confluences are regarded as auspicious places, but in Sangam, the confluence's significance is most pious because here, the holy Ganga, Yamuna, and the mythical Saraswati meet to become one. The Maha Kumbh Mela, celebrated once every 12 years, is one of India's largest religious congregations, attended by millions.

Main attraction: Allahabad Fort, Khusro Bagh, Chandrashekhar Azad Park, Allahabad Museum, Triveni Sangam, All Saints Cathedral, Swaraj Bhavan, Jawahar Planetarium, Akshayavat, Anand Bhavan, Saraswati Ghat, Sumitranandan Pant Park and many more.

BODH GAYA

Location: Bihar's northeastern state of Bodh Gaya is home to the village of Bodh Gaya.

Significance: Bodh Gaya is a religious site and place of pilgrimage associated with the Mahabodhi Temple Complex in the Gaya district in the Indian state of Bihar. It is famous as Gautama Buddha is said to have attained Enlightenment under what became known as the Bodhi Tree. As one of the most important Buddhist pilgrimage sites, it's dominated by the ancient brick Mahabodhi Temple Complex, built to mark the spot where the Buddha attained enlightenment under a sacred Bodhi Tree. Six other sacred sites, including a lotus pond, sit within the complex today, including a direct descendant of the tree.

Main attraction: 1. Vishnupad Temple · 2. **Gaya** pind daan · 3. Rajayatna Tree · 4. Pind Daan **Gaya** · 5. Mangla Gauri Temple · 6. Dungeshwari Cave Temples

GOKARNA

Location: Gokarna is a town on the Arabian Sea, in the southwestern Indian state of Karnataka.

Significance: Known for its idyllic beaches and pristine waters, Gokarna is a small temple town on the western coast of India in the Kumta taluk of Uttara Kannada district of the state of Karnataka. The main temple is Sri Mahabaleshwara Swamy Temple Gokarna and the chief deity is Shiva, also known as Mahabaleshwara. This temple houses what is believed to be the original image of Shiva's *linga* (Atmalinga).

Main attraction: Om Beach, Kudle Beach, Half Moon Beach, Paradise Beach, Namaste Cafe, Mahabaleshwar Temple, Gokarna Beach, Mirjan Fort, Koti Tirtha

BRAHMA TEMPLE

Location: Brahma Temple, Pushkar is a Hindu temple situated at Pushkar in the Indian state of Rajasthan, close to the sacred Pushkar Lake to which its legend has an indelible link.

Significance: There are over 500 temples in Pushkar, some very old, but the Brahma temple is the most important. According to legend, Brahma chose this location for his temple after coming down to earth to perform a yajna. Jagatpita Brahma Mandir is a Hindu temple situated at Pushkar in the Indian state of Rajasthan, close to the sacred Pushkar Lake, to which its legend has an indelible link. The temple is one of the very few existing temples dedicated to the Hindu creator-god Brahma in India and remains the most prominent among them.

Main attraction: Varaha temple is the largest and the most ancient temple of Pushkar. Constructed by the 12th century ruler,

King Anaji Chauhan, this temple is dedicated to the third incarnation of Lord Vishnu as a wild boar.

GANGOTRI

Location: Chota Char Dham Yamunotri Gangotri Kedarnath Badrinath Gangotri is a town and a Nagar Panchayat in Uttarkashi district in the state of Uttarakhand, India. It is 99 km from Uttarkashi, the main district headquarters. It is a Hindu pilgrim town on the banks of the river Bhagirathi – the origin of the river Ganges.

Significance: Gangotri is believed to be the abode of goddess Ganga. The river Ganga originates from the Gangotri glacier and is known as Bhagirathi. The striking presence of the snow-clad mountains in the vicinity and the pure crystal-clear water of the Ganges flowing around adds to the place's sanctity. Religious rituals are in full swing in the Gangotri temple, with the Arti ceremony performed by the pujaris of the Semwal family.

Main attraction: Places to **Visit** in **Gangotri** · Auden's Col Walk · Kedartal Patangini Pass Trip · Tapovan · Dayara Bugyal · Pandav Gufa · **Gangotri** National Park · Gaumukh Tapovan Trail.

SARNATH

Location: There is a town called Sarnath in Uttar Pradesh, India, located 10 kilometers northeast of Varanasi at the confluence of the Ganges and the Varuna rivers.

Significance: Sarnath is a Buddhist pilgrim spot located near Varanasi. The city is famous for being the first place where God Buddha preached for the first time after gaining enlightenment. Later, kings who followed Buddhism, like King Ashoka, built many stupas and structures focused on Buddhism. Sarnath temple is believed to be the first place where God Budha delivered His first sermon of the five principles that lead to Nirvana.

Main attraction: Sarnath's top sightseeing attractions include Chaukhandi Stupa, Ashoka Pillar, Thai Temple, Tibetan Temple, Archaeological Museum, Sarnath, Buddha Purnima.

MANIKARAN

Location: In the Kullu District of Himachal Pradesh, Manikaran is in the Parvati Valley on the river Parvati. With an altitude of 1760 meters, it is located 4 km from Kasol, 45 km from Kullu, and 35 km from Bhuntar.

Significance: Manikaran is a pilgrimage center for Hindus and Sikhs. A visit to the Manikaran Temple gives an inclusive mental and spiritual fulfillment to every devotee. This shrine of God Shiva is situated at the height of 2650 meters from sea level, in Manikarn town in the Kullu district of Himachal Pradesh. Every visitor is amazed to get freezing water in the Parvati River on one side and boiling hot water spring on the other.

Main attraction: Manikaran Attractions; Sri Guru Nanak Devji Gurudwara ; Kulant Pith ; Harinder Mountain and Parvati River ; Lord Ramchandra Temple ; Temple of Lord Shiva.

CHITRAKOOT

Location: 'Chitrakoot' means 'Hill of many wonders'. The Chitrakoot region lies in Uttar Pradesh and Madhya Pradesh along the northern Vindhya Range. There are two districts in this region: Chitrakoot in Uttar Pradesh and Satna in Madhya Pradesh. On 4 September 1998, Chitrakoot district was created in Uttar Pradesh.

Significance: Chitrakoot is a famous pilgrimage center in the Satna district in the state of Madhya Pradesh, India. It is a place of religious, cultural, historical, and archaeological importance, situated in the Bundelkhand region. It is a forested hill skirted all along its base by a chain of temples and is revered today as the holy

Main attraction: The top **attractions** to **visit** in **Chitrakoot** are: Ram Ghat · Gupt Godavari Caves · Kamadgiri Temple · Sati Anusuya Temple · Hanuman Dhara Temple.

Hemkund Sahib

Location: Hemkund Sahib is best known for its magnificent Gurudwara, the holiest shrine for Sikhs. Unlike conventional Sikh architecture, the Gurudwara is built on slopes since it is covered in snow most of the year. Gurudwara Hemkund Sahib is a Sikh place of worship and pilgrimage site in Chamoli district, Uttarakhand, India.

Significance: Situated in one of the country's most scenic locations, Hemkund Sahib adds charm to religious tours in India. Unlike other Sikh pilgrimages in India, Hemkund Sahib has a pentagonal structure. The scenic beauty of the place is worth mentioning as this shrine is nestled amidst lofty hills that are covered with snow.

Main attraction: 6 Magnificent Hemkund Yatra **Attractions** · 1. Govindghat · 2. Ghangaria · 3. **Hemkund Sahib** · 4. Hemkund Lake · 5. Lakshman Temple · 6. Valley of Flower.

Jwalamukhi Temple

Location: **Jwalamukhi** Temple · Location. 30-km from Kangra and 56-km from Dharamshala. The temple is in the scenic state of Himachal Pradesh and the main city is Dharamshala which is the home of the Dalai Lama.

Significance: Jwalamukhi is a famous temple to the Goddess Jwalamukhi, the deity of the flaming face. The temple is situated overlooking the Dhauladhar range and set amidst undulating hills. The temple consists of a copper pipe that emanates natural gas, lit by the temple's priest to form a flawless blue flame. The flame is worshiped as the manifestation of the Goddess Jwalamukhi.

Main attraction: Brajeshwari Temple (source) · Kangra Fort (source) · Baijnath Temple (source) · **Jwala** Devi Temple or **Jwalamukhi** Kareri Lake

KAMAKHYA TEMPLE

Location: In India, Kamrup Kamakhya has been the seat of the powerful tantrik cult for centuries. One of the 108 Adi-Shakti Peethas of the country, it is located on the Nilachal Hill in Guwahati. This temple is located on a hill that rises 562 feet above the mighty river Brahmaputra and commands a magnificent view of the entire city. In its vicinity are also several smaller shrines and temples dedicated to Kala Bhairava, Shiva, and other Hindu deities. The temple is dedicated to Maa Kamakhya, the goddess of power. Situated atop the Nilachal Hill in **Guwahati**, it is one of the 108 Adi-Shakti Peethas of the country. Rising to a modest height of 562 feet above the mighty river.

Significance: Contrary to the shaming treatment that menstruation gets elsewhere in India, at the Kamakhya Temple, it is worshiped as a woman's ability to conceive. Located on the

Nilachal Hill in the capital city of Guwahati, the deity of the temple, Kamakhya Devi, is revered as the 'Bleeding Goddess, considering this to be a woman's power to give birth. Every year, thousands of devotees from all over the world visit the temple because of its mystic powers. Tantriks and pandits provide blessings and guidance at the Kamakhya temple.

Main attraction: Navagraha Temple · Saraighat Bridge · Umananda Temple · Assam State Museum · Peacock Island

DEOGHAR

Location: Deoghar is a holy city beside the Mayurakshi River, in the east Indian state of Jharkhand. It is a significant Hindu pilgrimage site to visit the ancient Baba Baidyanath Temple complex. The ornate, stone-carved Naulakha Mandir temple has a shrine to Krishna. Sacred water tanks and a whitewashed Shiva temple can be found at Harila Jori, northeast of town.

Significance: Deoghar Vishnu Temple is also known as the Dashavatara temple indicating the ten incarnations of God Vishnu in Hindu mythology. It is among India's oldest stone temples and the earliest Panchayatan temple still existing. This place was under the rule of important dynasties like the Guptas, the Pratiharas, the Gondas, the Marathas. As a result of all these, the area has a tremendously rich architectural and archaeological history.

Main attraction: Places To **Visit** In **Deoghar** · 1. Baidyanath Dham · 2. Nandan Pahar · 3. Tapovan Caves and Hills · 4. Naulakha Mandir.

GOMUKH

Location: Gomukh, also known as "Gaumukh" or "Gomukhi", is the terminus or pout of the Gangotri Glacier and the source of the Bhagirathi River, one of the primary headstreams of the Ganga River. It is in the Uttarkashi District of Uttarakhand. **Gaumukh**, or **Gomukh**, is the source of the holy Bhagirathi River (Ganga). It is located 18km from **Gangotri**. The 18km trek is usually covered in 2 days.

Significance: Literally meaning "mouth of a cow," Gomukh is the glacier from where the Bhagirathi River originates. Gaumukh is one of the holiest places for Hindu pilgrims and Indian tourists who come here to witness the beauty and take blessings of Goddess Ganga. It is situated at the Gangotri glacier and is thronged by devotees mainly for its serenity and pious mythological history. It is a well-known pilgrimage site as well as a trekking location.

Main attraction: The **Gangotri** Glacier is one of the prominent **tourists' attractions** among them.

Devprayag

Location: In Uttarakhand, India, Devprayag is a town and a nagar panchayat situated near the city of New Tehri in the Tehri Garhwal district. It is the last of the Panch Prayag of the Alaknanda River, where it meets the Bhagirathi river and flows on as the Ganges river.

Significance: Devprayag is a beautiful showcase of traditions, myths, and mysticism. This is where the holy rivers Bhagirathi and Alaknanda meet, merge into one and take the name 'Ganga.' Devprayag is a pilgrimage center of great significance. The main temple of the town is the 'Raghunath Temple,' dedicated to God Rama.

Main attraction: **Places** near **Devprayag** · Tehri Dam · Tehri Lake · Koteshwar Dam · Teen Dhara · Chandrabadni Temple · New Tehri · Srinagar · Pauri.

Akshardham Mandir

Location: Swaminarayan Akshardham is a Hindu temple, and spiritual-cultural campus in **Delhi, India**. The temple is close to the border with Noida.

Significance: Akshardham Mandir, or the Swaminarayan Akshardham complex, in Delhi is a quintessential Hindu shrine epitomizing Indian culture, architecture, and spirituality. The exquisite temple is dedicated to Swaminarayan, an Indian yogi and spiritual soul who existed during the 18th century. Touted as the world's largest comprehensive Hindu temple by the Guinness World Record, Delhi's Akshardham is known for its aesthetic beauty, unique exhibitions, sprawling campus, and tranquility.

Main attraction: Top **Attractions** in New **Delhi**. Qutub Minar · Swaminarayan **Akshardham** · Gurudwara Bangla Sahib · Humayun's Tomb · Lodhi Garden etc..

PADMANABHASWAMY TEMPLE

Location: The Shree Padmanabhaswamy Temple is a Hindu temple, dedicated to Maha Vishnu, in Thiruvananthapuram, the capital of the state of Kerala, India.

Significance: Sree Padmanabhaswamy Temple, situated in Thiruvananthapuram, is dedicated to God Vishnu. It is one of the wealthiest temples in India. An inventory unveiled a significant priceless treasure. Massive piles of jewels, idols, and coins were uncovered. The temple is one of 108 centers of worship in Vaishnavism.

Main attraction: 1. Kovalam Beach · 11.05km. Recommended Sightseeing Time: ; 2. Shangumugham Beach · 3.52km. Address: ; 3. Magic Planet · 13.34km. Address: ; 4. Thiruvananthapuram Zoo.

Shani Shingnapur

Location: It is known for its popular temple dedicated to Shani, the Hindu god associated with Saturn's planet (graha) in Nevasa taluka in Ahmednagar district.

Significance: A one of a kind village in India, and probably the world, Shani Shingnapur is famous for the fact that no house here has any doors. Residents of the town feel little need for security, thanks to their belief in superior protection from the Hindu deity Shani, whose famous temple is located here.

Main attraction: Shani Shinganapur Temple · Bramhni Pushkarni · **Shani Shingnapur** · Pradyumna Mote Patil · Nagar Ves · Manjarsumba Waterfall · Ladmod Tekadi · Pimpalgaon Lake.

Dhakshineshwar Kali Temple

Location: In Kolkata, West Bengal, India, Dakshineswar Kali Temple or Dakshineswar Kalibari is a Hindu navaratna temple. Bhavatarini, a form of ParaAdi-Shakti Adya Kali, also known as AdiAdi-Shakti Kalika, presides over the temple on the eastern bank of the Hooghly River.

Significance: Located on the Hooghly River banks, the Dakshineshwar Kali Temple is one of the most popular places of worship not only in Kolkata but across eastern India. The

Dakshineswar Kali Temple is not just any other temple dedicated to Goddess Kali. The temple has also been an essential part of West Bengal's history.

Main attraction: Top Tourist Attraction in Dakshineswar, Kolkata · Dakshineswar Kali Temple · **Dakshineswar Skywalk** · Chaitanya Ghat · Nivedita Setu · Pc Mahalonibis Memorial Museum

TARAPITH

Location: Tarapith is a 13-century Hindu temple in Chandipur village Rampurhat II CD block in Rampurhat subdivision of Birbhum district of the Indian state of West Bengal, known for its Tantric temple and its adjoining cremation grounds where sādhanā are performed. Tarapith is a small temple town located near Rampurhat in Birbhum district, West Bengal. There is a temple dedicated to the Tantric goddess Tara in the city, as well as a crematorium next to it.

Significance: Tarapith is famous for the temple of Tara ma and sadhana pith of Sadhak – Bamakhyapa. The deity of Tara is enshrined inside the temple. It is a unique temple for more reasons than one. The worship here includes blood offerings. The intense rituals and the hymns sung here also contribute to make this temple an exceptional one.

Main attraction: Best **places** to **visit** in **Tarapith** include - **Tarapith** Temple, Bakreswar Temple, and Nalhateshwari Temple.

BELUR MATH

Location: Swami Vivekananda, the chief disciple of Ramakrishna Paramahamsa, founded the Ramakrishna Math and Ramakrishna Mission at Belur Math. The city lies on the west bank of the Hooghly River in Belur, West Bengal, India.

Significance: Belur math is a place of pilgrimage for people of different religious faiths. This place of religious importance is visited by people from all over India and abroad. The main gate of Belur math leads to the Ramkrishna Sarada Mandir. The awe-inspiring majesty of the temple coupled with its austere simplicity spontaneously kindles devotion

Main attraction: **Places** to **Visit** near **Belur Math** · Dakshineswar Kali Temple, West Bengal · Howrah Bridge, West Bengal · Writers Building, West Bengal · Armenian Church, Kolkata

17

BRIDAL ATTIRES AND
ITS SIGNIFICANCE

～∽～

Importance of Jewelry for Indian Women

Indian women hold a great deal of cultural, social, and personal significance when it comes to jewelry. Their lives are shaped by it in a variety of ways:

Rituals and Traditions: Jewelry plays an integral role in Indian culture. In many cases, it is passed down through generations, carrying the weight of ancestral customs with it.

Women's bridal trousseau include jewelry as a crucial component. As a symbol of prosperity, blessings, and family unity, it signifies prosperity and blessings.

Jewelry is considered an investment in many Indian households. As a result, it has value and can be liquidated when needed. Jewelry often serves as a status symbol for a woman, reflecting the social and economic standing of her family.

A gold mangalsutra, a toe ring, and a bangle have religious connotations and are considered auspicious items. A blessing and protection are believed to be brought by them. Rings, mangalsutra, and other jewelry items symbolize marital commitment and are worn as a symbol of love and commitment.

In addition to maintaining women's beauty and protecting their chastity, jewelry is an invaluable cultural inheritance. Rather than merely objects for display or pleasure, they are an important medium for providing a woman with Chaitanya (Divine Consciousness) and activating her divinity. Ornaments have a lot of spiritual significance. As well as reminding a woman to remain chaste and prevent infidelity, it reduces the black (negative) energy in her body, protects her from negative energy attacks; the parts of her body where ornaments are worn undergo spiritual healing like acupressure. Additionally, toe rings are said to have acupressure benefits. As a result, they press some nerves in the feet that are known to help the female reproductive system.

Jewelry enhances the overall look of Indian attire and adds a touch of elegance. Style and taste are reflected in different types of jewelry. During festivals and special events, women wear elaborate jewelry reflecting the celebratory nature of these events. Often, jewelry pieces have sentimental value, as they are associated with significant life events like weddings, birthdays, and anniversaries.

As a tangible representation of familial heritage, jewelry often serves as a link between generations and a link between mothers and daughters. Women in India often own their own jewelry, providing them with a sense of financial independence and security. While maintaining traditional elements, Indian jewelry designs have evolved over time to incorporate modern trends.

Jewelry plays a symbolic role in various rituals and ceremonies, emphasizing women's roles and status. Jewelry can hold memories, values, and stories that can be passed down from generations to generations beyond its material value.

For Indian women, jewelry is more than just adornment. A rich tapestry of traditions and values is intertwined with their cultural, social, economic, and personal lives.

Married women and multiple Ornaments significance

Tikka

Maang Tikkas are worn by brides across India. Maang Tikka on the forehead chakra represents the third eye or soul power. The ornament is worn between the middle part of the hairline. It symbolizes the ability to concentrate and control emotions.

Nose ring/Nath

The Nath is a common ornament worn by Indian brides. In honor of Goddess Parvati, this ornament signifies good health for husbands. In women, piercing a particular node on the nostril relieves or lessens the pain during monthly periods. The left nostril is the most common place for women to wear nose rings since the nerves leading from the left nostril are associated with female reproductive organs. Having the nose pierced at this position also aids in easing childbirth.

Necklace Choker

Gold chokers, crafted with intricate lacy designs, are a must-have in Bihari brides' kits, and they are paired with longer necklaces.

Chandrahar

This layered necklace, crafted from gold pearls, is one of the longer necklaces in the Bihari bride's collection and has two lockets on either side.

Tiklis, which are also studded with precious stones, are worn on the bride's central parting; they are like maang tikkas.

Panchlari

Traditionally crafted from pearls and colorful gems, the Panchlari necklace has five layers, and each layer contains a small locket.

Satlari

Satlaris are layered with seven necklaces containing lockets that contain pearls and precious stones, like saat lada haars.

Sita Haar

The Sita Haar necklace is a statement-making necklace that's forged out of gold and dangles down to the waist of the bride, making it a perfect pairing with other shorter necklaces.

Ring

Ring is wearing on the fourth finger from the thumb is connected to the neurons cells as the nerve passing through this finger is said to be connected to the brain and heart as the nerve passing through this finger is said to be connected to the neuron's cells. This finger is a metallic one, which provides a better stimulation of the nerve, which in turn contributes to achieving a feeling of good health and confidence to deal with emotions.

Belly Belt/Hip/ Kamar Bandh

Wearing it around the belly makes it look beautiful. As a result, belly fat (fat around the waist) is prevented from accumulating in the body.

Hindu Married women wear Sindoor

According to Science, sindoor enhances feminine grace to a large extent, lending it a divine beauty. On the forehead between the eyebrows is where the sixth chakra (third eye) is located. . Spirituality and mental power can be enhanced through it. A sindoor daan is an auspicious Hindu ritual worn by married women. Sindoor contains turmeric, lime, and mercury, as well as stimulating good health. In addition to alleviating stress, strain, and keeping the brain active and alert, it controls blood pressure, stimulates sexual drive, and increases libido. This enhances concentration power by absorbing bad water from the forehead region.

Bindi

Traditionally, they were made from vermilion, sandalwood paste, or turmeric paste. An Indian woman is characterized by her Bindi. It is not only worn by married women, but also by young girls and unmarried women. A Bindi is a small red or maroon dot worn by women between their eyebrows on their foreheads. Pottu, Bottu, Sindoor, Kumkum, etc... are some of the names given to Bindi. There are ready-made Bindis available in the market, which women can peel and stick on their foreheads. At the time of a wedding, the bridegroom applies vermilion to his bride's forehead. According to the Holy Vedas and scientific evidence, the forehead contains a lot of energy. It is the location of the Ajna chakra, where the Pineal gland is located. By activating this gland, Melatonin and other hormones are produced optimally for the body's well-being. Bindi activates the Pineal gland, which has enormous health benefits for women.

Why does Hindu married women wear Earrings?

Earrings made of gold cause friction and improved eyesight. Besides adding charm to your face, the ears also contain nerves that connect to your eyes and reproductive organs (only for women). Furthermore, wearing earrings also has an acupuncture effect on the body. Earrings are therefore recommended for both men and women. Menstrual problems can also be alleviated by pierced ears. The 'Hunger Point' is also said to exist in the ears. An earring helps curb your food cravings as well as keep your weight in check.

Earrings that sit on your earlobes are called studs. You can wear them daily since they are petite. Solitaires are a special type of stud earring. In addition to complementing the look, colored earrings are quite jewelry. Earrings with color make a great addition to any outfit.

A dangle earring extends beyond the earlobes and can range from a simple daily wear design to a fancy occasion wear item. It depends on your requirements whether you want lightweight or heavy designs. It is possible to wear hoop earrings to complete your formal meeting look or to go out with friends on a fun outing.

Why does Hindu married women wear Bangles?

As a symbolic representation of their Suhag, the husband/groom, they are a compulsory part of bridal wear. After marriage, different regions in the country wear different colored bangles. Red is the color of Punjab, green is the color of Maharashtra, ivory is the color of Bengal, gold is the color of Southern states, etc. Energy and prosperity are represented by red, while good luck and fertility are represented by green. White symbolizes a new beginning, while gold symbolizes prosperity and fortune. According to Ayurveda, bracelets release stress by pressing on certain nerves in the arm.

Mauri

The mauri is a headgear made from mango leaves or date leaves and worn by the bride during the wedding ceremony. Nowadays, it is also made from fancy papers.

Why do Hindu married women wear Mangal Sutra/Dholna Patwasi?

Dholna are not only worn on their wedding day, but also during festive occasions. They are adorned with an ornate gold drum-shaped locket. As the name suggests, it is auspicious jewelry, since 'mangal' means good or auspicious while 'sutra' means thread connecting/uniting two souls. It is made by threading black beads around a gold pendant with mustard-sized black beads giving the power to repel evil forces or bad omens. It helps in boosting heart function, developing the immune system, regularizing blood flow, keeping healthy and fresh by attracting cosmic waves from the surroundings. The pendant close to the heart helps to attract cosmic waves from the surroundings.

Why do Hindu married women wear Anklets/pajayab?

In Indian culture, anklets depict the marital status of women, so it is mandatory that women wear them after marriage. An Indian woman's Solah Shringaar consists of sixteen adornments. An anklet, also known as a Payal or a Pajeb, is a magnificent piece of jewelry worn around the ankle. Hindu culture attaches some religious significance to each adornment. The wearing of anklets is a symbol of good fortune for her husband and their relationship. Wearing anklets is thought to bring positivity into the house and ward off negative energies. As the women walk, the sonorous sound of the anklets fills the atmosphere with vibrant energy, and the melodious ringing of the bells attached to them catches everyone's attention. A maternal uncle presents a bride with silver anklets on the day of her wedding before Saptapadi or Saat phere. It is considered auspicious. The bride steps into her new house with the jingling of anklets, bringing prosperity and good omen into the home of her in-laws. Gold is considered a sacred metal in Hinduism, so married women prefer silver anklets over gold anklets. Wearing it at the lower part of the body is therefore considered disrespectful. Anklets are more than just jewelry. An Indian woman's beauty is enhanced by it. An adornment is one of sixteen that contributes to the attractive appearance of the garment. There are some health benefits associated with it and it is associated with a woman's well-being. It is scientifically proven that wearing silver anklets or ankle chains regulates blood pressure and reverts energy back to one's own body. As a result of constant friction between silver metal and ankles, ankle bones became stronger. An anklet made of silver is recommended for females in Ayurveda as a metal with medicinal properties. As a fashion statement, anklets or payals are also worn by young girls and unmarried women. It pairs well with skirts, jeans, and kurta salwars. Wearing anklets by married women is considered auspicious and a symbol of good fortune in Hindu culture. Anklets are available in different designs, colors, distinct beads, and pearls and have evolved according to the thinking of modern era's generation. It is not only adorned by women in India, but around the world as well.

Why do Hindu married women wear toe-rings?

A Bihari bride wears silver/gold toe rings on her middle toe, as do many other brides on the Indian subcontinent. Married women wear them on both second toes. Sometimes two sets are worn, one for the brother and one for the husband, and if either dies, one set is removed. If the husband dies, the brother will protect her. These ornaments are never worn by unmarried women. In addition to adorning the feet, the ring is supposed to regulate the flow of blood to the uterus, keeping it healthy so it can produce babies. Gold is never used to make it. As gold represents Goddess Laxmi, wearing gold on the feet would be disrespectful. As a good conductor, silver absorbs energy from the Earth and transfers it to the body, refreshing it. Each ornament worn by married women has a traditional meaning. However, they also have scientific reasons behind them which help increase their strength, concentration, and relieve pain.

Importance of saree?

Although the festival is celebrated in different ways throughout India, Sarees are the one common factor. The festival is celebrated by wearing banarasi sarees in the north and kanjivaram, upaada, etc in the south. While in the western part of the country, women wear bandhani and chanderi. Women wear jamdani in eastern parts of India. Sarees are loved by women and girls of all ages. It adds a vibrant touch to the festival when sarees of different colors and varieties are worn. For Navratri, special types of sarees are designed. As silk can imbibe positive energy from the cosmos, Indian women wear exquisite silk sarees during these nine days, which are charged with beautiful divine energy.

Importance of gajra

The beauty of a queen is captivated by a gajra made of jasmine, the queen of flowers. Hinduism attaches special significance to gajra. In olden times, women used to put Gajra in their hair when they did sixteen makeups. Gajra is worn by women in South India, whether it's for worship, functions, or festivals. Currently, there is a lot of fashion for applying Gajra to one's hair, especially on Karva Chauth, when women apply it to their hair. The fragrance of gajra made with jasmine flowers is not only beautiful but can make anyone crazy.

Religious significance of gajra

The flowers of the Gajra increase its growth. White and very soft Bela-Jasmine flowers are used in Gajra. Goddess Lakshmi likes these flowers. Offerings of jasmine flowers are made to Goddess Lakshmi. Women are also considered to be the forms of Goddess Lakshmi, which is why they apply Gajra to their hair.

Importance of Gajra on Karva Chauth

It is believed that placing Gajra in one's hair will bring good fortune and prosperity. Like Gajra in your hair, you should keep the fragrance in your relationship as well. The white flower, however, is a symbol of peace and happiness in the house. Goddess Lakshmi is believed to reside in the house when Gajra is applied to the hair. Smelting Gajra preserves love between husband and wife.

History of Gajra

Women of South Asia have worn Gajra as ornaments and adornments since ancient times. Planting Gajra is a tradition in worship, festivals, and weddings. Gajra is mainly made from jasmine flowers. Besides wearing Judah and hair, women also wear Gajra in their hands. Gajra jewelry is still worn by some people.

Hindu Men Traditions Value

Why do we wear marks (tilak, Pottu and the like) on the forehead?

A tilak covers the area between the eyebrows, where memory and thought are located. Yoga calls it the Ajana Chakra. Tilaks are thus blessings of the God as well as protection against wrong tendencies and forces. Every part of the body emits electromagnetic waves, especially the forehead and the subtle spot between the eyebrows. The reason worry causes a headache is because it generates heat. The tilak and Pottu cool the forehead, protect us, and prevent energy loss. Chandan or bhasma is sometimes applied to the entire forehead. Although they serve as decorations, plastic reusable "stick bindis" are not very beneficial.

Wearing tilaks or pottus instills a sense of sanctity in the wearer and others. Historically, there were four castes (based on varna or color) - Brahmanas, Kshatriyas, Vaishyas

To signify purity, the brahmin applied a white Chandan mark. The kshatriya applied a red

Kumkum mark signifying velour as he belonged to warrior races.

A Vaishya wore a yellow kesar or turmeric mark, symbolizing prosperity as a businessman or trader.

Sudras were marked with black bhasma, Kasturi or charcoal to signify their support for the other three divisions.

A Chandan tilak in the shape of "U" is applied by Vishnu worshippers and a tilak in the shape of "S" is applied by Shiva worshippers

Importance of dhoti kurta in Indian men?

The Dhoti is an Indian national and ethnic costume worn by men. It is also known as chaadra, mardani, dhotar, and panchey. Traditionally, a Dhoti is made from one rectangular piece of unstitched cloth. A typical length is around four and a half to five meters. Dhotis are worn like saris, which are wrapped around the waist. The Dhoti is a type of men's trousers that evolved from the Antriya, an ancient garment worn by tucking a cloth at the back of the waist through the legs. At the front, the Antriya fell into long pleats that covered one's legs. An Indian dhoti is a traditional garment that is worn primarily by men in South Asia, particularly in India, Bangladesh, and Sri Lanka. Cotton or silk cloth is draped around the waist and legs and is usually rectangular in shape. Dhotis typically range in length from 4 to 7 yards (3.7 to 6.4 meters). Regions and cultures have different ways of draping the dhoti. One end of the scarf is tucked in at the waist, while the other is draped over the shoulder or wrapped around the head. Depending on the style of the dhoti and the way it is draped, it can also be indicative of a person's social status, their religious affiliation, or other cultural factors. Often worn at weddings and religious ceremonies, dhotis can also be worn every day. South Asians often wear them with kurtas, which are long loose shirts. Dhotis are the equivalent of saris for Indian men, while women wear beautiful saris. Dhotis are common menswear items in India. Dhoti, which means to "cleanse or wash", refers to a garment that is frequently worn and is part of everyday wear. The main difference is that the Dhoti wraps around the waist and hips, with one end going between the legs and then being knotted into the waistband either at the front or the back. By wearing these trousers this way, one creates a similar fit and silhouette to their regular trousers. Dhoti bottoms drape loosely around the thighs or upper leg area and gradually narrow and taper down towards the hem. However, the way one wraps a Dhoti around the body to create a bottom garment varies greatly from region to region.

Commonly, it is worn over loincloth undergarments such as a kaupinam or langot.

Dhotis can be described as a hybrid between a sari and harem pants, but with a uniquely Indian flair.

In general, cotton and silk are used for the rectangular fabric of the Dhoti. Although black is arguably the most common color for trousers, plain white and solid cream are the most popular colors for Dhotis. With India's tropical climate, the Dhoti is a practical and comfortable garment to wear throughout the year. With a kurta or shirt, cotton dhotis are usually worn for daily wear and are more casual in style. Dhotis are not just for everyday wear, however. A formal celebration, a traditional event, or a religious ceremony can all be celebrated with them. For wedding ceremonies, men wear silk Dhotis with embroidered borders and angavasthrams for the upper body when it comes to formal wear, including Dhotis. Dhotis are also typically worn by Indian politicians as they convey authority, dignity, and respect. Indian men wear the Dhoti regardless of the occasion.

A Brief History of the Indian Dhoti

"Dhoti" is derived from the Sanskrit word "dhauta," which means cleansed or washed. In Indian culture, the dhoti has a long and rich history dating back thousands of years.

Here is a brief history of the Indian dhoti:

Ancient Times: Dhotis are believed to have originated in the Indus Valley Civilization around 2500 BCE. A single piece of cloth was draped around the waist and legs and worn by both men and women. In time, the dhoti evolved into a more refined garment for men, while sarees became more prevalent for women.

Vedic Period : During the Vedic period (1500-500 BCE), the dhoti became a symbol of purity worn by priests during religious rituals. To maintain its purity, it was washed and ironed before each use from pure white cotton or silk.

Medieval Times : The dhoti became more elaborate during the medieval period (600-1600 CE) and was worn by men of all social classes. Dhotis developed differently in different regions of India, with variations in length, draping style, and fabric.

British Colonial Period : During the British Colonial Period (1757-1947), Western-style clothing became more popular among the educated elite, but the dhoti remained a staple garment for many Indians, particularly in rural districts.

Modern Times : Dhotis are still worn by men in India today for both formal and casual occasions. A kurta or another traditional garment is often worn with it as a symbol of Indian culture and tradition.

What does Dhoti signify culturally?

Among Indian men, the dhoti holds great cultural and religious significance. The dhoti is important for the following reasons:

Tradition:

Dhotis have been worn by Indian men for centuries as a traditional garment. In India, it is regarded as a symbol of culture and heritage.

Religious Significance:

In Hinduism, the dhoti is often worn during religious rituals and ceremonies. During religious ceremonies, it is worn as a symbol of respect and devotion as it is considered to be a pure and sacred garment.

Social Significance:

Dhoti style and drape can indicate the wearer's social status, caste, or profession. Dhotis are draped differently by certain communities or castes in India, for instance.

Comfort:

Dhotis are comfortable and practical garments, especially in India's humid climate. Designed to provide relief from heat and allow for ease of movement, it features a loose, airy fit.

Identity:

Dhotis are worn by many Indian men to connect with their cultural and religious roots. The purpose is to preserve and promote Indian culture and tradition.

What are Dhotis made of?

Dhotis can be made from a variety of materials, but the most common ones are cotton and silk.

The Garment donned by the Gods

Yes, several Hindu gods are depicted wearing dhoti, which is considered a sacred and pure garment in Hindu culture. Here are some examples:

God Ganesha:

Often depicted wearing a dhoti and a sacred thread (upavita) around his torso, God Ganesha is the elephant-headed god of wisdom and prosperity. In this way, his status as a Brahmin or priest is symbolized.

God Vishnu:

The preserver of the universe, God Vishnu wears a dhoti with a long scarf or shawl draped over his shoulders (uttariya). As the protector of dharma (righteousness), he represents his royal status.

God Krishna:

Often depicted wearing a dhoti and a peacock feather, God Krishna is the god of love and compassion. As a result, he is playful and carefree.

God Rama:

God Rama, the hero of the Hindu epic Ramayana, is often depicted wearing a dhoti and a crown or turban. In this way, he symbolizes his status as a prince and his righteous and just nature.

Different ways to wear a Dhoti

There are various ways to wear a dhoti, and the style can vary depending on the region, occasion, and personal preference. Here are some common ways to wear a dhoti:

Nivi Style:

The cloth is wrapped around the waist and legs, then passed between the legs and tucked at the back, a popular dhoti style in southern India. Afterward, the remaining cloth is draped over the shoulder and wrapped around the waist.

Bengali Style :

West Bengal and Bangladesh are common places where the dhoti is draped like a lungi or sarong, tucked at the waist and pleated at the back. Afterward, the remaining cloth is draped over the shoulder and wrapped around the waist.

Gujarati Style :

Traditionally, the dhoti is wrapped around the waist and legs, and the excess cloth is tucked into the waistband, resulting in a loose, skirt-like look.

Maharashtrian Style :

In this style, the dhoti is wrapped around the waist and legs, and the excess cloth is tucked into the waistband. Over the left shoulder, the remaining cloth is draped.

Kerala Style :

A diagonal sash across the body is created by wrapping the dhoti around the waist and legs, then draped over the right shoulder. There are many ways to wear a dhoti, and each style may be worn differently depending on individual preference and cultural traditions.

3. Importance of wearing Turban/Topi/safa/pagdi?

There is nothing more beautiful for a bride than a veil. Grooms can also be glorified by their headgears. Among grooms and their immediate male relatives, turbans and headgears play an important role.

Originally, an Indian groom was expected to dress like a king in his entire ensemble. Perhaps therefore Indian grooms dress so elaborately. Crowns and turbans were symbols of pride and stature for Indian kings. In Indian wedding dressing, the turban is therefore indispensable.

The Indian subcontinent is a land of many cultures. Colors and textures of headgear may change due to these cultures. India has a large variety of turbans!

This important piece of clothing will take us on a journey through India! This turban is associated with many local beliefs. Bihari grooms wear red silk cloths on their heads. The groom wears a simple white turban in Jharkhand, where there are many tribes. Oriya grooms and brides wear the same turban, a magnificent crown embellished with multicolored stones, beads, and paisley patterns.

Many indigenous tribes live in the East, and their customs are very interesting. Assamese grooms are well known for their turbans. He either wears a tulsi mala or a fresh flower crown. In Manipur, the groom wears a white turban with golden braiding called a 'kokyet'. Turbans with beads, cowries, feathers, and bamboo spikes are also popular headgears. Marriages in tribes use these.

18

Common Hindu Traditions – Belief or Science behind

❦

Why do we worship Tulsi plants in Hindu culture?
Answer

Tulsi is also known as Holy Basil or Ocimum Sanctum. Tulsi has been worshipped by Hindus for thousands of years. A Tulsi plant must be placed in front of every Hindu house as it is considered a sacred plant.

Science

The Tulsi plant releases Ozone (O3) along with oxygen, which is essential for ecological balance. Tulsi plants are distributed in large numbers on World Ozone Day, which falls on 16th September every year. According to Ayurveda, Tulsi is a very important herb that has many medicinal uses. Our immune system is strengthened by tulsi leaves. Tulsi leaves are mainly used to treat fever, common cold, cough, sore throat, and respiratory disorders.

Why do Hindus worship some trees and not all the trees?

Answer

Even though Hindus honor all trees, some trees and plants are considered sacred and have been worshiped for thousands of years. Examples include the Peepal Tree (Ficus virginiana) and the Audumbar Tree (Ficus racemosa). Audumbar trees are associated with Guru Dattatreya, one of the main Hindu deities, and cutting them or dishonoring them is considered sinful.

Science

Neither of these trees can be planted manually since they produce oxygen 24 hours a day. Their fruits are eaten mainly by birds, which allow them to grow on their own. Ecological balance depends on both trees. By associating them with Hindu deities, they have been protected from being cut down.

Why do Hindus not eat meat on specific days?

Answer

Hinduism considers killing animals a sin. To preserve the sacredness of those particular days, people avoid eating meat at least on those auspicious days. Every Monday, Thursday, and Saturday of the week, Sankashti Chaturthi, Angarki Chaturthi, Ekadashi, Gudivada, Akshaytrutiya, Diwali (all days), and many more auspicious days. Religious reasons are given for not eating meat on certain days excluding weekly days. By assigning days to deities, Hinduism has placed some restrictions. By doing this, they limit the amount of meat in their diet, which is beneficial for their health.

Science: Since humans require only a small amount of meat to fulfill their needs for iron, vitamin B12, and other vital nutrients, we don't eat meat on weekdays, including Mondays, Thursdays, and Saturdays. In Hinduism, meat is not eaten on days, including, but not limited to. There are several diseases caused by it, including piles, kidney stones, colon cancer, high blood pressure, heart attacks, and more. People cannot also refrain from eating flesh.

What is 84 Lakh Yonis?

Answer:

We get the human body after our soul passes through 84,00,000 species.

According to Hindu belief, we acquire a human body after passing through 84,00,000 species. Initially, critics of Hinduism said that these species didn't exist, since they were just myths.

Science has revealed that there are about 84,00,000 species on earth. We humans are at the most advanced stage of evolution, so the above statement symbolizes the fact that a human being is born through evolution.

Chitragupta and the Near-Death Experience?

Answer:

During near-death experiences, people see a snapshot of their lives in a flash. In Hinduism, there is a god named Chitragupta who keeps track of people's good and bad karma and determines whether they will go to heaven or hell. Chitragupta means "one who takes pictures secretly". It implies that Hindus have been aware of this phenomenon since ancient times.

Why do we light diyas?

Answer:

"Knowledge Principle" (Chaitanya) is the source, enlivener, and illuminator of all knowledge. The lighting of diyas symbolically removes ignorance and light removes darkness. Our vaasanas or negative tendencies are symbolized by the oil or ghee in the lamp, and our ego is symbolized by the wick. The vaasanas slowly exhaust when lit by spiritual knowledge, and the ego finally perishes as well. As we acquire knowledge, we should strive to attain higher ideals. Traditionally, all auspicious events begin with the lighting of a lamp, which is kept burning throughout the event. The God's altar is lit daily in almost every Indian home. It is lit at dawn, twice a day - at dawn and dusk - in some houses, and in a few, continuously (Akhanda Deepa). Auspicious functions begin with the lighting of a lamp, which is usually maintained throughout the event. As light removes darkness, knowledge removes ignorance. Moreover, knowledge is a lasting inner wealth that can be obtained through all the outer accomplishments you can make. Therefore, we light the lamp in honor of knowledge, the greatest wealth.

Importance of doing namaste?

Answer:

Namaste. Nam – as – te. In its literal translation, namaste means "I bow to the same Divine within you." This one word encompasses the essential teachings of Hinduism despite its simplicity. In terms of its potential power, it transcends Hinduism and Hindus.

Science: In Hindu culture, the 'Namaskar' has a scientific reason. By joining both hands, all the fingers are touched together, which corresponds to pressure points in the eyes, ears, and mind. It is said that pressing them together activates them, helping us to remember that person forever.

Why do we not touch papers, books, and people with the feet?

Answer:

The Indian culture teaches us from an early age not to touch papers, books, or people with our feet. Children are told to touch their eyes after accidentally touching papers, books, musical instruments, or any other educational equipment with their feet. In Indian culture, knowledge is considered sacred and divine.

Knowledge is entrusted to the goddess Saraswati (Goddess of Learning). The act of touching books with your feet or kicking a school bag containing books is considered sinful. Saraswati is disrespected by this act. In the same way, one should not touch any musical or educational instrument with their feet. In Hinduism, every object that contains knowledge is respected. In Indian culture, the custom of not stepping on educational tools signifies the importance accorded to knowledge. When this happens accidentally, we apologize by touching the person's eyes with our fingers.

Why do we worship cows?

Answer:

According to Hinduism, is the veneration and protection of the cow as a symbol of divine and natural beneficence. Many deities have also been associated with the cow, including Shiva (whose steed is the bull Nandi), Indra (closely associated with Kamdhenu, the wish-granting cow), Krishna (a cowherd in his youth), and goddesses in general (because of their maternal characteristics). Cow veneration dates to the Vedic period (2nd millennium–7th century BCE). During the 2nd millennium BCE, Indo-Europeans came to India as pastoralists; cattle played a significant role in their religion. Although cows were sacrificed and their flesh was eaten in ancient India, the slaughter of milk-producing cows became increasingly prohibited. It is forbidden in parts of the Mahabharata, the great Sanskrit epic, and in the religious and ethical code known as the Manu-smriti ("Tradition of Manu"), and the milk cow was already said to be "unslayable" in the Rigveda. As a measure of the reverence accorded to the cow, the panchagavya, the five products of the cow, is used for healing, purification, and penance. As early as the 3rd century BC, cows were also associated with Brahmans or priests, and killing a cow was sometimes equated (by Brahmans) with killing a Brahman.

Why do we worship sun?

Answer:

Hinduism calls the Sun the soul of the world. It is impossible to imagine a day without it. As the sun rose, the ancestors offered water in a round copper utensil called a Lota (with a wide edge). A flowing film of water would create the seven colors of the spectrum through refraction, allowing indirect viewing of the sun. According to Hindus, this is beneficial to the eyes, vitalizes the body, and purifies the mind.

Science: Early morning sun rays are scientifically proven to be beneficial to human beings, after all, the human body is a bundle of energy. In the human body, there are five elements: air (Vayu), water (Jal), earth (Prithvi), fire (energy) and space (Aakash). All ailments of the body can be cured by these five elements alone, and the rising sun is one of them. The use of sun rays can cure many diseases, such as heart disease, eye disease, jaundice, leprosy, and weak mental health. Blood circulation is also improved, metabolism is balanced, and many body systems are restored.

Why are no new clothes worn during Pitrapaksha?

Answer:

During the Shraddhas/Pitra Paksha, their ancestors once lived in this area and were family heads. As a result of our respect for our ancestors and Pitra, we are called Shradh. According to Karma, hunger and thirst do not cease after death, so one should not forget their Pitras or dead relatives. Thus, Shradh or Pitra paksha is what God Hari arranges for dead souls.

Story:

Once, Yamraj Maharaj, the Mirtyu Devta, asked God Brahma ji for dead souls' agony because of their attachment to their relatives and families even after death. Hence, in Yamraj's version, God Brahma ji asked Sri Hari, Param Purush, Supreme God/Parmatma to find a solution. During the Krishna Paksha of the Ashwin month, Bhagwaan Vishnu immediately said that now all dead souls of Yamlok would be able to meet their near and dear ones on earth. In Krishna Paksha of Ashwin month, Bhagwan ordered Yamraj to leave free all dead souls, so that they (dead souls) could meet their relatives and observe how they react or offer them (dead) in Shradh or Pitra Paksha. In accordance with Param Purush's directive, Yamraj leaves Yamlok's dead souls free.

Why do we need to sleep keeping head towards north side?

Answer:

Blood circulation can also be disrupted by sleeping with your head pointing north. It is better to avoid sleeping with your head facing north to prevent such a scenario. Sleeping in the east and south directions is ideal.

What is the importance of Feeding cow?

Answer:

Cows proliferate energies that help people overcome anger and tension. By doing this, Rahu's negative aspects can be eliminated. The act of feeding a cow makes you feel peaceful and relaxed. A positive mindset and happy thoughts can also be achieved by feeding a cow.

What is the importance of Ganga jaal?

Answer:

Ganga Jal is used by Hindus from birth to death. According to religious beliefs, this destroys all sins and evil thoughts and purifies the body and mind. Ganga Jal is poured into a person's mouth on normal death.

In addition to being rich in oxygen, nutrients, and salts, Ganga Jal is also clean and safe. It can also be used for a long time and helps to cure chronic diseases. As a healthy drink, it will benefit their growth and development.

What is the importance of Rudra?

Answer:

Mantras of Rudra remove fear and clear the mind of confusion and vagaries. We all have fears. The Rudra mantra can help overcome all types of fears and stresses if chanted regularly in the prescribed manner with devotion and focus of mind.

What is the importance of waking during brahm mutra?

Answer:

The benefits of waking up during Brahma Muhurta have been researched. Oxyhemoglobin is formed when this nascent oxygen mixes with hemoglobin, providing the following benefits: Increases immunity. Enhances energy levels. Maintains the pH level of the blood in a balanced manner.

Importance of Swastik?

Answer:

Swastika is a Sanskrit word composed of the words 'su' (meaning 'good'), and 'asti' (meaning 'to exist').

A Swastika is a symbol of auspiciousness and good fortune, which is commonly translated as 'all is well.' The Swastika is usually worn on Hindu homes, businesses, printed materials, cars, temples, and ashrams as a sign of good luck and auspiciousness. A swastika is often adorning the threshold of the front entrance to the home of many Hindus. During Diwali, especially, swastikas are washed away and reapplied, or included in rangoli (which decorates courtyards with dyed powders, rice and grains, or flowers). Swastikas are often created by arranging clay lamps artfully.

What is the importance of washing hair on Friday?

Answer:

In Hinduism, women are considered incarnations of goddess Lakshmi. It is believed that people in the old days, and possibly even today, still took hair baths on festivals, birthdays, and other auspicious occasions. Traditionally, Friday is considered as the day of the goddess Lakshmi, hence if a woman takes a hair bath on this auspicious day, she is supposed to receive wealth, according to popular belief.

Can I go to Mandir on my period?

Answer:

The study found that many Hindu people believe menstruating women are so pure that they are 'worshipped' as living goddesses during that time of the month, so women who are currently in menstruation cannot enter a temple due to their energy attracting the energy of the murti, and the murti becoming lifeless as a result.

Why is 108 important in Hinduism?

Answer:

In Hindu tradition, there are 108 Mukhya Shiva Ganas (attendants of Shiva), so Shaiva religions, particularly Lingayats, use malas with 108 beads. In Gaudiya Vaishnavism, God Krishna had 108 followers known as gopis in Vrindavan.

Why can't we touch Tulsi on Sunday?

Answer:

As Goddess Tulsi fasts for God Vishnu on Sunday, offering her water on this day will break her fast. On a Sunday, it is also believed that if you water the Tulsi plant, negative forces will inhabit your home.

Why do Hindus walk around 7 times?

Answer:

The Saptapadi involves the couple walking seven steps clockwise around the Angi near the Mandap. The seven steps are called Pheras, and each Phere represents the seven promises and principles the couple made to one another during the exchange of vows.

Why do we have a prayer room/place?

Answer:

Meditation, worship, and chanting done there regularly have accumulated spiritual thoughts and vibrations. The prayer room is a calm, rejuvenating and spiritually uplifting place, even when we are tired or agitated.

Why do we prostrate before parents and elders?

Answer:

We invoke the good wishes and blessings of elders when we prostrate with humility and respect, which flow as positive energy around us. Because of this, the posture assumed, whether it be standing or prone, allows the entire body to receive the energy.

Pratuthana - rising to welcome a person is one form of showing respect.

Namaskaara - is a form of paying homage to another person.

Upasangrahan is touching the feet of elders or teachers.

Shaashtaanga - prostrating fully in front of an elder with the feet, knees, stomach, chest, forehead, and arms touching the ground.

Pratyabivaadana - greeting returned.

To touch another with the feet is considered an act of misdemeanor. Why is this so?

Answer:

It is believed that there is no more beautiful, breathing, living temple than that of man! Thus, touching another's feet disrespects their divinity. An apology is immediately needed, and it should be offered with reverence and humility.

Why do we apply the holy ash?

Answer:

The word bha implies the word bhartsanam ("to destroy"), while sma implies the word smaranam ("to remember").

Bhasma (holy ash) is ash from the homa (sacrificial fire) where wood and herbs are offered as sacrifices to the God. Deities are worshipped by pouring ash as abhisheka and then distributing bhasma. Ash from burnt objects is not considered holy ash. Ascetics rub it all over their bodies. By bhasma, we destroy our sins and we remember God. By applying bhasma, the evil is destroyed and the divine is remembered. Vibhuti means "glory" because it gives glory to the wearer, and raksha means "source of protection" because it protects the wearer from evil by purifying them. God Shiva associates Bhasma with His body, which he applies all over.

In many ayurvedic medicines, bhasma is used as a medicinal ingredient.

Why offer food to God before eating it?

Answer:

It is a tradition among the Indians to offer food to the God at the time of worship and to then take a portion of it as prasada - a holy gift from the God. As part of our daily ritualistic worship (pooja), we also offer naivedyam (food) to the God. Before consuming what we receive, we share it with others. As far as food quality is concerned, we don't complain, demand, or criticize it. The food is then offered to God, the life force, which is also present in us as the five physiological functions that provide life.

Why do we fast?

Answer:

During festivals or other special occasions, most devout Indians fast. On such days, we either do not eat at all, eat just once, or consume simple foods like fruits. In Sanskrit, fasting is called upavasa. In Sanskrit, upa means "near" and vaasa means "to stay."

As such, upavasa means staying close to (the God), which means achieving close mental proximity.

We are encouraged in the Bhagavad-Gita to eat appropriately - not too little nor too much - yukta-ahara, and to eat simple, pure, and healthy food (a sattvic diet) even when we are not fasting.

Why do we do pradakshina (circumambulate)?

Answer:

Pradakshina is important as we keep our deities in the center of our thoughts and recognize him as the focal point in our lives, while carrying our life duties. This is important to ensure we keep this thought in our mind while we visit temples and near our deities.

Shivling ½ round
Durga 1 round
Ganesh 3 rounds
Hanuman 3 rounds
Vishnu 4 rounds
Surya 7 rounds
All other Gods 5 rounds

Why is pradakshina done only in a clockwise manner?

Answer:

Our God always sits on our right side when we do pradakshina. It is customary to perform pradakshina around ourselves after traditional worship (pooja). We recognize and remember the supreme divinity within us, which alone we worship as the deities outside.

Why do we ring the bell in a temple? Is it to wake up God?

Answer:

The ringing of the bell is considered auspicious. Om, the universal name of God, is produced by it. Ringing the bell is part of the ritualistic aarti. Conch and other musical instruments are sometimes used to accompany it. Additionally, ringing the bell, conch, and other instruments helps drown out any inauspicious or irrelevant noises and comments that disturb or distract the worshippers' devotion, concentration, and inner peace.

What precautions are taken during the Solar and lunar eclipse?

Answer:

Eclipses or grahan are inauspicious according to the Hindu mythology. Well, there is a scientific reason why one should not cook/eat food during an eclipse. No food should be cooked during the eclipse. People believe that harmful rays are emitted during eclipse which harm cooked food. So, it is advised to eat raw food items. You can take a sattvic diet, raw vegetable salads, and fruits.

Also, it is believed still water or water stored long hours during an eclipse is harmful. To avoid any negative effects, you can add ginger powder to water. Also, one can take coconut water.

You can avoid pre-cooled food as ultraviolet rays can destroy good bacteria in food and give way to growth of microorganisms. Prepare fresh food and add basil to it to avoid harmful effects.

Also avoid alcohol and meat during the eclipse. It takes a lot of energy to digest this food, so it is suggested to avoid it.

Tulsi should be placed on all cooked foods. Pregnant ladies should be inside home and refrain from coming in open. All people take showers after the eclipse is over and give money or grains to the poor.

Why do we worship the kalasha?

Answer:

Kalasha is a pot filled with water made of brass, copper, mud, or mud. Mango leaves are placed in the pot's mouth, and a coconut is placed on top. A red or white thread is tied around its neck or sometimes all around in an intricate diamond-shaped pattern. It is possible to decorate the pot with designs of swastika.

Purnakumbha, when filled with water or rice, represents the inert body that when filled with life force can accomplish all the wonderful things that make life what it is. There are many traditional occasions for placing kalashas, including housewarmings, weddings, and daily worship. Kalashas symbolize the primordial water that gave rise to the entire universe. Leaves and coconuts are symbols of creation. In creation, the thread represents the love that binds everything together. Kalasas are therefore considered auspicious and worshiped. During the abhisheka, water from all the holy rivers, the knowledge of all the

Vedas, as well as the blessings of all the deities are invoked in the kalasha.

Why do we blow the conch?

Answer:

Conch blowing emits Om's primordial sound. People were briefly elevated to a prayerful attitude through the conch sound, even in the middle of their daily routines. Temples and homes place the conch on the altar as a symbol of the Vedas, Om, dharma, victory, and auspiciousness. To raise devotees' minds to the highest Truth, tirtha (sanctified water) is often offered.

What are the colors of the Surya horses?

Answer

Sun is the source of light and that is white light (VIBGYOR) =white Violet + indigo + blue + green +yellow + orange + red ==white So all 7—horses represent each color of the VIBGYOR. It is the seven colors of the sunlight which reach us on our earth, give us warmth, sustain our life, and balance our solar system.

Why do we offer a coconut?

Answer:

Coconuts are one of the most common offerings in Indian temples. Also, it is offered at weddings, festivals, when purchasing a new vehicle, constructing a bridge, building a house, etc. During homa, it is offered in the sacrificial fire. Coconuts are broken and placed before God. Many ayurvedic medicines and alternative medicines contain this ingredient. Coconut marks are even said to represent the three-eyed Lord Shiva, so it is a means to fulfill our desires.

Why do we chant Om?

Answer:

Universe's primordial sound is Om. Om is the beginning of most mantras and vedic prayers. There are three letters in it: A (phonetically "around"), U (phonetically "put"), and M (phonetically "mum"). Three letters represent the three states (waking, dreaming, and deep sleep), the three deities (Brahma, Vishnu, and Shiva), the three Vedas (Rig, Yajur, and Sama), and the three worlds (Bhuh, Bhuvah, Suvah). In this sense, Om symbolizes everything - the means and the end of life, the world and its purpose, the material and the sacred, the form and the formless.

Science: Om is the cosmic sound that initiated the creation of the universe, according to the Big Bang theory. It consists of the letters A (phonetically like "around"), U (phonetically similar to "put"), and M (phonetically similar to "mum"). Chanting OM stimulates the vague nerve through its auricular branches, sharpening the mind. Additionally, OM' chanting has been associated with limbic deactivation, according to a study.

Why do we do aarti?

Answer:

Aarti is done towards the end of every ritualistic worship (pooja or bhajan) of the Hindu God/Goddess. Aarti is accompanied by few musical instruments, ringing bell (ghanti), taal.

How to do: Aarti is done by a lighted lamp on the right hand and waves in clockwise circling movement to light the entire form of God. As light is waved, we either do mental or loud chanting of prayers. Post the aarti, we place our hands over the flame and gently touch our eyes and head.

Singing, clapping, ringing of the bell, etc., represent the joy and auspiciousness associated with God's vision. Camphor is often used in aarti. There is a spiritual significance to this. Camphor burns completely without leaving a trace when lit. As our vaasanas are lit by knowledge that illuminates the God (Truth), they burn out completely without leaving any trace of ego that separates us from the God. Camphor also emits a pleasant perfume while burning to reveal the glory of God.

Science: Dhoop reduces air pollution and bacteria in the air, and it generates positive energy in devotees. In the past, idols were in the basement of temples and in low light, so the Aartis were performed in the morning and evening so that all devotees could see the God

What are the 12 months in Hindu calendar?

Answer

Here the names are Chaitra, Vaisakha, Jyaistha, Asadha, Shravana, Bhadra, Ashwin, Kartika, Mārgasirsa (Agrahayana), Pausha, Magha, and Phalguna.

HINDU	GREGORIAN
Chaitra	March – April
Vaishaka	April – May
Jyeshta	May – June
Ashada	June – July
Shravan	July – August
Bhadrapada	August – Sep
Ashvina	Sep – October
Kartik	Oct – Nov
Margashirasha	November – Dec
Pausha	December – Jan
Magha	January – Feb
Phalgun	February - March

What are the types of Tilak?

Answer:

In Hindu culture, a tilak or bindi is applied on the forehead. There is a cultural, religious, and social significance to it. Tilaks come in several forms, each with its own meaning and application. Tilaks are often chosen based on personal preference, religious tradition, and the occasion or ritual. Additionally, different sects and communities within Hinduism may have their own variations and preferences for tilaks.

These are some of the most common types:

Ashtagandha Tilak: This type of tilak is made from eight fragrant ingredients. As a result, it is often used in rituals as it is considered auspicious.

Chandan Tilak: Made from sandalwood paste, it is applied as either a dot or a vertical line. In Hinduism, sandalwood is considered sacred.

Gopi Chandana: A yellow sandalwood paste tilak. Worshippers of Krishna commonly wear it.

Kumkum Tilak: Worn by Hindu married women in northern India, this red tilak is made from vermilion.

Namskar Tilak: A simple tilak with a dot in the center, usually made of sandalwood paste. In daily worship and greeting ceremonies, it is used.

A Navagraha Tilak, which represents each planet in the nine planetary deities (Navagrahas), is used for worship.

Rice Tilak: During ceremonies, such as weddings, rice grains are used as tilaks in some rituals.

Shrivatsa Tilak: It refers to the special mark associated with Vishnu, specifically Krishna. It is shaped like a diamond.

Tripundra: This is the name given to followers of Lord Shiva. There are three horizontal lines, usually made from sacred ash (vibhuti).

Urdhva Pundra: This type of tilak is worn by Vaishnavas, followers of Vishnu. There are two vertical lines or a 'U' shape with a red dot or a 'T' shape in the middle.

The Vibhuti Tilak is made from sacred ash and is associated with Shiva. There are three horizontal lines that are often used to represent it.

What is Bhagavan?

Answer:

The Bhagavan word denotes 5 elements of human existence.

B – Bhu / Earth

G- Gagan / Cloud

V – Vayu / Air

A – Agni / Fire

N – Neer / Water

Why do we open shoes outside the temple or sit on the floor?

Answer:

There is a scientific reason why we open shoes outside and enter bare feet inside the temple or sit on the floor while doing pooja. The floor of the temple radiates magnetic waves, and this energy is observed while we walk on it. This gives positivity to our body and mind. This aligns our energies with earth's energy and helps find a sense of balance and harmony within ourselves.

Why does Ganesh trunk in different directions?

Answer:

The trunk of Lord Ganesha represents a lot of things, and the curved side represents what the idol of Lord Ganesha represents and the way it should be worshipped.

The Left Trunk:

This is the most popular side for the trunk to be. Most householders always buy an idol with a trunk to the left. The trunk curving to the left is called a Vamamukhi (Facing the Northern direction). The left side of Lord Ganesha is believed to be aligned with and possess the qualities of the Moon, which makes that side peaceful and blissful. Hence, the left-sided trunk pays homage to Goddess Parvati and invokes her blessings. It brings about family bonding and happiness.

The Right Trunk:

The right trunk is not very common and almost rare. Ganesh idols with the right trunk are worshipped fervently and religiously. The Ganesh idol at the famous Siddhivinayak Temple in Mumbai has a right-curving trunk. Siddhi Vinayaka refers to the right-side trunk. The idol with a trunk curved to the right is called Siddhi Vinayaka because Siddhi is one of Ganpati's wives. Pingala Nadi, or the sun's energy, is also symbolized by the right-sided idol. The Ganpati can bring happiness if worshipped properly or destruction if uncared for, just as the sun creates and destroys. Valampuri Ganesha must be cared for according to Vedic customs.

The Straight Trunk:

This is the rarest of the lot and rarely found. The significance of this is also deep. There is a complete oneness between the body senses and the divinity now that the Sushma Nadi has opened. Having no burden and being completely transparent makes you feel totally unburdened. Ganpati of this type also needs to be worshipped, though the worship of this type is not as rigid as the worship of Right Trunk Ganesha. Even though they are extremely rare, these types of Ganesha make great gifts.

What is Mantra?

Mantras are sacred and powerful sounds, words, or phrases that have spiritual and transformative properties in Hinduism. Invoking specific deities, aligning with cosmic energies, or attaining spiritual goals can be achieved by chanting, reciting, or meditating on them. Typically, mantras are composed in ancient Sanskrit, but other languages are also acceptable.

Here are some key aspects of mantras in Hinduism:

♦ Sanskrit Origin: Most Hindu mantras are in Sanskrit, which is considered a sacred language. Sanskrit words are believed to have a direct impact on consciousness and the environment.

Sacred Formulas:

♦ It is common for mantras to be structured as concise and rhythmic formulas. In many cases, they are composed of a single syllable (for example, "Om"), or a single word (for example, "Aum Namah Shivaya").

Deity Invocation:

♦ Mantras dedicated to specific deities are called deity invocations. Devotees chant these mantras to connect with the deity and receive their blessings.

Meditative Practice:

♦ In meditation, mantras are used to focus the mind, quiet mental chatter, and cultivate a state of inner peace and spiritual awareness. Meditative states can be achieved through repetitive chanting.

Vibrational Power:

♦ Mantras emit vibrational frequencies that are believed to have a powerful effect. To align oneself with specific energies or cosmic forces, a mantra must be consistently chanted.

Japa:

♦ The practice of silently or audibly repeating a mantra is called "japa." This can be done individually or in groups.

Bija Mantras:

♦ Mantras composed of a single syllable are called Bija Mantras. A particular deity or energy is often invoked through them since they are considered the essence of that deity or energy.

Healing and Transformation:

♦ Mantras can be used to heal physical or mental ailments, remove obstacles, attract positive energies, and grow spiritually.

Mantra Initiation:

♦ Through a process known as "mantra diksha" or initiation, a spiritual teacher or guru imparts a mantra to a disciple. It is believed that this infuses the mantra with spiritual power.

Mystical Symbolism:

♦ Mystical Symbolism: Many mantras have symbolic meanings, such as the "Om" symbol or yantras (geometric diagrams). Mantras are more effective when they contain these symbols.

Mantras are central to Hindu spiritual practices, and they play a crucial role in rituals, meditation, and daily devotions. They are considered a direct path to experiencing higher states of consciousness and connecting with the divine.

In Sanatan Dharma, ethical behavior, compassion, and the interconnectedness of all beings are emphasized. Modern notions of ethics and morality align with these principles.

19

BRIEF ON HINDU SCRIPTURES

✦

Hindu scriptures (such as Vedas, Upanishads, Agamas, and Puranas), epics (Bhagavad Gita and Ramayana), lawbooks, and other philosophical and denominational texts have been transmitted orally and in writing for generations. Scriptural teachings are presented in a variety of ways to guide spiritual seekers. The Vedas and other sacred writings are regarded as valid sources of knowledge about God, but personal experience is also highly regarded.

There are two broad categories of Hindu scriptures: Shruti and Smriti.

The word Shruti literally means 'hear', and it is a collection of what Hindus believe to be eternal truths, akin to the laws of nature. The vibrations of the universe contain these truths, according to Hinduism. These eternal truths were realized by ancient sages through meditation, and then passed on orally. Shruti refers to the Vedas and includes the Upanishads, which are the fourth and final part of the Vedas. All other scriptural texts are considered Smriti by many Hindus.

In Smriti texts, teachings should be interpreted considering changing circumstances over kala (time), Desha (land), and Guna (personality). For these texts to serve as a structure for society, they must be flexible and adaptable to changes in history, geography, and community. Despite variations across Hindu denominations, we review the major Hindu scriptures, regardless of whether they are classified as Shruti or Smriti.

Approximately 1200 - 400 B.C.E. were the years when the Vedas were written. Between 700 - 400 B.C.E. were the years when the Upanishads were written. Rituals, customs, and applications are the focus of the Vedas. Spiritual enlightenment is the primary concern of the Upanishads.

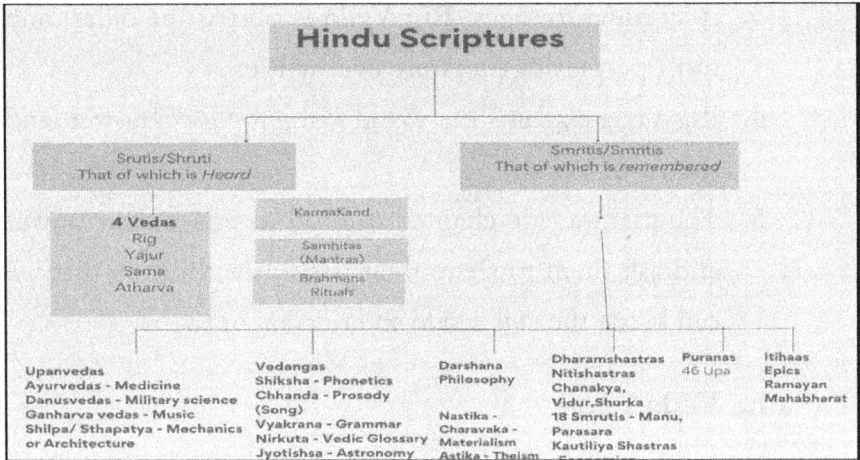

Hindu Scriptures

Srutis/Shruti
That of which is *Heard*

Smritis/Smritis
That of which is *remembered*

4 Vedas
Rig
Yajur
Sama
Atharva

KarmaKand

Samhitas
(Mantras)

Brahmana
Rituals

Upanvedas
Ayurvedas - Medicine
Danusvedas - Military science
Ganharva vedas - Music
Shilpa/ Sthapatya - Mechanics
or Architecture

Vedangas
Shiksha - Phonetics
Chhanda - Prosody
(Song)
Vyakrana - Grammar
Nirkuta - Vedic Glossary
Jyotishsa - Astronomy

Darshana
Philosophy

Nastika -
Charavaka -
Materialism
Aastika - Theism

Dharamshastras
Nitishastras
Chanakya,
Vidur,Shurka
18 Smrutis - Manu,
Parasara
Kautiliya Shastras

Puranas
46 Upa

Itihaas
Epics
Ramayan
Mahabharat

Vedas:

In ancient Indian society, Vedas had a significant influence, and these Vedas contributed to the formation of Hinduism. Though Vedic knowledge has always existed, Rishi Vyasa compiled it into four Vedas and passed it orally thousands of years ago.

Vedas are divided into four categories: Rigveda, Samaveda, Yajurveda, and Atharvaveda. Here are some interesting facts about Vedas.

Rig Veda Facts

1. In total there are 1028 mantras (or hymns) in Rig Veda, prayers to God. These are also called the *'Pancha Bhutani' alias* the five forces. Earth (Prithvi), water (jal), wind (Vayu), fire (Agni), sky (Akash)
2. In Rig Veda, all the mantras are compiled into ten books known as mandalas(circles)

3. According to sages, **Rig Veda** is one of the oldest and most perplexing literature ever written.

4. Rig Veda explains the world's origin, God's power, and the art of living.

5. The mantras are chanted to God to praise their power and ask them to share their passion with us so that we can battle the evil inside and outside of us.

Sama Veda Facts

1. Sama Veda consists of the same meaning and content as Rig Veda, but it is written to form a set of music. Hence, Sama Veda is known as the Veda of Melodies or as of chants.

2. Sama Veda is believed to have been written around 1000 BC. Some parts within the Sama Veda are said to be dated around 1700 BC.

3. Among all the four Vedas, **Sama Veda** is the shortest Veda. There are 1875 verses in Sama. Among them, around 1771 verses are from Rig Veda. The remaining 99 verses are their own.

4. As the Veda of Melodies, it is the oldest music composition, in the world that contains all types of music: meter, mantras, chhandas, and lastly, the linguistics

5. The Sama Veda was compiled so that it could be sung during the ceremonies of "soma-sacrifices,". This is a ritual where chopped vegetables or animal sacrifice were offered to Gods to please them.

Udgatar Priests used to sing them, and it reflected their point of view.

Yajur Veda Facts

1. Yajur Veda is all about the religious rituals. It is said to be a step-by-step guide which describes the correct way of doing religious ceremonies and rituals. However, few claim that this never talks about the right way but instead, guides people in thinking about the rituals.

2. Hence, when someone goes deeper into the Yajur Veda, one can find a much deeper meaning than just the list of ceremonies

3. As compared to Rig Veda, Yajur Veda has a much simpler language to understand

4. Between the four Vedas, Yajur Veda was the most used Vedic scripture by the ancient scholars and priests

5. Yajur Veda develops the level of consciousness among people and it is linked to the yogic practice of purifying mind, body, and soul. This helps people to awaken the consciousness within and open to the study of life with an open mind.

Atharva Veda Facts

1. Atharva Veda is the most diverse in nature compared to the other three vedas

2. Classic Atharva Veda is related to socio-cultural aspects of society, religion and provides knowledge on the same

3. Atharva Veda is related to the cult of occult science (Mantra-Tantra-Yantra (Tone Totke and Keelam Method). This is the opposite side of science – the ones related to death, spirits, and the afterlife.

4. Scholars disregard **the Atharva Veda** as part of the Vedas.

5. God Indra is considered the most popular deity in Atharva Veda, followed by Agni and Soma as similar to Rig Veda.

Karmakand:

Karma Kāṇḍa (Sanskrit: कर्मकाण्ड) describes the rites and rituals performed by Brahmins to receive Dakshina for performing rituals and sacrificial rites for material benefits or for liberation. KARMA-KĀṆḌA refers to all the ritual practices of Hindus.

1. **Daily rituals** like bath, dress, food, pūjā, Japa, meditation, and the Five Great Sacrifices (Pancha-maha yajña).

2. **Periodic rituals** like festivals, vratas, fasts, etc.

3. **Occasional rituals** like attending and celebrating temple festivals, pilgrimages, etc. Also included here are the rituals known as **iṣṭha-pūrta** - such as charitable works and endowments for the public

good - digit wells, building rest houses, gardens, schools, and clinics, etc.

Samhitas:

Samhitas are the oldest Hindu and yogic texts, which are part of the Vedas. Mantras, prayers, litanies, and hymns are found in the Samhitas. Hindus believe that the texts were handed down orally for thousands of years after being received directly from God by scholars.

Upanishads:

In Hindu philosophy, Upanishads are the most important religious texts. Humanity's place in Brahman's plan, the supreme force of the universe, is explained in Hindu cosmology. Upanishads emphasize the connection between Brahman, the supreme force in the universe, and humanity.

Upavedas:

There are four traditional arts and sciences called Upavedas (usually considered smriti).

- ♦ Ayurveda (medicine), associated with Athrvaveda
- ♦ Gandharva-Veda (music and dance), associated with Samaveda
- ♦ Dhanur-Veda (warfare), associated with Yajurveda
- ♦ Shilpa-Veda (architecture), associated with Rigveda

Vedangas

Vedangas literally means limbs of the Vedas. There are six of them. Their purpose is to support, preserve, and protect the Vedas and Vedic traditions, like the limbs of the body. Among the six Vedangas are Siksha, Chhanda, Vyakarana, Nirukta, Jyotisha and Kalpa. The Vedas and Vedic traditions are supported, preserved, and protected by them, just like the body's limbs. Vedangas have existed since ancient times, and the Brihadaranyaka Upanishad includes them as part of Vedic literature's Brahmana layer. As a result of the compilation of the Vedas in Iron Age India, several ancillary areas of study emerged. The date on which the six Vedangas were first conceived is unknown. Most likely, the Vedangas emerged towards the end of the Vedic period, around the middle of the first millennium BCE. As the language of Vedic writings became too archaic for the people of the period, several supplementary branches of Vedic studies emerged.

The six Vedangas are Siksha, Chhanda, Vyakarana, Nirukta, Jyotisha and Kalpa.

Chandas = meter

Kalpa = ritual

Jyotishya = astronomy

Nirukta = etymology

Shiksha = phonetics

Vyakarana = grammar

Darshanas:

A Darshana is a school of philosophy based on the Vedas. Darshana literature is philosophical in nature and is intended for scholars endowed with intellect, understanding, and acumen. Unlike the Itihaas, Puranas, and Agamas, which appeal to the heart, the Darshanas appeal to the intellect. Each of the six Darshanas aims to remove ignorance and its effects of pain and suffering, as well as to attain freedom, perfection, and eternal bliss through the union of the individual soul with the Supreme Soul. Mithya Jnana is what Nyaya calls ignorance. Aviveka, or non-discrimination between the real and the unreal, is the term used by the Sankhyas. In Vedanta, it is called Avidya or nescience. Through knowledge or Jnana, each philosophy aims to eradicate ignorance and achieve eternal bliss.

- **The Mimamsa:** Sage Jaimini was a disciple of the great sage Vyasa and he composed the Sutras of the *Mimamsa* school. This is based on the ritual sections of the Vedas

- **The Nyaya:** Sage Gautama created the principles of *Nyaya* or the Indian logical system. This is considered as a prerequisite for all philosophical inquiry

- **The Sankhya:** Sage Kapila created the Sankhya system.

- **The Vaiseshika:** This is a supplement of the Nyaya. Sage Kanada composed the *Vaisheshika Sutras.*

- **The Vedanta:** The Vedanta is the fulfillment of the Sankhya. It was composed by Sage Badarayana as *Vedanta-Sutras* or *Brahma-Sutras* which describes the teachings of the Upanishads.

- ♦ **The Yoga:** The Yoga supplements the Sankhya. Sage Patanjali systematized the Yoga school and composed the yoga sutras

Dharma-shastra:

Dharma-shastra is an ancient Indian body of jurisprudence that provides the basis, subject to legislative modification, for Hindu family law, both within India and across other countries in the globe. As a primary concern, Dharma-shastra does not deal with legal administration, though courts and their procedures are discussed extensively, but it is about the right course of action in any given situation. There are more than 5,000 titles in Sanskrit Dharma-shastra literature. Three categories can be distinguished: (1) sutras, (2) smritis, (3) nibandhas, which digest smriti verses from a variety of sources, and (4) vrittis, which comment on smriti verses individually. Nagandhas and vrittis, legal works intended for legal advisers, demonstrate considerable skill in harmonizing divergent sutras and smritis.

Puranas:

The Puranas are a collection of literary texts written in Sanskrit verse, which are believed to date from the 4th century BCE to around 1000 AD. They are generally considered to follow the epics chronologically, but sometimes the Mahabharata, which is considered a work of history, is also called a Purana.

In addition to 18 major puranas, there are a similar number of minor or subordinate puranas. Traditionally, Puranas are classified according to the three qualities of purity (sattva), impurity (tamas), and passion (rajas). There are also puranas in which the quality of sattva is said to predominate, and there are six of them in all: the Puranas of Vishnu, Narada, Bhagavata, Garuda, Padma, and Varaha. In another scheme of classification, Vishnu appears as the Supreme Being in these puranas. In another set of six Puranas, Shiva is the God to whom devotion is rendered: Matsya; Kurma; Linga; Shiva; Skanda; and Agni. Among the third set of six puranas, rajas appear to prevail: Brahma, Brahmanda, Brahmavaivarta, Markandeya, Bhavishya, and Vamana. Vayu Purana and Harivamsa are sometimes included in the list of eighteen. Although neither Vishnu nor Shiva is exclusively referred to in any of the puranas, this mode of classification is clearly inadequate. Accordingly, the Vishnu Purana and the Bhagavata Purana (also known as the Bhagavatam) are preeminent works of devotional literature; the Bhagavata Purana is even the supreme work of Krishna devotional literature. There are eighteen major puranas, each of which enumerates all the others, so it is reasonable to assume that all the puranas have been revised at some point. Among them, the Skanda Purana has 80,000 couplets, while the Brahma and Vamana Puranas each have 10,000 couplets.

Itihaas:

Ramayana is the first poem. Mahabharata being the longest poem ever written in human history. The *Ramayana* is an ancient epic written originally in Sanskrit which describes Prince Rama's quest to rescue his beloved wife Sita from Ravana. Ram took help of an army of monkeys including Hanuman. This is traditionally attributed to the authorship of the sage Valmiki and it dates around 500 BCE to 100 BCE.

Comprising 24,000 verses in seven cantos, this epic contains the teaching of the very ancient Hindu sages. This is one of the utmost literary works of ancient India. This has greatly influenced art, culture and traditions in the Indian subcontinent and Southeast Asia. The story of Rama has constantly been rewritten and retold in poetic and dramatic versions by some of India's greatest writers. This is also in narrative sculptures on the walls of temples of India and parts surrounding India. It is one of the staples of dramatic traditions, re-enacted in dance-dramas, village theater, shadow-puppet theater and the annual *Ram-lila* (Rama-play).

Story of *Ramayana*

Here is a condensed version of the Ramayana:

- ◆ Birth and Childhood of Rama: Rama was born into the royal family of King Dasharatha and Queen Kausalya in the city of Ayodhya. As the eldest of four brothers, he was greatly admired for his noble qualities. The stepmother of Rama, Kaikeyi, was manipulated by her maid, Manthara, to demand that her son, Bharata, be crowned king instead of Rama. In return for an old promise, Dasharatha banished Rama for fourteen years to the forest.

- ◆ Sita's Swayamvara: Rama and Sita, along with their brothers Lakshmana and Lakshmana, went into exile. The demon king Ravana abducted Sita in the forest with the help of the powerful rakshasa (demon) Maricha. Despite his best efforts, Jatayu, a noble vulture, was killed while trying to save Sita.

Hanuman and the Monkey Army:

Rama and Lakshmana encountered the monkey-god Hanuman on their quest to find Sita. To reach Sita, Hanuman leaps across the ocean to Lanka (modern-day Sri Lanka). Assuring Sita that they were on the verge of being rescued, he gave her Rama's ring.

- ◆ **Battle Against Ravana:** Under the leadership of Hanuman and Sugriva and Angada, Rama formed an army of monkey tribes to fight Ravana. Using Hanuman's intelligence and reconnaissance, they fought a great battle against Ravana's forces. After a fierce battle between Rama and Ravana, Rama defeated the demon king and won the epic climax.

Sita's Purity and Agni Pariksha:

- ◆ Rama had doubts about Sita's chastity during her captivity after his victory. The Agni Pariksha (trial by fire) Sita underwent to prove her purity vindicated her honor.

Return to Ayodhya:

- ◆ Rama, Sita, and Lakshmana returned to Ayodhya with Hanuman and their army of monkeys. The celebration of their return was filled with joy and festivity.

Rama's Reign and the Golden Age:

♦ Rama ruled Ayodhya as a benevolent and just king, known for his devotion to dharma (righteousness) and compassion for all creatures. The kingdom under his rule is often called Ram Rajya, an epitome of what a prosperous and ideal kingdom should be.

Exile of Sita and Birth of Lava and Kusha:

♦ It was unfortunate that there continued to be rumors questioning Sita's purity. Even though he loved Sita deeply, Rama sent her away despite his love for her. The sage Valmiki offered Sita refuge in his hermitage, where she gave birth to twin sons, Lava and Kusha.

♦ Return and departure: Rama sought to bring his sons back to Ayodhya after discovering their existence many years later. Rama was overjoyed to be reunited with Lava and Kusha after they proved their royal lineage. In a final test of her purity, Sita chose to return to the earth, her mother. Then she disappeared into the ground, asking Mother Earth to take her back.

Rama's Ascension:

Rama ruled for several more years before realizing his divine mission on earth had been completed. Upon entering the Sarayu River, he symbolically returned to his celestial abode, leaving behind a legacy of righteousness and dharma.

In Hindu culture and literature, the Ramayana remains a testament to the ideals of duty, love, sacrifice, and righteousness.

Mahabharata narrates the period when war between Kauravas and Pandavas for the throne of Hastinapur was fought. The war is also popularly known as the Kurukshetra war. One of the utmost important and respected books, Bhagavad Gita, is also a part of Mahabharata's great epic. It is one of the longest epic poems in the world, comprising over 100,000 verses.

Mahabharata primarily tells the story of the Kurukshetra War, but it also contains many philosophical and moral teachings. Here is a condensed version of the Mahabharata.

The Kurukshetra Conflict:

One of the main themes of the Mahabharata is the Kurukshetra conflict between two groups of royal cousins, the Pandavas, and the Kauravas, for control of the kingdom of Hastinapur. Duryodhana, the eldest Kauravas, is envious of Yudhishthira, the skilled and virtuous leader of the Pandavas.

The Game of Dice:

Duryodhana plans to cheat the Pandavas out of their kingdom through a rigged dice game. The Pandavas lose everything in the game, including their wife Draupadi, with the help of their cunning uncle Shakuni and their blind father Dhritarashtra.

Exile and Return:

The Pandavas are exiled to the forest for thirteen years, followed by an incognito year. It is during this time that they encounter numerous sages, learn valuable lessons, and acquire powerful weapons.

The Kurukshetra War:

Duryodhana refuses to give the Pandavas their kingdom upon their return. The two factions prepare for war after diplomatic efforts fail. A countless number of warriors and heroes fight at Kurukshetra, including Lord Krishna, who serves as Arjuna's charioteer and guide.

Bhagavad Gita:

Before the battle begins, Arjuna, the key figure among the Pandavas, has doubts and moral conflict about fighting his own kin and mentor. Bhagavad Gita provides Arjuna with profound spiritual teachings and guidance on righteous action and the nature of reality, addressing his doubts and providing guidance on righteous action.

The Fall of the Kauravas:

Eighteen days pass before the Kauravas are defeated. The sons of the Pandavas, Bhishma, Drona, and Karna are among the heroic figures who meet their ends on both sides. In the end, the Pandavas triumph, but at a high price.

The Final Reckoning: After the war, the Pandavas return to Hastinapur and ask for their kingdom. Despite being crowned king, Yudhishthira is deeply affected by the war's immense casualties and its moral complexities.

The Ascension and Death: At the conclusion of the Mahabharata, the Pandavas retire from their kingdom and embark on a pilgrimage to the holy land. Eventually, they renounce their thrones and embark on a final journey to the Himalayas with a dog representing the god Dharma. The sages and celestial beings they meet along the way provide them with guidance. Only Yudhishthira and the dog reach the gates of heaven, where Yudhishthira is reunited with his brothers and the celestial beings are revealed.

It is not just a narrative of a great war, but also a compendium of philosophical, moral, and spiritual teachings. Several complex themes are explored, including duty, righteousness, morality, and dharma. It also includes many sub-stories and teachings from various characters, making it a comprehensive guide to life and ethics.

Bhagavad Gita:

The Bhagavad Gita is considered the most sacred book in Hindu tradition and it describes the conversation between Arjuna, a supernaturally gifted warrior about to go into battle, and Lord Krishna, who chose to be his charioteer for the war. While imparting spiritual and material advice, Krishna explains *karma*, the self, the Supreme Self, the purpose of yoga, the difference between our self and our material body, how our environment affects our consciousness, and how to attain the perfection of life.

EPILOGUE

At the end of this journey through the rich tapestry of Hinduism in Bihar, we find ourselves at a crossroads of ancient wisdom and modern existence. Bihar, a land steeped in history, has revealed its secrets, revealing a profound connection between its people and their spiritual heritage.

Through dusty alleys of ancient temples, fragrant offerings of incense, and resonant echoes of devotional chants, we have traced the contours of faith that have endured. Throughout each chapter and verse, devotion, resilience, and deep reverence for the cosmic dance of creation and destruction are vividly depicted.

At the sacred city of Bodh Gaya, where the Bodhi tree stands as a living witness to enlightenment, we observed seekers from all over the world drawn together by a universal quest for truth and self-realization. As the Ganga's gentle flow through Patna and the temples of Vaishali reminded us, the sacred river is more than just water; it is a living embodiment of purity, purifying both body and soul along its journey.

By exploring the colorful festivals and rituals of Bihar, we witnessed how the rhythms of life are intertwined with the celestial calendar. Rajgir Dance Festival and Chhath Puja, with their soul-stirring devotion to the sun god, provided glimpses into the Bihari spiritual landscape's fusion of devotion and artistic expression.

We encountered a wide variety of people along this journey and their lives were woven into the vast tapestry of Hinduism in an incredibly intricate way. Throughout their lives, the stories of their devotion, sacrifice, and unwavering faith have been woven into the fabric of their existence, a testament to the power of tradition that has endured for thousands of years.

With the sounds of temple bells and the scent of marigolds, we bid farewell to Bihar and carry its wisdom with us. As Hinduism has been shown to be not just a religion but a philosophy that celebrates the interconnectedness of every living being, we are reminded that Hinduism is not just a religion.

We hope that the lessons learned along the way will find resonance in our hearts, reminding us to seek the divine in every corner of existence, to honor tradition while embracing change, and to walk the path of the dharma with grace and compassion.

Thus, as the final chapter closes, let us continue to carry on the torch of respect and understanding, knowing that the traditions of Bihar are not limited to its borders, but resonate across the universe, uniting all seekers in the quest for truth and enlightenment.

ACKNOWLEDGMENTS

Throughout my journey to write this book, I have been deeply inspired and supported by many individuals and organizations. The unwavering support and encouragement I have received from my family have been a constant source of strength for me.

I am deeply blessed and would like to thank my mother Mrs. Shobha Sinha, Father Mr. Umesh Sinha, all my teachers, and to my God for their immense blessings on me, because of them I exist.

To the folks who raised me and gave me the best childhood – my mother

Mrs. Shobha Sinha, my dadi late Sonamati Devi. My father/Papa Mr. Umesh Sinha whose guidance and timely advice helped me throughout the journey of writing my first book.

Also, I would like to thank my Nana Late Jamuna Lal, Nani Late Radha, Dadaji Late Nageshwar and Dadi Late Sonamati Devi for leading life by example.

To the loves of my life: Shriya, Om, and Aadhya, the three musketeers, who are the reason for my daily smiles and inspiration for this book.

To my husband Mr. Rajeev Sinha, for having my back and promising me an interesting journey. To

my brother Mr. Yashwant Sinha for supporting me. And to my vast extended family who made the festivals and celebrations so joyous and more memorable.

Thanks a bunch, to my circle of strong women, who always lift me, my loyal family, and friends, who showered their love and blessings on me immensely.

This book would not have been possible without the professionalism, guidance, and enthusiasm of the team at Thanx A. Mills, LLC. This process has been made easier by Ayanna Mills Ambrose and the entire publishing team.

Experts and colleagues in the field generously shared their insights and knowledge during my research for this book. Thanks for taking the time and sharing your expertise with me.

Thank you for being a constant source of motivation for me and for providing unwavering support and encouragement.

I would also like to thank the readers who will join me on this literary journey for their curiosity and engagement. My hope is that you will find this book valuable and that it resonates with you.

The book represents the culmination of many people's efforts and kindness. My heartfelt thanks go out to all of you who contributed to this work.

With heartfelt thanks,

Bishakha Sinha

ABOUT AUTHOR

Author Name: Bishakha Sinha

As a first-time author, Bishakha Sinha is passionate about exploring the depths of Hindu philosophy. As someone with a background and origin from India, Bishakha brings a fresh perspective to ancient wisdom, making it accessible to everyone.

During her writing, Bishakha draws inspiration from years of intensive study and personal experience to provide timeless truths and practical insights for modern living, which she reveals in her reflections on the Hindu scriptures. As a writer, she strives to bridge the gap between ancient wisdom and contemporary challenges, providing readers with a path to inner peace, purpose, and fulfillment.

Bishakha Sinha is deeply committed to sharing the profound teachings of Hinduism with her upcoming generations and everyone, believing that they hold the potential to inspire positive transformation in individuals and communities alike. Her debut book, "Roots and Rituals- Bihari Kayastha Traditions in Hinduism" is a testament to her dedication to making these profound teachings accessible and relevant in today's fast-paced world.

When not immersed in her writing, Bishakha enjoys wall paintings, cooking, and baking for her family. She resides in Georgia, USA with her husband and kids, finding solace in the beauty of nature and the wisdom of ancient texts. The responsibility of being a mother of three children entails a strong commitment to her family. Having a career in IT implies that she is involved in the field of information technology. She loves to travel and explore different cultures and traditions.

References

https://www.exoticindiaart.com/blog/dhoti/

https://pujayagna.com/blogs/hindu-fasting-days/ekadashi-fast

https://thisismyindia.com/culture/bihari-wedding/index.html

https://www.byarcadia.org/post/the-4-yugas-of-the-endless-time-hinduism

https://www.hindufaqs.com/4-stages-life-hinduism/

https://pujayagna.com/blogs/hindu-fasting-days/guruvar-vrat-thursday-fast

https://www.weddingwire.in/wedding-tips/bihari-wedding--c2615

https://www.prathaculturalschool.com/post/16-sanskaras-in-hinduism

https://vedicfeed.com/facts-about-vedas/

https://pujayagna.com/blogs/hindu-fasting-days/shanivar-vrat-saturday-fast

https://www.hinduamerican.org/blog/5-things-to-know-about-vasant-panchami

https://symbolgenie.com/symbols-diwali-meanings/

https://atoday.org/suggested-disclaimer-for-all-websites-and-publications-sponsored-byreligious-denominations-and-parareligious-evangelistic-organizations/

https://myoksha.com/bhoomi-pooja/

https://pujayagna.com/blogs/hindu-fasting-days/purnima

https://pujayagna.com/blogs/hindu-fasting-days/amavasya

https://www.khanacademy.org/humanities/approaches-to-art-history/understanding-religionart/hinduism-art/a/hindu-deities

https://en.wikipedia.org/wiki/Shiva

https://www.asiahighlights.com/india/janmashtami

https://www.happywedding.app/blog/post-marriage-rituals/

https://rgyan.com/blogs/why-hindus-perform-pind-dan-at-gaya

https://www.tourmyindia.com/blog/top-25-religious-tourism-places-in-india/

https://pujayagna.com/blogs/hindu-fasting-days/budhwar-vrat-wednesday-fast

https://hindupad.com/jitiya-puja-katha-story-jitiya-vrata/

https://blog.wego.com/50-pilgrimage-destinations/

https://southasia.ucla.edu/religions/texts/puranas/

https://pujayagna.com/blogs/hindu-fasting-days/pradosh-fast

https://en.wikipedia.org/wiki/Rishikesh

https://pujayagna.com/blogs/hindu-fasting-days/ravivar-vrat-sunday-fast

http://www.pujaservices.com/festival-view/Dussehra/15/

https://pujayagna.com/blogs/hindu-fasting-days/shravan-somvar-vrat-monday-fast

https://www.britannica.com/topic/sanctity-of-the-cow

https://comparativereligion.com/god.html

https://www.india.com/news/india/do-you-know-why-some-ganpati-idols-have-their-trunkon-the-right-some-left-and-some-straight-1454930/

https://www.hinduamerican.org/wp-content/uploads/2019/12/Scriptures2.0_0.pdf

https://www.easemytrip.com/blog/sapta-puri-7-holy-cities-in-india

360

https://www.learnreligions.com/the-darshanas-an-introduction-to-hindu-philosophy-1770582

http://www.bhaidooj.org/chitragupta-puja.html

https://pujayagna.com/blogs/hindu-fasting-days/shukravar-vrat-friday-fast

https://en.wikipedia.org/wiki/Vishnu

https://en.wikipedia.org/wiki/Adityas

https://www.soultree.in/blogs/makeup/learn-the-ancient-recipe-of-kajal-made-using-3000-year-old-process

https://pujayagna.com/blogs/hindu-fasting-days/mangalvar-vrat-tuesday-fast

https://www.hindu-blog.com/2009/09/jivitputrika-vrat-katha-story-of-jitiya.html

https://www.lettrlabs.com/post/40-heartfelt-thank-you-note-examples-for-friends-family-andco-workers-greeting-card-inspiration-for-any-occasion

https://www.magicbricks.com/blog/griha-pravesh-puja-tips/127093.html

https://www.hindustantimes.com/more-lifestyle/navratri-2019-significance-and-importanceof-the-festival/story-A0BiRogyVDuxx4kriWgYeL.html

https://www.himalayanacademy.com/readlearn/basics/karma-reincarnation

https://medium.com/@amy1924a/title-exploring-the-rich-tapestry-of-hinduism-a-journeyinto-the-worlds-oldest-religion-959b1ec21ca4

https://en.wikipedia.org/wiki/Saṃsāra_(Buddhism)

https://www.nature.com/articles/s41599-022-01109-4

https://www.livescience.com/who-was-siddhartha-gautama-the-buddha

https://en.wikipedia.org/wiki/Vedas

https://99pandit.com/blog/hartalika-teej/

https://parenting.firstcry.com/articles/your-complete-diwali-puja-vidhi-guide/

https://www.india.com/travel/articles/murudeshwar-temple-5-interesting-facts-about-templewith-worlds-second-largest-shiva-statue-3227996/

https://www.trafalgar.com/real-word/diwali-story/

https://medium.com/@privatedriverinindia/sapta-puri-the-seven-sacred-cities-of-indiafe9b9df723b8

https://bhagwanbhajan.com/stories/read-story.php?my-story=four-ashramas-of-vedic-lifethe-4-stages-of-life-in-hinduism-926147

https://www.oprahdaily.com/life/a34520345/diwali-celebrations/

https://en.wikipedia.org/wiki/Brahma_Temple,_Pushkar

https://www.businessinsider.in/thelife/news/maha-shivratri-2020-dos-and-donts-you-mustknow-to-celebrate-it-in-the-right-way/articleshow/74219387.cms

https://rigbiswas.com/blog/bihari-wedding-rituals

https://www.hinduismfacts.org/science-in-hinduism/

https://sanskritdocuments.org/articles/Hindu_Rituals.pdf

https://www.ecraftindia.com/blogs/articles/how-to-perform-shri-krishna-janmashtami-pujavidhi-at-home

https://aanmeegam.co.in/blogs/kalasha-significance/

https://prayagpandits.com/faqs-ancestors-rituals/

https://mirchi.in/stories/lifestyle/ways-to-do-navratri-puja-at-home/99097839

https://www.theholidayspot.com/shivratri/origin.htm

https://en.wikipedia.org/wiki/Hindu_cosmology

https://www.travelworldplanet.com/gomukh/

https://wanderlog.com/tp/1874/vrindavan-trip-planner

https://www.tourism-of-india.com/kamakhya.html

https://vedicfeed.com/16-samskara-rites-of-passage/

https://indusscrolls.com/pumsavana-the-age-old-wisdom-of-ayurveda-for-healthy-pregnancyand-for-healthy-baby

https://www.artofliving.org/mahashivratri/what-to-do-on-mahashivratri

https://hinduism.stackexchange.com/questions/10898/what-is-the-exact-way-of-doing-faston-shivratri

https://www.fitsri.com/articles/samskaras

https://planningahinduwedding.com/therefore-hindu-brides-throw-rice/

https://www.jagranjosh.com/general-knowledge/what-is-the-story-behind-makarsankranti-1673705183-1

https://mumbaicity.gov.in/tourist-place/siddhivinayak-temple/

https://en.wikipedia.org/wiki/Bodh_Gaya

https://www.samagre.com/2023/09/hinduism-journey-of-spirituality.html

https://www.radha.name/news/philosophy/gotras-a-simple-explanation

https://99pandit.com/blog/what-is-gand-mool-nakshatra-shanti-puja-cost-vidhi-benefits/

https://medium.com/@neelamsharma202222/the-haldi-ceremony-a-time-honored-traditionwith-beautiful-significance-f3f70e2ebe09

https://en.wikipedia.org/wiki/Jagannath_Temple,_Puri

https://srisailamtourism.com/places-to-visit

https://en.wikipedia.org/wiki/Manikaran

https://www.sanskritimagazine.com/why-do-we-do-aarati/

https://www.vedanet.com/the-ancient-yoga-of-the-sun/

https://www.mysanskruti.in/shubh-navratri/

https://traveltriangle.com/blog/places-to-visit-near-golden-temple/

https://en.wikipedia.org/wiki/Khajuraho_Group_of_Monuments

https://tamarindweddings.com/blog/multi-turban-indian-grooms/

https://www.hinduismfacts.org/dashavatara/

https://desifavors.com/blogs/news/dos-and-donts-for-housewarming-rituals

https://medium.com/@sunilkeshari/jivitputrika-vrat-katha-in-hindi-603f53530b04

https://ritsin.com/chitragupta-puja-dawaat-puja-yam-dwitiya.html/

https://mythiclibrary.com/hindu/the-myth-of-vishnu-and-the-eternal-cycle/

https://krishijagran.com/others/what-is-navratri-and-why-is-it-celebrated/

https://traveltriangle.com/blog/meenakshi-temple/

https://www.astroved.com/astropedia/en/temples/north-india/khajuraho-temples

https://housing.com/news/holi-pooja-procedure-and-significance/

https://mangoandmarigoldpress.com/blogs/blog/rakish-bandhan

https://www.weddingsutra.com/bride/bridal-fashion/traditional-jewelry-guide-for-the-biharibride/

https://krishna.com/topic-term/bhagavad-gita

https://www.pratidintime.com/lifestyle/thank-you-for-your-support

https://medium.com/philosophicalmusings/things-that-shaped-my-life-8a8d59d38269

https://economictimes.indiatimes.com/news/new-updates/chitragupta-puja-2022-date-timepuja-methods-and-significance/articleshow/95098505.cms

https://iskconeducationalservices.org/HoH/further-information-and-teaching-resourcessecondary/fact-sheets/hindu-birth-and-childhood-ceremonies/

https://jasmineflowers.in/blog/makar-sankranti/

https://www.karnataka.com/festivals/ayudha-puja/

https://vajiramias.com/current-affairs/what-is-the-chhathfestival/654231a65483f34a0dda0c29/

https://www.india.com/travel/articles/history-of-puri-jagannath-rath-yatra-how-it-allbegan-3233251/

https://www.thebetterindia.com/114044/the-legend-of-kamakhya-temple-assam-bleedinggoddess-assam/

https://culturalatlas.sbs.com.au/religions/hinduism/resources/hinduism-rituals-and-practices

https://sage-answer.com/on-which-day-mahishasura-was-killed/

https://hicare.in/blog/top-3-importance-of-house-cleaning-in-diwali/

https://dranshublog.com/bhai-dooj-the-bihar-version/

https://prathamdarshan.com/religious/gurdwara-harmandir-sahib/

https://karnatakatourism.org/tour-item/shravanabelagola/

https://en.wikipedia.org/wiki/Gomukh

https://aavartana.com/vamana/

https://hindumediawiki.com/hn/story.php?id=486

https://bengalics.org/the-ramayana/

https://www.wikiwand.com/en/Kayastha

https://wedbuddy.com/taiwan-wedding-traditions/

https://pinddaangaya.co.in/pitru-paksha-shradh-gaya/

https://www.hinduismfacts.org/hindu-gods-and-goddesses/devi-sati/

https://www.timesnownews.com/spiritual/religion/article/basant-panchami-puja-samagri-listand-rules-everything-you-need-to-know/855394

https://anamikamishra.com/how-i-do-krishna-janmashtami-puja-at-home/

https://isha.sadhguru.org/mahashivratri/shiva/maha-mrityunjaya-mantra/

https://en.wikipedia.org/wiki/Konark_Sun_Temple

https://theculturetrip.com/asia/india/articles/must-visit-temples-in-kanchipuram-india

https://nandyal.ap.gov.in/temple-tourism/

https://www.sanskritimagazine.com/why-we-dont-touch-books-and-people-with-feet/

https://www.indiaparenting.com/chhathi-ceremony.html

https://www.thebridalbox.com/articles/haldi-ceremony_0051007/

https://greatindiantours.com/destinations/kanchipuram/

https://prayagraj.nic.in/tourist-place/sangam/

https://gayajipurohit.com/ekodrishti-shradh.php

https://www.indiatoday.in/information/story/ayudha-puja-2021-date-time-history-andsignificance-1864628-2021-10-14

https://en.wikipedia.org/wiki/Kedarnath_Temple

https://www.keralatourism.org/kerala-article/2010/sabarimala-pilgrim-centre/84

https://anamikamishra.com/how-i-do-ganesh-chaturthi-puja-at-home/

https://www.shaktipatinternational.com/about-ujjain/

https://brilliantio.com/what-is-spiritual-empowerment/

https://www.indusage.com.au/diwali-2020-lakshmi-puja-muhurat-how-to-do-diwali-puja-athome/

https://www.britannica.com/place/Varanasi

https://wanderlog.com/tp/1316/shirdi-trip-planner

http://www.ganesh.us/rituals/why-do-wear-tilak.html

https://timesofindia.indiatimes.com/religion/web-stories/four-kumaras-who-are-sanakadirishis-lord-brahmas-manasputras/photostory/104909799.cms

https://www.smartpuja.com/blog/rudra-homam/

https://apcohandlooms.com/drape-these-nine-colours-of-divinity-for-this-navrathri/

https://prayagpandits.com/how-to-perform-pind-daan-poojan/

https://www.india.com/festivals-events/hartalika-teej-2022-date-timings-puja-muhurat-andrituals-know-all-details-here-5599554/

https://atmajyotifoundation.org/article/shukravar-vrat

https://www.travel-history.com/2021/04/somnath-temple-history-somnath-mahadev.html

https://www.tripoto.com/tamil-nadu/trips/tamilnadu-place-of-rajni-anna-5cf6c79ca94cc

https://www.rajasthantourplanner.com/Monuments-Citywise/Brahma-Temple-Pushkar.html

https://www.tourism.rajasthan.gov.in/pushkar.html

https://en.wikipedia.org/wiki/Belur_Math

https://www.academia.edu/50963403/Was_Lord_Rama_of_Ramayana_a_Devraja_and_an_In_spiration_to_Cambodian_Kings

https://www.tirthpurohit.org/special-events/science-behind-pind-daan-why-should-weperform-this-ritual/

https://www.jagranjosh.com/general-knowledge/sawan-maha-shivaratri-history-andsignificance-1564467535-1

https://wanderlog.com/tp/914/tirupati-trip-planner

https://en.wikipedia.org/wiki/Badrinath

https://en.wikipedia.org/wiki/Shravanabelagola

https://timesofindia.indiatimes.com/readersblog/my-voices/manikaran-shiva-temple-3159/

https://www.sanskritimagazine.com/why-do-hindus-ring-the-bell-in-temple/

https://www.outlooktraveller.com/experiences/heritage/a-step-back-in-time-in-biharhistorical-sites-to-see

https://www.mapsofindia.com/bihar/geography-and-history.html

https://krishijagran.com/blog/5-things-everyone-should-know-about-basant-panchami/

https://www.britannica.com/place/Mathura

https://devilonwheels.com/gangotri-the-most-complete-guide/

https://blog.yatradham.org/devprayag/

https://www.facebook.com/deyorcamps/posts/residents-of-the-village-feel-little-need-forsecurity-thanks-to-their-belief-in/1751211728231634/

https://timesofindia.indiatimes.com/travel/kolkata/dakshineshwar-kalitemple/ps47798885.cms

https://science-atlas.com/science/women-still-made-to-sleep-outdoors-in-menstruation-hutsthroughout/

http://journeyintohinduism.org/

https://medium.com/@jagadekavya/unveiling-the-rich-tapestry-of-hinduism-a-journeythrough-its-storied-history-6543fa54c47

https://en.wikipedia.org/wiki/Narasimha

https://www.nortonsimon.org/art/detail/F.1975.16.06.S

https://en.wikipedia.org/wiki/Sati_(Hindu_goddess)

https://www.crooked-compass.com/travel-blog/travel-photo-diary-the-mist-magic-of-india/

https://www.astroved.com/astropedia/en/temples/north-india/jwalamukhi-temple

https://en.wikipedia.org/wiki/Swaminarayan_Akshardham_(Delhi)

https://thetempleguru.com/listing/padmanabhaswamy-temple/

https://www.mangalparinay.com/blog/jewellery-clothing/anklets-a-traditional-bridal-jewellery

http://360hinduism.com/why-do-we-blow-the-conch/

https://www.hinduwebsite.com/hinduism/concepts/vedangas.asp

https://www.babycenter.in/a1018734/igodh-bharaii-indian-baby-shower

https://www.babycenter.in/a1016889/annaprashan-first-rice-eating-ceremony

https://en.wikipedia.org/wiki/History_of_Nashik

https://nashiktouristplaces.com/about-nashik-tourist-places/

https://en.wikipedia.org/wiki/Amarnath_Temple

https://en.wikipedia.org/wiki/Gangotri

https://www.boldsky.com/yoga-spirituality/housewarming-be-aware-of-these-dos-anddonts-146465.html

https://www.drikpanchang.com/navratri/durga-puja/ayudha-puja-date-time.html?year=2025

https://www.doyou.com/maha-mrityunjaya-mantra/

https://www.news18.com/news/lifestyle/dussehra-2017-aprajita-puja-shami-pujasignificance-rituals-and-shubh-muhurat-1532105.html

https://abcm.co.in/dawat-puja/

https://www.tripsavvy.com/shirdi-guide-to-sai-baba-pilgrimage-1539705

https://wanderlog.com/tp/976/kanchipuram-trip-planner

https://www.britannica.com/place/Vrindavan

https://www.thrillophilia.com/destinations/gokarna/places-to-visit

https://uttarakhandtourism.gov.in/yamunotri-gaumukh

https://www.lashkaraa.com/blogs/lashkaraa/dhoti

https://www.nhsf.org.uk/2006/09/why-do-we-light-a-lamp/

https://timesofindia.indiatimes.com/religion/mantras-chants/rudra-mantra-mantra-meaningand-benefits/articleshow/68205205.cms

https://sakalapuja.com/samskar/simanta-or-godhbharai/

https://www.mamasmiles.com/world-culture-mukhe-bhaat-ceremony-in-west-bengal-india/

https://www.spotlightnepal.com/2020/11/17/chhath-puja-2020-bidhi-significanceimportance-and-history/

https://blog.yatradham.org/ghats-and-temples-of-nashik/

https://allindiaroundup.com/festival/why-some-ganapati-idols-have-their-trunk-on-right-sidesome-left-and-some-straight/

http://acecontent.apexlearning.com/online/cr_eng_II_sem_1_c_2016/Unit_3/Lesson_3/Activity_18322/printables/Reading_Materials918326.htm

https://hinduism.stackexchange.com/questions/9380/how-did-the-rumor-started-that-thereare-33-crore-gods-in-hinduism

https://www.mypoojabox.in/blogs/articles/how-to-do-navratri-puja-at-home

https://www.easyayurveda.com/2015/11/01/shami-tree-banni-tree-prosopis-cinerariamedicinal-uses/

https://www.holidify.com/pages/chhath-puja-1323.html

https://indianastrology.co.in/5654-chhath-puja-history-who-is-chhathi-maiya/

https://www.gujaratpackage.com/blogs/a-guide-to-planning-your-perfect-dwarka-andsomnath-tour-itinerary/

http://www.saibabaofindia.com/important-festivals-events-program-accomodation-shirdisamadhi-mandir-in-shirdi-ramanavami-vijayadashami-gurupurnima.htm

https://www.holidify.com/places/gaumukh/

https://www.fabhotels.com/blog/akshardham-temple-delhi/

https://www.hindu-blog.com/2023/11/history-of-dakshineswar-kali-temple.html

https://sciencebehindindianculture.in/tulsi-hindu-culture-sacred-plant/

http://360hinduism.com/why-do-we-light-a-lamp/

https://www.sanskritimagazine.com/why-do-we-touch-feet/

https://www.trafalgar.com/real-word/diwali-story/#:~:text=After he slayed the demon, Lord Krishna declared,also celebrate the Hindu Goddess Lakshmi during Diwali.

https://whyhindu.com/hindu-fasting-days/

https://www.hellotravel.com/stories/amazing-facts-about-jagannath-puri-temple-odisha

https://www.trulyindiatours.com/the-pristine-beaches-of-gokarna-a-hidden-gem-inkarnatakas-coastline/

https://en.wikipedia.org/wiki/Chitrakoot,_Madhya_Pradesh

https://tripsaround.in/chitrakoot-madhya-pradesh-the-hill-of-many-wonders-a-spiritual-placeto-rest-your-soul/

https://en.wikipedia.org/wiki/Gurdwara_Hemkund_Sahib

https://en.wikipedia.org/wiki/Margram

https://sciencebehindindianculture.in/why-hindus-do-not-eat-non-veg-on-some-particulardays/

https://www.herzindagi.com/web-stories/society-culture/reasons-to-not-touch-tulsi-plant-onsunday-ws-18761

http://www.chinmayaupahar.in/blog/why-do-we-prostrate-before-parents-and-elders/

https://allindiaroundup.com/news/different-types-of-ganesh-idol-trunks-explained/

https://www.thestatesman.com/india/from-bond-between-lord-krishna-and-draupadi-tobengal-partition-and-tagores-mass-call-for-rakhi-1503217016.html

https://svastika.in/blogs/blog/how-to-worship-lord-krishna-and-its-benefits

https://www.facebook.com/holisticbasket/posts/diwali-vibes-have-already-kicked-in-festivalseason-is-the-one-where-there-are-1/1268889950230147/

https://atmajyotifoundation.org/article/ravivar-vrat

https://whc.unesco.org/en/list/246

https://en.wikipedia.org/wiki/Dakshineswar_Kali_Temple

https://www.hindujagruti.org/hinduism/importance-of-jewelry

https://testbook.com/ias-preparation/rig-veda-upsc-notes

https://inews.co.uk/news/world/maha-shivaratri-2021-what-meaning-hindu-festival-whendate-celebrations-908515

https://www.calendarr.com/india/janmashtami/

https://vajiramias.com/current-affairs/what-is-the-chhathfestival/654231a65483f34a0dda0c29/#:~:text= The rituals surrounding Chhath Puja are supposedly harsher,'prasad' to the Sun during sunrise and sunset.

https://en.wikipedia.org/wiki/Golden_Temple

https://blog.templesofindia.org/post/5-temples-of-sabarimala-pilgrimage-circuit/

https://belurmath.org/sri-ramakrishna-temple/

https://timesofindia.indiatimes.com/life-style/health-fitness/de-stress/why-you-should-neversleep-with-your-head-facing-north/articleshow/75347715.cms

https://www.ptaufiqphotography.com/saptapadi-seven-steps-indian-wedding-ceremony/

https://www.nhsf.org.uk/2006/09/why-do-we-apply-the-holy-ash/

https://www.templepurohit.com/the-six-vedangas/

https://www.lastjourney.in/blog/why-do-the-hindus-believe-in-immersing-the-ashes-in-theholy-river-ganga/

https://www.wikiwand.com/en/Vaishno_Devi

https://en.wikipedia.org/wiki/Badrinath_Temple

https://wanderlog.com/tp/5780/sabarimala-trip-planner

https://dbpedia.org/page/Allahabad

https://en.wikipedia.org/wiki/Sarnath

https://www.holidify.com/places/sarnath/sightseeing-and-things-to-do.html

https://www.holidify.com/places/chitrakoot/

https://www.vibrant-gujarat.com/why-do-hindu-wear-marks-tilak-pottu-and-the-like-on-theforehead.htm

http://www.chinmayaupahar.in/blog/why-do-we-not-touch-papers-books-and-people-withthe-feet/

https://gunatitjyot.org/about/beliefs/who-do-we-do-pradakshina/

https://www.yogapedia.com/definition/9056/samhita

https://iasbaba.com/wp-content/uploads/2019/09/TLP-Plus-2019-Comprehensive-Mock-1.pdf

https://www.psychnewsdaily.com/spiritual-awakening-process/

https://www.vyasaonline.com/encyclopedia/satya-or-krita-yuga/

https://www.bbc.co.uk/bitesize/guides/zkkck2p/revision/1

https://www.ndtv.com/india-news/raksha-bandhan-2023-is-rakhi-on-august-30-or-31-knowhere-4290420

https://indiashine.net/char-dham/

https://en.wikipedia.org/wiki/Rameswaram

https://www.srisailadevasthanam.org/en-in/about/general-information/sakshi-ganapathi

https://www.templefolks.com/temple-pedia/jwalamukhi-devi-temple

https://iskcondesiretree.com/profiles/blogs/the-glories-of-gopi-chandana-tilaka

https://en.wikipedia.org/wiki/108_(number)

https://www.nhsf.org.uk/2006/09/why-do-we-do-aarati/

https://en.wikipedia.org/wiki/Pumsavana

https://indianexpress.com/article/religion/dussehra-vijayadashami-2017-celebration-historyimportance-and-significance-of-this-festival-4867019/

https://oneminutesaree.in/blogs/news/navaratri-colors-and-their-significance-in-sareeselection

https://news.abplive.com/astro/chhath-puja-2023-day-1-live-updates-chhath-mahaparvanahay-khay-puja-muhurat-vidhi-pujan-samagri-1643242

https://vedics.in/chhath-puja/

https://www.holidify.com/pages/jagannath-puri-temple-facts-60.html

https://en.wikipedia.org/wiki/Mallikarjuna_Temple,_Srisailam

https://www.rvatemples.com/listings/tarapith-temple/

https://www.hinduamerican.org/blog/the-power-of-namaste

https://momababyetc.com/significance-and-procedure-of-annaprashan-ceremony/

https://www.volunteerforever.com/article_post/what-is-holi-festival-and-why-is-it-celebrated/

https://www.sumadhwaseva.com/wp-content/uploads/2010/06/Vata-Savitri-English.pdf

https://www.sanatan.org/en/a/281.html

https://templesinindiainfo.com/legend-of-chhath-puja-legend-of-chhath-pooja-chhath-poojastory/

https://en.wikipedia.org/wiki/Vaishno_Devi

https://revolvingcompass.com/meenakshi-amman-temple-madurai-things-to-know-beforeyou-go/

https://www.thetilesofindia.com/global-architects/the-beauty-of-the-akshardham-temple/

https://deoghartourism.com/tarapith/

https://belurmath.org/

http://www.ganesh.us/rituals/ring-bell-in-temple.html

https://templesinindiainfo.com/why-do-we-worship-kalasha-kalasam/

https://en.wikipedia.org/wiki/Karma_Kāṇḍa

https://study.com/learn/lesson/the-upanishads-history-religion-oral-tradition.html

https://www.ancient-origins.net/myths-legends-asia/mahabharata-indian-epic-familyfighting-0010153

https://philonotes.com/2023/06/the-mahabharata

https://poemverse.org/rumi-poems-about-life/

https://aavartana.com/kalki/

https://www.britannica.com/topic/Narasimha

https://www.caleidoscope.in/art-culture/traditional-food-of-bihar

https://joshitours.org/pind-daan-in-gaya-varanasi-allahabad/

https://www.eastrohelp.com/blog/shivaratri-puja-vidhi-at-home/

https://www.theholidayspot.com/shivratri/shiva-tales/shiva-as-neelkantha.htm

https://www.floweraura.com/blog/article/what-is-dussehra-and-why-it-is-celebrated

https://www.antaryami.com/hinduism/the-eight-vasus-of-hindu-mythology/

https://purekayastha.weebly.com/history-of-chitragupta-maharaj.html

https://selectvenue.in/blog/chhath-puja-2021-know-what-is-chhath-puja-the-rituals-andsignificance-associated-with-it/

https://alchemlearning.com/chhath-puja-festival/

https://www.thedivineindia.com/nageshvara-jyotirlinga-mandir/5955

https://blog.yatradham.org/tirupati-darshan-10-interesting-facts/

https://en.wikipedia.org/wiki/Kedarnath

https://www.forbes.com/sites/jimdobson/2015/11/13/a-one-trillion-dollar-hidden-treasurechamber-is-discovered-at-indias-sree-padmanabhaswam-temple/

https://www.wikihow.com/Ring-on-Finger-Meaning

http://360hinduism.com/wear-marks-tilak-pottu-like-forehead/

https://religion.fandom.com/wiki/Vibhuti

https://www.studyiq.com/articles/types-of-vedas/

https://iskconeducationalservices.org/HoH/tradition/doctrine-and-scripture/shruti-the-fourvedas/

https://hindutemples.info/books/vedas

https://hindupad.com/ashta-vasus/

https://www.indiadivine.org/hindus-gotra-system-scientific-meaning-of-gotra-in-vedas/

https://en.wikipedia.org/wiki/Tarpana

https://timesofindia.indiatimes.com/life-style/events/happy-makar-sankranti-2022-top-50-wishes-messages-and-quotes-to-share-with-your-loved-ones/articleshow/88853062.cms

https://www.colorsexplained.com/color-white-meaning-of-the-color-white/

https://www.news18.com/news/lifestyle/chhath-puja-2022-date-time-in-india-tithi-shubhmuhurat-significance-6223357.html

https://www.britannica.com/money/topic/globalization

https://en.wikipedia.org/wiki/Haridwar_district

https://www.holidify.com/places/ujjain/

https://en.wikipedia.org/wiki/Dwarka

https://famoustemplesofindia.com/dwaraka-tirumala-temple-chinna-tirupati/

https://en.wikipedia.org/wiki/Somnath_temple

https://www.gujarattourism.com/saurashtra/gir-somnath/somnath-temple.html

https://www.tourmyindia.com/states/maharashtra/nashik-tourist-attractions.html

https://www.2indya.com/why-shiva-is-called-shambhu-or-shankar/

https://templesinindiainfo.com/why-do-we-wear-tilak-pottu-bottu-on-forehead/

https://drishtiartcentre.com/drishti-art-centre/magazine/issue-9/timeless-indian-traditionswhy-do-we-not-touch-papers-books-and-people-with-the-feet/

https://hindupad.com/upvaas-significance/

https://hinduism.stackexchange.com/questions/156/why-do-we-perform-pradakshinamcircumambulation-clockwise

https://www.indiatoday.in/lifestyle/culture/story/total-solar-eclipse-indian-hindu-mythssupersitions-rahu-surya-grahan-religious-rituals-lifest-1030644-2017-08-21

https://www.revesery.com/2023/03/how-to-read-hindu-calendar-explained.html

https://isha.sadhguru.org/en/wisdom/article/mahabharat-ep59-war-meanness-continues

https://yogadura.com/what-is-the-bhagavad-gita/

https://www.academiabees.com/acknowledgement-for-research-paper/

https://www.india.com/photos/news/char-dham-yatra-to-kedarnath-halted-amid-heavyrain-240763/why-one-should-do-sacred-pilgrimage-yatras-240766/

https://www.hinduismtoday.com/magazine/july-august-september-2008/2008-07-quotesand-quips/

https://theverandahclub.com/article/indian-married-woman-and-the-meaning-behind-theirsymbolic-accessories-654

https://www.sanskritimagazine.com/bindi-meaning-and-significance-of-the-dot-on-forehead/

https://www.artofliving.org/in-en/lifestyle/tips/know-about-brahma-muhurta

https://www.researchgate.net/publication/361149208_A_REVIEW_OF_THE_EFFECT_OF_OMK_AR_MANTRA_CHANTING_ON_THE_NERVOUS_SYSTEM_AND_ITS_BENEFITS